REMAPPING BIBLICAL STUDIES

BIBLICAL SCHOLARSHIP IN NORTH AMERICA

Number 31

REMAPPING BIBLICAL STUDIES

CUREMP at Thirty

Edited by

Stephanie Buckhanon Crowder and Mary F. Foskett

SBL PRESS

Atlanta

Library of Congress Control Number: 2023945284

Contents

Part 2. Fusion of the Critical/Political and Biblical/Geopolitical

Part 3. Intercultural Readings and Transborder Cultural Readings

Abbreviations

ABS	Archaeology and Biblical Studies
AHR	*The American Historical Review*
ANEM	Ancient Near East Monographs
BASOR	*Bulletin of the American Schools of Oriental Research*
BibInt	*Biblical Interpretation*
BibInt	Biblical Interpretation
BIPOC	Black, Indigenous, and People of Color
BSNA	Biblical Scholarship in North America
BTB	*Biblical Theology Bulletin*
BW	Bible and Women
BZAW	Beihefte zur Zeitschrift für die alttestamentliche Wissenschaft
CHANE	Culture and History of the Ancient Near East
CRT	Critical Race Theory
CurBR	*Currents in Biblical Research*
CUREMP	Committee on Underrepresented Racial and Ethnic Minorities in the Profession
DEI	Diversity, Equity, and Inclusion
GPBS	Global Perspectives on Biblical Scholarship
HvTSt	*Hervormde Teologiese Studies* (*HTS Teologiese Studies/HTS Theological Studies*)
IECOT	International Exegetical Commentary on the Old Testament
JAAR	*Journal of the American Academy of Religion*
JBL	*Journal of Biblical Literature*
JCS	*Journal of Cuneiform Studies*
JFSR	*Journal of Feminist Studies in Religion*
JNES	*Journal of Near Eastern Studies*
JSNT	*Journal for the Study of the New Testament*
JSOT	*Journal for the Study of the Old Testament*

JSOTSup	Journal for the Study of the Old Testament Supplement Series
LAI	Library of Ancient Israel
LHBOTS	Library of Hebrew Bible/Old Testament Studies
LPTh	Library of Philosophy and Theology
NAACP	National Association for the Advancement of Colored People
NEA	*Near Eastern Archaeology*
NITGC	New International Greek Testament Commentary
NTS	*New Testament Studies*
Or	*Orientalia*
OtSt	Oudtestamentische Studiën
PEQ	*Palestine Exploration Quarterly*
RenQ	*Renaissance Quarterly*
SemeiaSt	Semeia Studies
SHBC	Smyth & Helwys Bible Commentary
SHR	Studies in the History of Religions
SWBA	Social World of Biblical Antiquity
VT	*Vetus Testamentum*
ZAW	*Zeitschrift für die alttestamentliche Wissenschaft*

Introduction

STEPHANIE BUCKHANON CROWDER AND MARY F. FOSKETT

In *Moral Leadership: Integrity, Courage, and Imagination*, Robert Franklin defines integrity as centering down, courage as stepping forward, and imagination as dreaming up.[1] For decades scholars of African, African American, Asian, Asian American, Latino/a/x, and Native American heritage have employed their central core—their intellect, histories, and lived experience—as a means to live courageously and imagine greater in the Society of Biblical Literature. We each initially found ourselves as the only or one of a few minoritized scholars in a white, Eurocentric, male-dominated guild. Our efforts to push the academic metes and bounds and insist on the worthiness of scholarship rooted in social location, cultural identity, and contextual studies proved arduous. Yet, we persisted.

With this volume, the Society of Biblical Literature marks thirty years since the founding of the Committee on Underrepresented Racial and Ethnic Minorities in the Profession (CUREMP). According to the Society's website, CUREMP was "constituted to assess the status and encourage the participation of underrepresented racial and ethnic minorities in all professional areas of biblical studies."[2] In this light the committee seeks to advance the representation of racial and ethnic minorities in scholarly and biblical professions while focusing on areas of mentoring and networking.

The Committee first met in 1992, the same year the Status of Women in the Profession Committee was formed. Some of the early trailblazers and CUREMP founders include: Randall C. Bailey, Lydia Lebron-Rivera, Fernando F. Segovia, Henry T. C. Sun, Vincent L. Wimbush, and Gale A. Yee, to name a few. Wimbush would later serve as the first chair of CUREMP.

1. Robert Franklin, *Moral Leadership: Integrity, Courage, and Imagination* (New York: Orbis Books, 2020), 6.

2. https://www.sbl-site.org/SBLcommittees_CUREMP.aspx.

He, along with Segovia and Yee, were each elected to serve as president of the Society of Biblical Literature.

In 2019, an estimated 15 percent of the Society's more than 7,000 members self identified as African, African American, Asian, Asian American, Pacific Islander, Indigenous, Native American, or Latino/a/x.[3] These figures are significant for a Society founded in 1880 by an initial group of forty-five scholars, unsurprisingly all white, Protestant men working in the United States.[4] While there are areas for growth on its publishing boards, the Society's Council and various committees reflect elements of CUREMP's original intent and the Society's values of diversity, inclusivity, and equity. In 2023, the same year that Musa Dube served as president of Society of Biblical Literature, the Society called Steed Davidson as its first executive director from an underrepresented racial and ethnic minoritized group. Such is the thirty-year fruit of CUREMP.

The guild has come a long way, but still has miles to go. Both this Society and society writ large need scholars who will ashamedly marry who-ness with what-ness for the sake of justice, love, and mercy. This volume, *Remapping Biblical Studies*, not only honors the four presidents who have helped lead the intellectual community that CUREMP fosters; it also recognizes the longstanding prowess of the committee and all those who participate in and advance its work.

There are four pivot points to this volume highlighting the presidential addresses of CUREMP members. Each section opens with a presidential address, which is followed by reflections and essays noting personal points of engagement and/or challenge. The first section centers on the 2010 presidential address of Vincent L. Wimbush, "Interpreters—Enslaving/Enslaved/Runagage." Wimbush is the first African-American to have taken the helm of the Society. His address calls the guild to freedom to mine not just biblical texts but all interpretations of Scripture. Biblical scholars Gay L. Byron, Jacqueline M. Hidalgo, Velma E. Love, and Andrew Mbuvi offer thoughts on Wimbush's work while noting their own

3. This percentage is an estimate based only on members who completed their membership profile and indicated that the United States was the country of birth. The exact percentage is likely higher. See Society of Biblical Literature, "2019 SBL Membership Data," https://www.sbl-site.org/assets/pdfs/sblMemberProfile2019.pdf. A more recent report has yet to be published.

4. See Ernest Saunders, *Searching the Scriptures: A History of the Society of Biblical Litearture, 1880–1980*, BSNA 8 (Atlanta: Scholars Press, 1997).

relationship with Wimbush and journeys with CUREMP and the Society of Biblical Literature.

The second section opens with Fernando F. Segovia's 2014 president address, "Criticism in Critical Times: Reflections on Vision and Task." Segovia is the first person of Latino descent to lead the Society of Biblical Literature. His message on geopolitical contexts urges a pushing of the geographical borders for more inclusive scholarly engagement. Respondents Tat-siong Benny Liew, Yak-hwee Tan, Abraham Smith, and Ekaputra Tupamahu share their contextuality and connect to Segovia's clarion call for a *respons*ible approach to biblical studies from the Global South.

In honor of Brian K. Blount's 2018 presidential address, "The Souls of Biblical Folks and the Potential for Meaning," scholars note his call to a hermeneutics aligning with social locus. Contributors Gregory L. Cuéllar, Raj Nadella, and Angela N. Parker expound on the role of language and location and embodied interpretation in their research. Referencing Blount, together the scholars' work evidences the personal paths taken to interpretive means.

The final section of this volume is dedicated to Gale A. Yee's 2019 presidential address, "Thinking Intersectionally: Gender, Race, Class, and the Etceteras of Our Discipline." Yee is the first person of Asian descent to serve as the president of the Society of Biblical Literature. Recounting her narrative as a Chinese scholar, Yee highlights the significance of self and story in academic pursuits. Writers Leslie D. Callahan, Janette H. Ok, Ahida Calderón Pilarski, and Jin Young Choi reflect on the matters Yee addresses in relation to their own career paths and in light of the ongoing work that minoritized biblical scholars are pursuing.

There are synergistic themes in the four presidential addresses aligning with the purpose of CUREMP. Identity and intellectual pursuits must be correlates. How society works is worth the work of the Society. This volume seeks to capture such tenets. In various ways, minoritized scholars in Society of Biblical Literature have remapped biblical studies by asking new questions; by interrogating the field's presumptions, methods, and aims; and by making connections between biblical scholarship and the lived realities of marginalized communities.

We have and continue to center down, step forward, and dream up. It takes integrity, courage, and imagination to do this work. We honor those who have led and are leading the way, and we look forward to the work and the new readings, methods, and insights that lie ahead.

Bibliography

Franklin, Robert. *Moral Leadership: Integrity, Courage, and Imagination.* New York: Orbis Books, 2020.

Saunders, Ernest. *Searching the Scriptures: A History of the Society of Biblical Litearture, 1880–1980.* BSNA 8. Atlanta: Scholars Press, 1997.

Society of Biblical Literature. "2019 SBL Membership Data." https://www.sbl-site.org/assets/pdfs/sblMemberProfile2019.pdf.

Part 1
Signifying on Scripturalization

Interpreters—Enslaving/Enslaved/Runagate

VINCENT L. WIMBUSH

The colonial world is a Manichean world.
—Frantz Fanon, *The Wretched of the Earth*

Big Jim Todd was a slick black buck
Laying low in the mud and muck
Of Pondy Woods when the sun went down
In gold, and the buzzards tilted down
A windless vortex to the black-gum trees
To sit along the quiet boughs,
Devout and swollen, at their ease.
....
Past midnight, when the moccasin
Slipped from the log and, trailing in
Its obscured waters, broke
The dark algae, one lean bird spoke.
....
"Nigger, your breed ain't metaphysical."
The buzzard coughed. His words fell
In the darkness, mystic and ambrosial.

"But we maintain our ancient rite,
Eat the gods by day and prophesy by night.
We swing against the sky and wait;
You seize the hour, more passionate
Than strong, and strive with time to die—
With Time, the beak-ed tribe's astute ally.
....
Nigger, regard the circumstance of breath:
'Non omnis moriar,' the poet saith."
Pedantic, the bird clacked its gray beak,
With a Tennessee accent to the classic phrase;

> Jim understood, and was about to speak,
> But the buzzard drooped one wing and filmed the eyes.
> ....
>
> —Robert Penn Warren, "Pondy Woods"

> Negro folklore … [was] not … a new experience for me.… But it was fitting me like a tight chemise. I couldn't see it for wearing it. It was only when I was … away from my native surroundings, that I could see myself like somebody else and stand off and look at my garment.
>
> —Zora Neale Hurston, *Mules and Men*

I am not unaware that, on occasions such as this, references to the personal and even embodiment are quite rare. Yet I can hardly avoid transgressing in this and likely other regards before the end of this address. In spite of what may be the testimonies of my remaining parent and other elders, and notwithstanding the certifications the state may present, my beginnings are not here in this city in the sixth decade of the twentieth century. In respects more profound and disturbing and poignantly ramifying for professional interpreters, my beginnings should be understood to be in that more expansive period and fraught situations of the North Atlantic worlds between the fifteenth and nineteenth centuries, moments and situations in which "the West" and "the rest" were coming into fateful first contact. With such contact many social and political formations, sentiments and orientations of the West were (re)forged and (re)defined. *Contact* is, of course, studied euphemy, rhetorical repression meant to veil the violence and hegemony of the West's large-scale triangular Atlantic slave trading in dark peoples.

This is the time and situation of my beginning and the framework for the consciousness that I bring to this podium. And almost all of you have beginnings like my own. The dynamics of this period now still largely determine, even haunt, our sometimes different but also often common positionalities and orientations, practices and discourses, ideologies and politics and social formations. Included in the haunting are the profound shifts in the understandings of the self, including ideas about freedom and slavery of the self that mark the period.

Although differently named and tweaked from decade to decade since 1880, those practices and discourses that define this professional Society have always been and are even now still fully imbricated in the general politics and emergent discourses of the larger period to which I refer. And the cultivated obliviousness to or silence about—if not also the ideological reflection and validation of—the larger prevailing sociopolitical currents and dynamics marks the beginning and ongoing history of this Society (among other learned and professional societies, to be sure). With its fetishization of the rituals and games involving books and THE BOOK, its politics of feigning apolitical ideology, its still all too simple historicist agenda (masking in too many instances unacknowledged theological-apologetic interests), its commitment to "sticking to the text," its orientation in reality has always contributed to and reflected a participation in "sticking it" to the gendered and racialized Others. The fragility of the fiction of the apolitical big tent holding us together is all too evident in the still mind-numbingly general and vapid language we use to describe our varied practices and ideologies and orientations.

Of course, there have been challenges to the Society and its orientations in some periods of our history.[1] You know what they have been. And you will not be surprised if I suggest that the challenges have been too few and too tepid—and always belated. The fact that we cannot document the membership and participation of a single African American in this Society before the fifth decade of the twentieth century, the fact that the most recent history of the Society (in observance of the centennial)[2] does not even mention black folks, the fact that we cannot point to the official regularly scheduled gathering of two or three African Americans in discourse before the eighth decade of the last century, is shocking. Only with the initiatives of Thomas Hoyt Jr. and John W. Waters—which led to the *Stony the Road We Trod* discussion and book project in the late 1980s, which in turn led to the establishment of the first honestly ethnically marked program unit, which paved the way for all such units today—only with such initiatives do black peoples and other peoples of color appear in numbers to make a point at all about diversity in the Society. This is the period of my initiation and participation in the Society. This suggests much about the timing of someone of my tribe standing before you today. Perhaps, it could

---

1. I am thinking here of Robert W. Funk (Society of Biblical Literature president, 1975) and his colleagues in the 1960s and 1970s; and Elisabeth Schüssler Fiorenza (Society of Biblical Literature president, 1987) and colleagues in the 1980s. Their addresses can be found in Harold W. Attridge and James C. VanderKam, eds., *Presidential Voices: The Society of Biblical Literature in the Twentieth Century*, BSNA 22 (Atlanta: Society of Biblical Literature, 2006).

2. Ernest W. Saunders, *Searching the Scriptures: A History of the Society of Biblical Literature, 1880*–1980, BSNA 8 (Chico CA: Scholars Press, 1982).

not have been otherwise. I do not presume that such folk were between the 1880s and the 1980s always and everywhere barred from membership and participation in the meetings of the Society. I do not imagine the chairs of the Synoptic Gospels or the Prophetic Texts units standing at the doors yelling "Whites only!" There is no doubt about the sick views of some, but I think something deeper was and, perhaps, remains even today at issue: given the state of emergency in which they have lived (emergencies that would give Walter Benjamin pause), given the onset of the second slavery in the post–Civil War era when the industrial liberal North threw black folk under the wagon and the South embraced racial violence, the worst practices of Jim Crowism and economic peonage and slavery,[3] black membership in the decades past would have required the Society, in the vernacular of the folk, to "be talkin' 'bout something.'" Notwithstanding all the historical and some continuing stumbling blocks in the way, I suggest that the paucity of black membership is due ultimately not to the bad faith and manners of members of the Society in the past but to something more profound—the (unrecognized, unacknowledged) racialized discursive practices and politics that have defined it.

It is imperative that we recognize, even if belatedly, those few black pioneers of the decades before the initiatives of Hoyt and Waters—the likes of Leon Edward Wright (1912–1996), Charles B. Copher (1913–2003), G. Murray Branch (1914–2006), and Joseph A. Johnson (1914–1979).[4] We must inscribe them and a few others into our full organizational con-

---

3. See the riveting and unsettling book by Atlanta bureau chief of the *Wall Street Journal* Douglas A. Blackmon, *Slavery by Another Name: The Re-establishment of Black Americans from the Civil War to World War II* (New York: Doubleday, 2008). It provides irrefutable evidence of the perduring effects of slavery among black peoples into this century.

4. Leon Edward Wright, *Alterations in the Words of Jesus, as Quoted in the Literature of the Second Century*, Harvard Historical Monographs 25 (Cambridge: Harvard University Press, 1952), a revision of his PhD thesis, Harvard University, 1945; Charles B. Copher, "Isaiah's Philosophy of History" (PhD thesis, Boston University, 1947); Copher, *Black Biblical Studies: An Anthology of Charles B. Copher; Biblical and Theological Issues on the Black Presence in the Bible* (Chicago: Black Light Fellowship, 1993); R. C. Bailey and J. Grant, eds., *Recovery of Black Presence: An Interdisciplinary Exploration. Essays in Honor of Dr. Charles B. Copher* (Nashville: Abingdon, 1995); George Murray Branch, "Malachi: Prophet of Transition" (MA thesis, Drew University, 1946); Joseph A. Johnson, "Christianity and Atonement in the Fourth Gospel" (PhD thesis, Vanderbilt University, 1958).

sciousness and memory. These few are no longer with us; they have yet to be fully claimed and recognized. They struggled mightily to figure out how to speak to the challenges and pressures of the different worlds they intersected as black male intellectuals on the peripheries of the field. They were not always understood by members of their own tribes. They were severely limited in terms of professional appointments. Because so many parts of society and the academy accepted racial segregation as a given, simply the way things were and were supposed to be, they all worked in black institutions, mostly in Atlanta and Washington. And the Society did not recognize them and did little to support them or resist the polluted status quo. They must surely have exhausted themselves. They surely had stories to tell, lessons for our edification. And, of course, that our sisters of color, who faced even more layered intersecting stumbling blocks to their participation emerged at all only in the 1980s and are here among us in their numbers is tribute to their strength and commitment and further evidence of the Society's fraught and frayed history.

Now after having left home in that flatter sense of the term or, in Zora Neale Hurston's terms, having loosened the grip of that hyper-racialized garment I was made to wear, with growing awareness of what I gain from the pioneers listed above, and through engagement of that fraught period of contact as an intense excavation of consciousness, I stand before you this evening with yet another challenge, imploring the Society—and by extension, all critical interpreters—to start and to sustain "talkin' 'bout something.'" Here is the challenge plainly put: there can be no critical interpretation worthy of the name without coming to terms with the first contact—between the West and the rest, the West and the Others—and its perduring toxic and blinding effects and consequences. The challenge remains for this Society and all collectivities of critical interpreters in general to engage in persistent and protracted struggle, not symbolic or obfuscating games around methods and approaches, to come to terms with the construal of the modern ideologization of language, characterized by the meta-racism[5] that marks the relationship between Europeans and Euro-Americans and peoples of color, especially black peoples. What might it mean to address in explicit terms the nature and consequences of first contact for the unstable and fragile big tent that is our Society? What might it suggest for the ongoing widely differently prioritized and oriented

5. See Joel Kovel, *White Racism: A Psychohistory* (New York: Pantheon Books, 1970).

work we do in our widely different settings and contexts with our nonetheless still widely shared absolutist and elitist claims and presumptions about such work? It would make it imperative that we talk about discourse and power, slavery and freedom, life and death.

In addition to the persons quoted at the beginning of this address, I have given myself permission to conjure one of those booming haunting voices from an earlier moment and situation from the period of first contact, a voice belonging to one among those peoples heavily "signified," one of the "voices from within the veil."[6] Unlike Robert Penn Warren's Big Jim (referred to in his poem used as part of the epigraph above), Frederick Douglass speaks and writes his mind. In his first autobiographical work, his 1845 *Narrative of the Life of Frederick Douglass, an American Slave, Written by Himself*,[7] he looks back on an incident from his youthful years when he was a slave. The incident was seemingly a recurring one, but he makes the reader experience it as a singular, pointed one for narratological effect. It is an incident that Douglass, the recently escaped and young but emerging lion-voiced abolitionist, remembers and recounts for the (assumed) mostly white abolitionist-minded readers. What he touches upon and opens up in an astonishing display of romanticist and critical-reflexive communication are several issues that likely escaped the review of or were not (or could not be) fully understood by the Garrisonians, the abolitionist patron/izers of the young exslave. These were issues that still offer pointed challenge to all moderns, especially those interested and invested in thinking about something—about the enslaved, enslaved thinking, critical and free thinking and interpretation.

---

6. "Voices from within the Veil" is the subtitle of W. E. B. Du Bois's collection of essays entitled *Darkwater: Voices from within the Veil* (New York: Harcourt, Brace & Howe, 1920). The subtitle represents a theme that is taken up in his most famous work *The Souls of Black Folk: Essays and Sketches* (Chicago: McClurg, 1903). The essays in *Darkwater* are said to represent Du Bois's most mature, certainly some of his more sharp-edged, writings. See Manning Marable's introduction to the Dover Thrift Edition (Mineola, NY: Dover, 1996). For "signified," see Charles H. Long, *Significations: Signs, Symbols, and Images in the Interpretation of Religion* (Philadelphia: Fortress, 1986), 4.

7. Reprinted in William L. Andrews, ed., *The Oxford Frederick Douglass Reader* (New York: Oxford University Press, 1996). All subsequent references to Douglass's text, cited as *Narrative*, are from this edition.

> The slaves selected to go to the Great House Farm, for the monthly allowance for themselves and their fellow-slaves … would make the dense woods, for miles around, reverberate with their wild songs, revealing at once the highest joy and the deepest sadness. They would compose and sing as they went along, consulting neither time nor tune. The thought that came up, came out—if not in the word, in the sound; and—as frequently in the one as in the other. They would sometimes sing the most pathetic sentiment in the most rapturous tone, and the most rapturous sentiment in the most pathetic tone. Into all of their songs they would manage to weave something of the Great House Farm. Especially would they do this, when leaving home. They would then sing most exultingly … words which to many would seem unmeaning jargon, but which, nevertheless, were full of meaning to themselves. I did not, when a slave, understand the deep meaning of those rude and apparently incoherent songs. I was myself within the circle; so that I neither saw nor heard as those without might see and hear.[8]

In this recounting Douglass names many issues for consideration—subjectivity and consciousness, discourse and power, power and knowledge, knowledge and positionality, knowledge and the center, knowledge and centers. He names or at least assumes at least three different categories of persons or groups as different types of knowers or interpreters produced by that world of first contact—first, the slave singers, those who through their songs provide evidence that they have some knowledge and some agency of communication but are nonetheless not allowed to communicate their knowledge and sentiment beyond their own circle; second, those outside the circle (of the slaves), the world associated with the Great House Farm and all that it represents, those who if they hear the slave songs at all hear them only as jargon, as "mumbo jumbo";[9] and third, Douglass himself, the one who although technically at first "within the circle" (who as such did not/could not know), later, as reflected in his writerly self, outside the circle of slavery, begins to understand not only what the slaves felt and

8. Douglass, *Narrative*, 27–38.

9. This is the title of Ishmael Reed's most famous and challenging and sometimes unfathomable novel (New York: Scribner, 1972). For his purposes, Reed traced "mumbo jumbo" to Mandingo *ma-ma-gyo-mbo*, "magician who makes the troubled spirits go away" (7). This tracing suggests that which has meaning within a larger structure of meaning. Obviously, in the hyper-racialized West defining itself over against the black world, the works and discourses of such a magician would be translated as nonsense, so much jumbled mumbling.

communicated but also something more, something about communicating, knowing.

Using African slaves to think with, Douglass thinks in terms of "site" sanctioning "insight,"[10] that is, in terms of types of consciousness and interpreters who are differently positioned—the enslaving, the enslaved, and the runagate. These categories I submit—and I think Douglass thought—are not always totally mutually exclusive; they can be and in history have been complexly intertwined, yet there is justification for their isolation for the sake of analysis. There is no escape from the consequences set in motion by that contact that was turned into violent conquest for some and long-term subordination for the many others. Douglass's wrenching passage about the black slaves he knew and the types of interpreters and consciousness that could be identified with them challenges all interpreters to seek a way out, a way to run. His analysis begins—complexly, emotionally—with those whose very identity as human agents was questioned and denied; he begins with physical black enslavement as a way to the problematization of the "black (w)hole,"[11] to a profound understanding of the larger complex of slavery and freedom that defines and marks black peoples to be sure, but nearly all of us in more general terms. To the three categories of interpreters I briefly turn.

First, the enslaving. Those participating in and profiting from the structure of dominance generated by the Great House Farm were understood by Douglass to be oblivious to the plight of others. They are imagined to be those who, like Warren's buzzard, lifted their wings so as to avoid seeing and hearing the others. They were also characterized, according to Fanon, as those who had fallen prey to a Manichaean psychology and epistemics: the world was understood to be black and white, the latter signifying light and purity and life, the former dirt and pollution.[12] Of course, we now know more about what subtends such psychology and epistemics. Since

10. See Kimberly W. Benston, *Performing Blackness: Enactments of African-American Modernism* (New York: Routledge, 2000), 293.

11. For a fascinating exploration of this term and the phenomenon to which it points, see literary and cultural critic Houston A. Baker Jr. in *Blues, Ideology, and Afro-American Literature: A Vernacular Theory* (Chicago: University of Chicago Press, 1984), 155 and passim.

12. See this argument developed by Frantz Fanon in his *Wretched of the Earth*, trans. Constance Farrington (New York: Grove, 1968), 41. Also see the discussion in Abdul R. JanMohamed, "The Economy of Manichean Allegory: The Function of Racial Difference in Colonialist Literature," *Critical Inquiry* 12 (1985): 59–87.

Melville and other raging mad sensitive souls, we know now that it represents a horrific splitting of the self—into the blankness of whiteness and the foreboding threatening overdetermined markedness of blackness—and the hardened essentialization of the parts. The splitting is traumatic; it is not recognized or acknowledged; it is part of the phenomenon of the "hidden brain."[13] It results in, among other things, the meta-racist regime that pollutes all of us, infects our discourses, our work and play, including our philological games.

It was at work in Thomas Jefferson's convoluted denial of Phillis Wheatley's brilliant artistry;[14] in Georg W. F. Hegel's disavowal of the successful struggle of those black folk in Saint-Domingue-turned-Haiti against their enslavers and the meaning of such struggle as the backdrop for his own theorizing about the dialectics of struggle between master and slave and the further disavowal of the meaning of this struggle for universalism and the turn to modernity;[15] in John Locke's "purification of language" project, part of the "metadiscursive formation" aimed to deny the right to public speech to any one—women; serfs and slaves; subaristocrat whites—who could not speak properly.[16] It was at work when Tony Perkins, head of the evangelical and corporatist Family Research Council, declared on CNN in the heat of the last presidential election with great authority and without a whiff of qualification—much like Warren's buzzard—that the jeremiads of the urban black pastor named *Jeremiah* Wright against corporatist and

13. See the compelling development of this concept by Shankar Vedantam in *The Hidden Brain: How Our Unconscious Minds Elect Presidents, Control Markets, Wage Wars, and Save Our Lives* (New York: Spiegel & Grau, 2010).

14. Thomas Jefferson, *Notes on the State of Virginia*, ed. with introduction and notes by Frank Shuffelton (repr., New York: Penguin Books, 1999).

15. Susan Buck-Morss (*Hegel, Haiti and Universal History*, Illuminations [Pittsburgh: University of Pittsburgh Press, 2009]) and Sibylle Fischer (*Modernity Disavowed: Haiti and the Cultures of Slavery in the Age of Revolution* [Durham, NC: Duke University Press, 2004]), advance compelling arguments concerning Hegel's denial of the universal implication in the Haitians' struggle to be free and to establish the first modern society with aspirations to universal nonracialized freedoms.

16. For general historical cultural background, focusing mainly on Britain, see Olivia Smith, *The Politics of Language, 1791–1819* (Oxford: Clarendon, 1984). For a discussion of John Locke and the dramatic ensuing consequences in many domains and contexts in the twenty-first century in the United States, see Richard Bauman and Charles L. Briggs, *Voices of Modernity: Language Ideologies and the Politics of Inequality*, Studies in the Social and Cultural Foundations of Language 21 (Cambridge: Cambridge University Press, 2003).

racializing/racist "America" were simply "unscriptural."[17] Can we doubt that Perkins's utterance comes out of the still regnant Manichaean world? Is it hard to see that in Perkins's mind—buried far in that hidden brain where meta-racism thrives—there is an assumption that he and his tribesmen own the Bible and that they are invested with all rights and privileges appertaining thereto, meaning control of the discourses about the Bible? Who cannot see that behind his outburst were exegetical arguments, no doubt legitimized by the scholarship of our membership, that conjure the ancient Near Eastern world as a white world in seamless historical development with the modern white world?

These and other such examples of disavowals and tortured silences and twisted arguments and declarations reflect the pollution and veiling of the humanity and consciousness that is the Manichaean psychology and epistemics, infecting all peoples.[18] It is arguable that it is no longer possible for those who are subject to such a construction or regime to argue freely what they see, think, or feel. Having to make black always signify the same thing—always signify the negative—represents a tremendous psychosocial and intellectual commitment and burden.[19]

This mentality of denial and disavowal, the most trenchant reflection of the Manichaean psychology, has been powerfully imaged in the frontispiece to Jesuit scholar Joseph-François Lafitau's 1724 multivolume work *Moeurs des sauvages Ameriquains comparées aux moeurs des premiers temps.*[20]

Following Michel de Certeau's interpretive glosses,[21] we see the racialized and gendered but otherwise unmarked writer/inscriber/historian of the world and interpreter of events and truth. She is complexly situated—in relationship to the anthropomorphized Father time and death. She writes within and for the larger framework that is Europe ascendant. But she must

17. See http://www.cnn.com/TRANSCRIPTS/0803/14/acd.02.html.

18. See Camara Jules P. Harrell, *Manichean Psychology: Racism and the Minds of People of African Descent* (Washington, DC: Howard University Press, 1999), for discussion of the way black peoples have been infected.

19. On this point, see Christopher L. Miller, *Blank Darkness: Africanist Discourse in French* (Chicago: University of Chicago Press, 1985), 246.

20. Joseph-François Lafitau, *Moeurs des sauvages Ameriquains comparées aux moeurs des premiers temps* (Paris: Saugrain l'aine et Charles Etienne Hochereau, 1724).

21. See Michel de Certeau, "Writing vs. Time: History and Anthropology in the Works of Lafitau," in *Rethinking History: Time, Myth, and Writing*, ed. Marie-Rose Logan and John Frederick Logan, Yale French Studies 59 (New Haven: Yale University Press, 1980), 37–64.

Frontispiece to the 1724 edition of Joseph-François Lafitau, *Moeurs de sauvages Ameriquains comparées aux moeurs de premiers temps.* Engraving signed by I. B. Scotin. Bibliothèque nationale de France. https://tinyurl.com/SBL1130j.

write in order to clarify in light of the contact with the Others and the changes in the world how now things must mean. She writes about the truth as Europeans must see it, tell it, know it. So notice along the bottom of the image the objects, trinkets, fetishes, representing the Others. The history, the truth that is to be told about these "savages" and "primitives" must now be told in the terms of the method of bricolage—assembling, choosing this and that part, this or that thing, from this or that world of savagery, in order to place the Others within the canonical framework that reflects Manichaean psychology and epistemics. The "savage" is assumed not to be able to communicate, at least, not in purified language, so deserves no hearing, demands no respectful gaze. But Europeans can and should inscribe the Other into reality and interpret and interpellate them.

Who enslaves whom? Douglass implied that those far outside the circle—those in some respect participating in the ways of the Great House Farm, those who, like the woman in Lafitau's frontispiece representing Euro-America or the West writing up the Rest—can hardly see or hear, much less understand, the Rest represented by the slaves. Like the poignantly named Nehemiah who "writes up" Dessa in Sherley Williams's *Dessa Rose*, the writer makes up a truth, like "science," a writing that represents a kind of violence done to her body.[22] The woman who is Euro-America who writes up the savages actually does not even look at the objects and symbols assumed to represent them. Her gaze redefines what it means to see straight.

Second, the enslaved. Their situation was not romanticized by Douglass, at least not without some resistance or qualification. In his view, they were denied any but overdetermined identification with and participation in the world that was represented by the Great House Farm. They were denied the main currents of communication and social exchange. They were considered chattel, and so it was assumed that they were unable to think, to communicate, except in the way of the "swinish multitude."[23] They

---

22. Sherley Williams, *Dessa Rose* (New York: Morrow, 1982). See Michel de Certeau, *The Practice of Everyday Life*, trans. Steven Rendall (Berkeley: University of California, 2002), part 4, ch. 10.

23. The language of Edmund Burke, found in his *Reflections on the Revolution in France, And on the Proceedings in Certain Societies in London Relative to That Event; In a Letter Intended to Have Been Sent to a Gentleman in Paris* (London: J. Dodsley, 1790). It provoked much reaction in England and beyond. See also Smith, *Politics of Language*, ch. 3.

were presumed not to be able to read and write—at least, not in canonical/cosmopolitan European languages or modes.[24]

Douglass knew that the black enslaved could make meaning or make things mean, but not beyond their small and rigidly contained circle. Outside their circle they experienced little or no intersubjectivity, which provokes what might be thought of as the "anxiety of ethnicity."[25] This phenomenon was understood to be one of the most important meanings and consequences of enslavement.[26] Slaves' communication was reduced to an "anti-language,"[27] unrecognized and unacknowledged by others. This is what Douglass called "unmeaning jargon." They were rendered silent and invisible. Ralph Ellison's character in *Invisible Man* put the phenomenon in riveting terms:

> I am invisible ... simply because people refuse to see me. Like the bodiless heads you see sometimes in circus sideshows, it is as though I have been surrounded by mirrors of hard, distorting glass.... They see only my surroundings, themselves, or figments of their imagination—indeed, everything and anything except me.[28]

The evidence of the silencing and rendering invisible the presence of the black Atlantic and contributions is everywhere to be seen. Consider Rebecca Protten, an eighteenth-century pioneer Moravian missionary and evangelist and founder of one of the first African American Protestant congregations

---

24. On this matter of canonical or conventional discourses, see Grey Gundaker, *Signs of Diaspora, Diaspora of Signs: Literacies, Creolization, and Vernacular Practice in African America* (New York: Oxford University Press, 1998). On more conventional history of conventional literacy among blacks, see Janet Duitsman Cornelius, *"When I Can Read My Title Clear": Literacy, Slavery, and Religion in the Antebellum South* (Columbia: University of South Carolina Press, 1992).

25. So David Van Leer, "Reading Slavery: The Anxiety of Ethnicity in Douglass's Narrative," in *Frederick Douglass: New Literary and Historical Essays*, ed. Eric J. Sundquist (New York: Cambridge University Press, 1990), 129.

26. See Orlando Patterson's works on slavery and freedom: *Freedom* (New York: Basic Books, 1991); Patterson, *Slavery and Social Death: A Comparative Study* (Cambridge: Harvard University Press, 1982); Patterson, *Rituals of Blood: Consequences of Slavery in Two American Centuries* (Washington, DC: Civitas, 1998), among others.

27. Ann M. Kibbey and Michele Stepto, "The Anti-Language of Slavery: Frederick Douglass's 1845 *Narrative*," in *Critical Essays on Frederick Douglass*, ed. William L. Andrews (Boston: Hall, 1991), 166–91.

28. Ralph Ellison, *Invisible Man*, 2nd ed. (New York: Vintage, 1995), 3.

in the North Atlantic world.[29] The establishment politics of "church" / "religious" history has contributed to her being largely forgotten. Note the woman known as "sister Francis" or as the "Blackymore maide." Her well-known charismatic leadership in the establishment of the seventeenth-century radical Protestant formation that became the establishment Church of Christ in Broadmead, later Broadmead Baptist Church, Bristol, England, was erased by Edward Terrill's establishmentarian revisionist history. Her leadership was reduced to overdetermined categories—of appellation and sentimentality. She was by exegetical sleight of hand erased out of her rightful place in history, as founding figure—and then flattened into a black pious maid.[30]

And Douglass's own situation as writer is worth mentioning. The abolitionist William Lloyd Garrison provided the preface to Douglass's 1845 *Narrative*. Whatever may be said about the substantive comments made in it, it is clear that this preface functioned primarily to translate Douglass, that is, to provide the metacommentary for all that is to follow. This is an example of enslavement as a kind of "framework."[31] A discerning reader can determine whether Garrison ever really understood Douglass's text. Douglass later severed ties with Garrison and the Garrisonians. He came to understand how slavery could continue to work—way up North—as discursive framing.

Perhaps, the most famous description, if not the final analysis, of the phenomenon of the enslaved as the framed is found in W. E. B. Du Bois's works. In his famous *Souls of Black Folk*, the Manichaean world, the world structured around what he termed the *veil*, is defined by racial division and alienation and ignorance that affects all: "there is almost no community of intellectual life or point of transference where the thoughts and feelings of one race can come into direct con- tact and sympathy with the thoughts and feelings of the other."[32]

---

29. See Jon F. Sensbach, *Rebecca's Revival: Creating Black Christianity in the Atlantic World* (Cambridge: Harvard University Press, 2005).

30. See Edward Terrill, *The Records of a Church of Christ in Bristol, 1640–1687* (Bristol Record Society, 1974). For historical-interpretive context, see Peter Linebaugh and Marcus Rediker, *The Many-Headed Hydra: Sailors, Slaves, Commoners, and the Hidden History of the Revolutionary Atlantic* (Boston: Beacon, 2000), ch. 3.

31. On Garrison's persistent liberal-abolitionist paternalism in relationship to Douglass, see Houston A. Baker Jr., *The Journey Back: Issues in Black Literature and Criticism* (Chicago: University of Chicago Press, 1984), 148–49.

32. From "IX. Of the Sons of Master and Man" in *Souls of Black Folk*, reprinted in *The Norton Anthology of African American Literature*, ed. Henry Louis Gates Jr. and Nellie Y. McKay (New York: Norton, 1997), 700.

As Douglass looks back to the Great House Farm, he does not romanticize the situation of the slaves. He indicates that he has come to understand that the chief dilemma that slaves faced was not the physical domination, as demeaning as it was, but the not being seen, not being heard, not being understood, not being communicated with in broad terms befitting the dignity of humanity, not being able to communicate the complexity of sentiments and feelings, and being cut off from everything—except, ironically, the Great House Farm. Enslavement meant being able to sing, perhaps, but only within the Manichaean-prescribed circle in which black was overdetermined as, among other things, unmeaning jargon. This was for Douglass intolerable. He would escape it.

Third, runagate. The term is an alternate form of "renegate," from Middle Latin *renegatus*, meaning "fugitive" or "runaway." It has come to carry the meaning of a more transgressive act than mere flight. It is marronage, running away with an attitude and a plan, a taking flight—in body, but even more importantly in terms of consciousness.[33] We know that Douglass literally runs away from enslavement. It is as a runagate that he writes his first autobiography. And in this part of the story about the slaves on their way to the Great House Farm, Douglass distinguishes himself from the others who are slaves. He seems to experience being in and out of solidarity with and consciousness about them. He knows them, but he is also alien to them. That he once occupied a similar psychic position with them but now assumes a different position is excruciatingly painful for him. He registers acute anxiety experienced over the need to step outside the circle, outside the framed experience, the framed consciousness that is slavery. It is a scary place. It is psychosocial and discursive marronage. He is a runagate *before* he runs away.

33. See Jean Fouchard, *The Haitian Maroons: Liberty or Death*, trans. A Faulkner Watts (New York: Edward Blyden, 1981); Alvin O. Thompson, *Flight to Freedom: African Runaways and Maroons in the Americas* (Kingston, Jamaica: University of West Indies Press, 2006); Hugo Prosper Learning, *Hidden Americans: Maroons of Virginia and the Carolinas*, Studies in African American History and Culture (New York: Garland, 1995); Mavis Christin Campbell, *The Maroons of Jamaica, 1655–1796: A History of Resistance, Collaboration and Betrayal* (Granby, MA: Bergin & Garvey, 1988); and Richard Price, ed., *Maroon Societies: Rebel Slave Communities in the Americas*, 3rd ed. (Baltimore: Johns Hopkins University Press, 1996). See also Houston A. Baker Jr.'s recontextualization arguments in *Modernism and the Harlem Renaissance* (Chicago: University of Chicago Press, 1987), 71–82.

There is a long history of this phenomenon of the runagate—long before and long after Douglass—among the people who have become and whom we now call African Americans. The runagate not only involved heroic individuals such as Douglass but everyday collective folk who showed themselves to be a people on the run, a marooned people, a people intent on migrating from deserts and fields of enslavement to other psychic places, with high purpose. Taking flight, running away, in the several different respects of meaning and experience, was the watchword. It brought some of my relatives to this city and took some others into other parts of the country. That other philosopher called Locke (as in Alain) in his 1925 edited volume *The New Negro: Voices of the Harlem Renaissance* vividly captured the impetus and drama of one of the waves of migration in the twentieth century:

> The wash and rush of this human tide … is to be explained primarily in terms of a new vision of opportunity, of social and economic freedom, of a spirit to seize, even in the face of an extortionate and heavy toll.… With each successive wave of it, the movement of the Negro becomes more and more a mass movement toward the larger and the more democratic chance … a deliberate flight not only from the countryside to city, but from medieval America to modern.[34]

The critical sign of Douglass having already become runagate before reaching the North is his acquisition and critical use of thinking about literacy. Learning to read had to do with more than learning the letters, having been given the "inch," as he called it. No, his reading involved taking the "ell," involving a much more complex phenomenon with profound consequences, including those and more that were feared by the masters. Douglass's command of the text is like Maurice Blanchot's notion of reading as reading past the text to something more or other, a reading of the self—a historicized collective self.[35] This self that Douglass began to read seems to be the result of a splitting of a different sort from, but with great implications and ramifications for, the engagement of the Manichaean psychology.

34. Alain Locke, ed., *The New Negro: Voices of the Harlem Renaissance* (repr., New York: Touchstone, 1999), 6.

35. See Michael Holland, ed., *The Blanchot Reader* (London: Blackwell, 1995), especially on the concept of "the work."

Du Bois continues to provide perspective. His references in *Souls of Black Folk* to the term *veil* as a metaphor to name the nature of the construction of the Manichaean world and his understanding of the consequences and impact of such include that most famous remark—"a peculiar sensation ... double-consciousness, this sense of always looking at one's self through the eyes of the others."[36] This remark is generally assumed to apply simply and universally to all black peoples in the United States. This interpretation is questionable as applied to *Souls of Black Folk*: in the latter he was focused on explaining (to a mixed readership) those black folks who were physically and increasingly psychically removed from the world of the Great House Farm and were now facing the negotiation of larger miscegenated worlds and consciousness. Du Bois understood that for such persons—like himself and like Douglass outside the circle—what was experienced most acutely is a splitting, an acute self-alienation, dissociation. This was what he termed existence behind the "Veil of Color."[37] Douglass's miscegenated and alienated consciousness led him to wage battle. It was the fight with Covey the infamous "nigger-breaker" that sharply reflected Douglass's struggle with alienation and anxiety. Douglass understood the fight with Covey to be more than physical contact. In Covey, Douglass comes face to face, so to speak, with the more tangible manifestations of meta-racism—the slave system and its imbrication of Christian ideology. But it also occasioned opportunity for Douglass to represent his confrontation with the world of the slave, more specifically, African traditions, in the form of Sandy the root doctor. Like Jacob's wrestling with the angel, Douglass fights an existential battle: he fights against aspects of himself that have been forced to split on account of Manichaean meta-racism; he fights the white side of himself represented by Covey and his absent father, which derides and demeans and

36. Du Bois, *Souls of Black Folks*, in Gates and McKay, *Norton Anthology of African American Literature*, 615.

37. Of course, the debate about what this means or when and how this was experienced and what should be the response to it rages on. Although it was not Du Bois's proposed analysis of or proposed solution to the problem, many critics of black existence have argued that enslavement has meant above all alienation to the point of the loss of a ("sense of") past and that only the future remained as basis for organization and orientation. For informative discussion, see Frank M. Kirkland, "Modernity and Intellectual Life in Black," *Philosophical Forum* 24 (1992–1993): 136–65; and Orlando Patterson, "Toward a Future That Has No Past: Reflections on the Fate of Blacks in the Americas," *Public Interest* 27 (1972): 25–62.

denies him and his blackness; and he fights the black side of himself, represented by Sandy, with his limited agency and communication skills and timidity if not also perfidy. He shows himself to be conscious of the tightly coiled constructedness of both worlds. In the end, his fight results in his becoming a subjectivity that was miscegenated, not merely a blending in literal/ physical terms, but an independent self that is unstable, fluid, protean, embattled, split from the violent framing.

It was this splitting and the anxiety over it that Du Bois considered a paradox, an opportunity and a gift to the black subjects and through them to the world. The forced splitting provides opportunity for cultivation of heightened critical consciousness: "Once in a while," he indicated, noting that the phenomenon was not guaranteed but had to be cultivated and exploited, "through all of us"—that is, those forced behind the veil, that "thick sheet of invisible … horribly tangible plate glass" limning "a dark cave" within which black folks are "entombed souls … hindered in their natural movement, expression, and development"[38]—"there flashes some clairvoyance, some clear idea, of what America really is. We who are dark can see America in a way that America can not."[39] In learning to read—not merely texts but texture and the world, including what Covey represented in the world and in the same larger scene, what Sandy represented in the world—Douglass had escaped. He had escaped from the cave, from the tight circle.

What might these arguments and perspectives mean for this Society? How could its discourses and practices not be fully implicated in and reflective of the Manichaean ideology and epistemics? In what respect is its epistemics different from that of Tony Perkins or Thomas Jefferson? How can the ever more sophisticated methods and approaches of the operations of its diverse members focused on a single text tradition or, at most, two complexly related text traditions, avoid functioning as apologetics—for the nation or empire and satellite orders? How can the Society avoid making and keeping the Scriptures and all characters in them white

38. See Du Bois's mature, somewhat autobiographical work *Dusk of Dawn: An Essay Toward an Autobiography of a Race Concept* (New York: Schocken Books, 1968), 130–31; see esp. ch. 5, "The Concept of Race." For larger historical and political-discursive context, see Thomas C. Holt, "Political Uses of Alienation: W. E. B. Du Bois on Politics, Race, and Culture, 1903–1940," *American Quarterly* 42 (1990): 308–9.

39. W. E. B. Du Bois, "Criteria of Negro Art," *Crisis* 32 (1926): 290–97. Printed in Gates and McKay, *Norton Anthology of African American Literature*, 753.

like Ahab's whale, like Perkins's white Euro-American Protestant/Catholic ancient Near Eastern world?

Douglass hints at a way out. His reflection on his own life story continues to be instructive. He argues that the critical interpreter must seek to escape, must run, must be oriented outside the circle. His own experience as a Scripture-reader is a direct challenge to us. Before he escaped he started a secret seminary/religious studies program—a "Sabbath school"—for groups of slaves from various plantations. Douglass indicated—in somewhat veiled terms—that his motive had to do with more than teaching letters—"We were trying to learn how to read the will of God," that is, read life and death, slavery and freedom. He helped establish a safe zone within which the students could learn, think for and talk among themselves apart from the slavers. In direct opposition to the expectations and interests of the masters and as a practice reflecting "mimetic excess,"[40] this Scripture-reading practice reflected self-reflexivity, a heightened consciousness of imitation of the other—with a difference. He knew that the reading of the Scriptures was hardly ever mere reading about the ancient Near East, about the life and times of Jesus or the prophets, that the reading of Scriptures in the modern world was a reading of the world as constructed by the splitting that made black signify in an ever tighter circle of reference. So having psychosocially positioned himself outside the circle of the world of slave culture and outside the Great House Farm, Douglass positioned himself to read—and help others read—the world as it had been and might be ordered. He was a runagate.

Can the members of this Society claim such consciousness? Douglass was not so much reading Scriptures as he was signifying on scripturalization, on the regime that creates and enforces uses of Scriptures for the sake of domination. Like Kafka's ape ape-ing high-minded humans,[41] he showed his thinking about thinking. He showed his understanding of the political constructedness of Scripture-reading and that such reading ought to result in talking and thinking about life and death, slavery and freedom. Surely, here is a challenge to a different critical orientation—an orientation to Scripture study as part of the human sciences with investment in critical histories that aim to make sense of what subtends the practices, the forms of expressivity, the relations of discourse and power.

---

40. Michael Taussig, *Mimesis and Alterity: A Particular History of the Senses* (New York: Routledge, 1993), 233, 246, 249, 252–55.

41. Taussig, *Mimesis and Alterity*, xiv, xvii, 254–55.

It makes sense, according to Du Bois, with all the pain and trauma involved, for the black self to want to run, to let go: there is no advantage, no life, in not running. Such sentiment and conviction regarding the relationship between alienation and freedom was powerfully expressed by Richard Wright: "I have no race except that which is forced upon me. I have no country except that to which I'm obliged to belong. I have no traditions. I'm free. I have only the future."[42]

But the impetus to run away, to let go, is not very strong for those strongly positioned within or benefitting from the Manichaean order. Such hidden-brain fundamentalism around which the Euro-American world is built is so deeply buried, so tightly coiled, so persistent, that nothing less than shock can dislodge it. Although a renegade member of a different academic professional society, Michael Taussig makes of himself a poignant and painful example and lesson for consideration of members of this Society. He accepts himself as a white man from the world of the Great House Farm who looks and listens to the other as the other constructs and projects an image of the white man. Note his reaction to such an image created by those associated with the Mabari shrine in Nigeria:

> He frightens me, this African white man. He unsettles. He makes me wonder without end. Was the world historical power of whiteness achieved through its being a sacred as well as profane power? It makes me wonder about the constitution of whiteness as global colonial work and also as a minutely psychic one involving psychic powers invisible to my senses but all too obvious, as reflected to me, now, by this strange artifact.... It is ... the ... West now face to face with its-self ... the white man ... facing himself.... Such face-to-faceness no doubt brings its quotient of self-congratulation. "They think we are gods." But being a god is okay as long as it isn't excessive. After all, who knows—in imagining us as gods, might they not take our power?[43]

Douglass's insurgent seminary sessions and Taussig's training in an African school of arts and social criticism suggest for the Society the imperative of seeing Scripture-reading as part of mimetic systems. The critic should see his or her own critical practices as part of such systems

---

42. Richard Wright, *Pagan Spain* (repr., New York: Harper, 2008), 21.

43. Taussig, *Mimesis and Alterity*, 237–38. Image originally from Julia Blackburn, *The White Men: The First Responses of Aboriginal Peoples to the White Man* (London: Orbis Books; New York: New York Times Books, 1979).

Mabari shrine in Nigeria. Photograph: Herbert M. Cole, 1966.

and remain open to influences toward greater self-reflexivity and the destabilization and vacancy of identity.

How could the Society not be so oriented in the twenty-first century? How can we be students of Scriptures in this century at this moment without making our agenda a radically humanistic science or art, excavating human politics, discourse, performances, power relations, the mimetic systems of knowing we may call scripturalization? How can we remain a Society *only* of *Biblical* Literature and not of comparative Scriptures? How can we in this big international tent in this century of globalization not include as our focus the problematics of Scriptures of all the other major social-cultural systems of the world as well the older dynamic systems of scripturalizing of the so-called smaller societies? How exciting and compelling and renegade would be a Society of interpreters that excavates all representations of Scriptures in terms of discourse and power!

Such orientation requires letting go—of unmarked or blank whiteness and of forced essential blackness. It means running away from all—the white text, the black essential—that has sought for several centuries to bind us. Clearly, the claim need not be made that only African America shows the way out. But African America certainly offers the gift of challenge, the model of the imperative of running for life to a zone of discursive and ideological marronage. On account of forced placement in a zone of nonsubjectivity, this tribe, after all, has given birth to artists/poets/shamans/diviners who model the runagate and challenge us to imitate them. They show us the way of the double-sighted, the way of those who know that knowing requires occupying a zone where there is "constantly shifting authorial consciousness" and the "piercing" of "cultural authority,"[44] a site on which radical translation and transformation are always to be worked on, a site where according to Ralph Ellison "black is and black a'int," because "black can make you and unmake you."[45] It means letting go of closed systems of cultural authority and of claims to be overseers of texts. Those folk who have been placed behind the veil challenge all of us to run, in fact to run continuously from the cave into the zone of marronage.

In his poem "Runagate, Runagate," Robert Hayden has woven together perhaps the classic expressions and images of the black cultural sentiments regarding the runagate:[46]

I.
Runs falls rises stumbles on from darkness into darkness
and the darkness thicketed with shapes of terror
and the hunters pursuing and the hounds pursuing
and the night cold and the night long and the river
to cross and the jack-muh-lanterns beckoning beckoning
and blackness ahead and when shall I reach that somewhere
morning and keep on going and never turn back and keep on going
    Runagate
        Runagate
            Runagate
....

II.
....
Wanted   Harriet Tubman   alias The General
alias Moses   Stealer of Slaves

44. Benston, *Performing Blackness*, 292, 294.

45. Ellison, *Invisible Man*, 9–10.

46. Robert Hayden, "Runagate, Runagate," in Gates and McKay, *The Norton Anthology of African American Literature*, 1506–8.

In league with Garrison   Alcott Emerson
Garrett   Douglas   Thoreau   John Brown

Armed and known to be Dangerous

Wanted   Reward   Dead or Alive

....

Come ride-a my train
Oh that train, ghost-story train
through swamp and savanna movering movering,
over trestles of dew, through caves of the wish,
Midnight Special on a sabre track movering movering,
....

Come ride-a my train
    Mean mean mean to be free

The folk who are dark challenge us to run—away from the feigned solid canonical self, onto "the ghost-story train," into a "disrupting blackness,"[47] down into what Howard Thurman called a "luminous darkness"[48] where the process of the hard work of self-criticism can take place. They also warn us that ultimately there is no other way out. That must have been what the song-poets meant when they crafted and sang:

[It's] so high, you can't get over [it],
[It's] so low, you can't get under [it],
So round, you can't get around [it],
You must go right through the door.

We may not, need not, all "talk that talk" or "talk like dat," but we all, for the sake of being a compelling force as a learned society—focused on the ultimate problematics of discourse and power—must start and sus-

47. Toni Morrison, *Playing in the Dark: Whiteness and the Literary Imagination*, William E. Massey Sr. Lectures in the History of American Civilization (Cambridge: Harvard University Press, 1992), 91.

48. See Howard Thurman, *The Luminous Darkness: A Personal Interpretation of the Anatomy of Segregation and the Ground of Hope* (repr., Richmond, IN: Friends United Press, 1999).

tain "talkin' about somethin'"—about slavery and freedom, about life and death.

Bibliography

Andrews, William L., ed. *The Oxford Frederick Douglass Reader.* New York: Oxford University Press, 1996.

Attridge, Harold W., and James C. VanderKam, eds. *Presidential Voices: The Society of Biblical Literature in the Twentieth Century.* BSNA 22. Atlanta: Society of Biblical Literature, 2006.

Bailey, R. C., and J. Grant, eds. *Recovery of Black Presence: An Interdisciplinary Exploration. Essays in Honor of Dr. Charles B. Copher.* Nashville: Abingdon, 1995.

Baker, Houston A., Jr. *Blues, Ideology, and Afro-American Literature: A Vernacular Theory.* Chicago: University of Chicago Press, 1984.

———. *The Journey Back: Issues in Black Literature and Criticism.* Chicago: University of Chicago Press, 1984.

———. *Modernism and the Harlem Renaissance.* Chicago: University of Chicago Press, 1987.

Bauman, Richard, and Charles L. Briggs. *Voices of Modernity: Language Ideologies and the Politics of Inequality.* Studies in the Social and Cultural Foundations of Language 21. Cambridge: Cambridge University Press, 2003.

Benston, Kimberly W. *Performing Blackness: Enactments of African-American Modernism.* New York: Routledge, 2000.

Blackburn, Julia. *The White Men: The First Responses of Aboriginal Peoples to the White Man.* London: Orbis Books; New York: New York Times Books, 1979.

Blackmon, Douglas A. *Slavery by Another Name: The Re-establishment of Black Americans from the Civil War to World War II.* New York: Doubleday, 2008.

Branch, George Murray. "Malachi: Prophet of Transition." MA thesis, Drew University, 1946.

Buck-Morss, Susan. *Hegel, Haiti and Universal History.* Illuminations. Pittsburgh: University of Pittsburgh Press, 2009.

Burke, Edmund. *Reflections on the Revolution in France, And on the Proceedings in Certain Societies in London Relative to That Event; In a*

Letter Intended to Have Been Sent to a Gentleman in Paris. London: J. Dodsley, 1790.

Campbell, Mavis Christin. *The Maroons of Jamaica, 1655–1796: A History of Resistance, Collaboration and Betrayal*. Granby, MA: Bergin & Garvey, 1988.

Certeau, Michel de. *The Practice of Everyday Life*. Translation by Steven Rendall. Berkeley: University of California, 2002.

———. "Writing vs. Time: History and Anthropology in the Works of Lafitau." Pages 37–64 in *Rethinking History: Time, Myth, and Writing*. Edited by Marie-Rose Logan and John Frederick Logan. Yale French Studies 59. New Haven: Yale University Press, 1980.

Copher, Charles B. *Black Biblical Studies: An Anthology of Charles B. Copher; Biblical and Theological Issues on the Black Presence in the Bible*. Chicago: Black Light Fellowship, 1993.

———. "Isaiah's Philosophy of History." PhD thesis, Boston University, 1947.

Cornelius, Janet Duitsman. *"When I Can Read My Title Clear": Literacy, Slavery, and Religion in the Antebellum South*. Columbia: University of South Carolina Press, 1992.

Du Bois, W. E. B. "Criteria of Negro Art." *Crisis* 32 (1926): 290–97.

———. *Darkwater: Voices from the Veil*. New York: Harcourt, Brace & Howe, 1920.

———. *Dusk of Dawn: An Essay Toward an Autobiography of a Race Concept*. New York: Schocken Books, 1968.

———. *The Souls of Black Folk: Essays and Sketches*. Chicago: McClurg, 1903.

Ellison, Ralph. *Invisible Man*. 2nd ed. New York: Vintage, 1995.

Fanon, Frantz. *Wretched of the Earth*. Translated by Constance Farrington. New York: Grove, 1968.

Fischer, Sibylle. *Modernity Disavowed: Haiti and the Cultures of Slavery in the Age of Revolution*. Durham, NC: Duke University Press, 2004.

Fouchard, Jean. *The Haitian Maroons: Liberty or Death*. Translated by A Faulkner Watts. New York: Edward Blyden, 1981.

Gates, Henry Louis, Jr., and Nellie Y. McKay, eds. *The Norton Anthology of African American Literature*. New York: Norton, 1997.

Gundaker, Grey. *Signs of Diaspora, Diaspora of Signs: Literacies, Creolization, and Vernacular Practice in African America*. New York: Oxford University Press, 1998.

Harrell, Camara Jules P. *Manichean Psychology: Racism and the Minds of People of African Descent*. Washington, DC: Howard University Press, 1999.

Holland, Michael, ed. *The Blanchot Reader*. London: Blackwell, 1995.

Holt, Thomas C. "Political Uses of Alienation: W. E. B. Du Bois on Politics, Race, and Culture, 1903–1940." *American Quarterly* 42 (1990): 308–9.

JanMohamed, Abdul R. "The Economy of Manichean Allegory: The Function of Racial Difference in Colonialist Literature." *Critical Inquiry* 12 (1985): 59–87.

Jefferson, Thomas. *Notes on the State of Virginia*. Edited with introduction and notes by Frank Shuffelton. Repr. New York: Penguin Books, 1999.

Johnson, Joseph A. "Christianity and Atonement in the Fourth Gospel." PhD thesis, Vanderbilt University, 1958.

Kibbey, Ann M., and Michele Stepto. "The Anti-Language of Slavery: Frederick Douglass's 1845 *Narrative*." Pages 166–91 in *Critical Essays on Frederick Douglass*. Edited by William L. Andrews. Boston: Hall, 1991.

Kirkland, Frank M. "Modernity and Intellectual Life in Black." *Philosophical Forum* 24 (1992–1993): 136–65.

Kovel, Joel. *White Racism: A Psychohistory*. New York: Pantheon Books, 1970.

Lafitau, Joseph-François. *Moeurs des sauvages Ameriquains comparées aux moeurs des premiers temps*. Paris: Saugrain l'aine et Charles Etienne Hochereau, 1724.

Learning, Hugo Prosper. *Hidden Americans: Maroons of Virginia and the Carolinas*. Studies in African American History and Culture. New York: Garland, 1995.

Linebaugh, Peter, and Marcus Rediker. *The Many-Headed Hydra: Sailors, Slaves, Commoners, and the Hidden History of the Revolutionary Atlantic*. Boston: Beacon, 2000.

Locke, Alain, ed. *The New Negro: Voices of the Harlem Renaissance*. Repr., New York: Touchstone, 1999.

Long, Charles H. *Significations: Signs, Symbols, and Images in the Interpretation of Religion*. Philadelphia: Fortress, 1986.

Marable, Manning. Introduction to *Darkwater: Voices from the Veil*, by W. E. B. Du Bois. Dover Thrift Edition. Mineola, NY: Dover, 1996.

Miller, Christopher L. *Blank Darkness: Africanist Discourse in French*. Chicago: University of Chicago Press, 1985.

Morrison, Toni. *Playing in the Dark: Whiteness and the Literary Imagination*. William E. Massey Sr. Lectures in the History of American Civilization. Cambridge: Harvard University Press, 1992.

Patterson, Orlando. *Freedom*. New York: Basic Books, 1991.

———. *Rituals of Blood: Consequences of Slavery in Two American Centuries*. Washington, DC: Civitas, 1998.

———. *Slavery and Social Death: A Comparative Study*. Cambridge: Harvard University Press, 1982.

———. "Toward a Future That Has No Past: Reflections on the Fate of Blacks in the Americas." *Public Interest* 27 (1972): 25–62.

Price, Richard, ed. *Maroon Societies: Rebel Slave Communities in the Americas*. 3rd ed. Baltimore: Johns Hopkins University Press, 1996.

Reed, Ishmael. *Mumbo Jumbo*. New York: Scribner, 1972

Saunders, Ernest W. *Searching the Scriptures: A History of the Society of Biblical Literature, 1880*–1980. BSNA 8. Chico, CA: Scholars Press, 1982.

Sensbach, Jon F. *Rebecca's Revival: Creating Black Christianity in the Atlantic World*. Cambridge: Harvard University Press, 2005.

Smith, Olivia. *The Politics of Language, 1791–1819*. Oxford: Clarendon, 1984.

Taussig, Michael. *Mimesis and Alterity: A Particular History of the Senses*. New York: Routledge, 1993.

Terrill, Edward. *The Records of a Church of Christ in Bristol, 1640–1687*. Bristol Record Society, 1974.

Thompson, Alvin O. *Flight to Freedom: African Runaways and Maroons in the Americas*. Kingston, Jamaica: University of West Indies Press, 2006.

Thurman, Howard. *The Luminous Darkness: A Personal Interpretation of the Anatomy of Segregation and the Ground of Hope*. Repr., Richmond, IN: Friends United Press, 1999.

Van Leer, David. "Reading Slavery: The Anxiety of Ethnicity in Douglass's Narrative." Pages 118–40 in *Frederick Douglass: New Literary and Historical Essays*. Edited by Eric J. Sundquist. New York: Cambridge University Press, 1990.

Vedantam, Shankar. *The Hidden Brain: How Our Unconscious Minds Elect Presidents, Control Markets, Wage Wars, and Save Our Lives*. New York: Spiegel & Grau, 2010.

Williams, Sherley. *Dessa Rose*. New York: Morrow, 1982.

Wright, Leon Edward. *Alterations in the Words of Jesus, as Quoted in the Literature of the Second Century*. Harvard Historical Monographs 25. Cambridge: Harvard University Press, 1952.

Wright, Richard. *Pagan Spain*. Repr., New York: Harper, 2008.

Presidential Reflection

VINCENT L. WIMBUSH

Consistent with my own intellectual orientation and the challenge it models, these reflections will be metatextual and psycho-political. The arguments of my presidential address I gladly own, but they are not my focus here.

It was 2010. The Society of Biblical Literature was in a somewhat insecure situation—there was a change in long-standing generational administrative leadership, and it was in the middle of the messy divorce from the American Academy of Religion. There was a sense among some that the Society was without purpose or clear and compelling direction for the times, that our standing among peer learned societies was precarious, that hyper-religious groups were defining the Society by their numbers and through their seeming obliviousness to a direction beyond learned apologetics. The generation—European or greatly European-influenced—that had held command during the twentieth century, with its confusion of mostly unacknowledged, hardly problematized commitments to religious life and scholarship—was leaving the stage. And, rather poignantly, this was the time in which the Others—women; racial-ethnic underrepresented types—were beginning to present themselves.

I was during that period in what I now understand to have been the advanced middle of my career arc. That meant for me that the honor of being nominated and elected as the Society's president for 2010 occurred at a point when I had developed sharp clarity about my intellectual-programmatic orientation, about projects, about initiatives to pursue. All such involved a commitment to "seeing through" black-fleshed peoples the complexities and dynamics and problems having to do with the Bible or, more broadly and more crucial for comparative analytics, Scriptures. This was the period on the other side of my piloting of the 1990s African Americans and the Bible project and the 2003 founding of the disciplinarily transgressive and explosive Institute for Signifying Scriptures. (Doubtless, only a very few noticed then or notice even now that the ISS was intended to "signify on"—critique, with attitude, reflecting sensibilities on the peripheries—the internationally known Claremont-based, German-imitating Institute for Antiquity and Christianity [IAC]). What I had stepped into involved some risk-taking, to be sure, as is the case with all ex-centric orientations. Who would come around to play in a new intellectual playpen for which space was theorized by one whose very representative presence in the academic guild of biblical scholars was so recent and in the minds of some so counter-intuitive? With such initiatives I was signaling the need for and commitment to model a different orientation—to a cultural-critical program for the study of scriptures. Fitting in, making the Europeanist-colonial school programs and guilds comfortable, competing merely to find the most radical/Afro-centric interpretation of the presumed sacred texts—these were off the table for me. I was given the honor of nomination and election to office anyway.

2010 was also the Obama era. Obama, deemed Black in the United States, had taken the biggest power stage in the world. This meant many things, of course. But I suggest that Obama's ascendancy in politics also had its complex effects within politics (Tea [Party], anyone?) and beyond, on how other domains—social and cultural, including academic-intellectual, even in the Society's little corner of the playpen—that operated through naturalized notions were destabilized. (A *Black* president of the United States?!! Then why not …???)

Back to the Society of Biblical Literature. What I take to have been in the 2010 address—accompanied and supported by academic protegees and cobuilders of the new ISS, with extended friends and family in the session audience (the Annual Meeting being held in my hometown, Atlanta)—my unqualified commitment to making use of Black expressivities or performances as the foregrounding of the critical inquiry of the scriptural in culture was not lost on many. Perhaps, many did not care (originalists know well how to burrow and tune out); but I think the problem for some was the point made that the study of the Bible should be focused on a different "problem-space" (*pace* ancient-made-modern-colonial-white worlds), and in terms of excavation, not exegesis, on textures and gestures, on psycho-social-cultural politics and dynamics. The presence of black-fleshed peoples disrupts the naturalized (Western dis)course. Before three words had been drawn together in the way that is today widely recognized, I think that the 2010 address performed a disturbing and disruptive and insistent point—that the guild that is the Society of Biblical Literature, in its discourse and its psycho-politics, must henceforth come to terms with "Black Flesh Matters." Was this an end or a beginning?

On Being a Black Biblical Scholar—and So Much More: A Reflection

GAY L. BYRON

In November 2010, at the Annual Meeting of the Society of Biblical Literature held in Atlanta, Georgia, I realized that the professional context through which colleagues shared their latest research and connected over meals and libations was in the midst of a radical transformation. This year marked the first time that a person of African descent delivered the presidential address. At this point, with ten years of teaching experience under my belt, I had become accustomed to the Saturday evening presidential address as something to attend out of respect for the colleagues being recognized for their contributions to the field, but usually this was more of a pit stop before my annual round of reception-hopping or other social engagements. But now, for the first time—since 1880—in the long history of the guild, there was someone showing up as a self-embodied runagate with a new message, a novel approach for delivering it, and a nuanced invitation for "the Society—and by extension, all critical interpreters—to start and to sustain 'talkin' 'bout somethin.'"[1]

Vincent Wimbush was not new to me. Indeed, he joined the faculty of Union Theological Seminary in New York City during the final year of my MDiv program and intervened fortuitously as I was discerning the possibility of graduate studies with a focus on the New Testament and Christian origins. His presence on the faculty, his course offerings, and his overall encouragement sparked a possibility that I could barely imagine at the time. Union Seminary with all of its tangible and intangible claims as a bastion of liberal theological education stumbled in the area of bibli-

1. Vincent L. Wimbush, "Interpreters—Enslaving/Enslaved/Runagate," *JBL* 130 (2011): 9.

cal studies. So, it was not until Wimbush arrived on campus in 1991 and stayed through the early 2000s that a small cadre of African American and Latinx students began to cross the finish line with PhD's in New Testament.[2] Several of his former Union students transferred and completed their studies after his relocation and establishment of the Institute for Signifying Scriptures at Claremont Graduate University.[3]

As a result of his mentoring I had a number of unique opportunities to see the inner workings of the Society of Biblical Literature as a graduate student, supporting his service as the first chairperson of the Committee on Underrepresented Racial and Ethnic Minorities in the Profession (CUREMP) and as a member of the Committee on the Status of Women in the Profession (CSWP). Both of these committees were formed at the same time, in 1992, to address inherent inequities for women and "minorities" (the nomenclature used at the time) within the guild. In addition to this, I had the opportunity to experience first-hand the scholarship and teaching of an African American biblical critic whose exegetical reach extended beyond the New Testament by excavating Africans buried in late ancient Christian hagiographic narratives such as Ethiopian Moses, who was the subject of "color-ful" language due to the world-making symbolism associated with his blackness.[4] This illumination of *blackness* as related to ascetic piety and behavior helped shape my hermeneutic of recovery (or rather discovery) of silenced discourses in early Christian writings and set me upon a quest to develop a taxonomy of ethnopolitical rhetoric related to Egyptians, Ethiopians, blacks, and blackness in early Christian literature.[5]

Even with the freedom to extend beyond canonical sources and historical critical methods, the journey through my PhD program was not without a struggle. Raising questions about ethnic-othering and racialized discourses in biblical texts was still not fully accepted at the time as

---

2. It was only in 1999 that the first African Americans earned PhD's in New Testament at Union Seminary: Gay L. Byron, Cottrell Ricardo "Rick" Carson, and Ann Holmes Redding; and later in 2006, Davina Lopez and David Sanchez.

3. Velma E. Love (2005), Robin Owens (2007), Fontella White (2009), and Jacqueline Hidalgo (2010).

4. Vincent L. Wimbush, "Ascetic Behavior and Color-ful Language: Stories about Ethiopian Moses," *Semeia* 58 (1992): 81–92.

5. Gay L. Byron, *Symbolic Blackness and Ethnic Difference in Early Christian Literature* (London: Routledge, 2002).

curricular structures and norms were well entrenched to uphold Eurocentric readings of Scripture despite the presence of faculty like Wimbush, James Cone, James Melvin Washington Jr., and Delores Williams at Union during the 1990s. But with other supportive mentors (including several of the contributors to the *Stony the Road We Trod* volume)[6] and financial support from the Fund for Theological Education, the Graduate Fund of the PC(USA), and the Ford Foundation, I persevered, completed my studies, and accepted my first appointment as a professor of New Testament at Colgate Rochester Crozer Divinity School.

Context matters. Colgate has both a Black Church Studies program and a Women And Gender Studies program, so I was able to continue in actively developing two undergirding foci of my scholarship, spiritual traditions of the Black church and womanist readings of the Bible.[7] I was also able to realize during these early years of teaching and research that the tools (philological and methodological) that had equipped me to complete my degree in New Testament and Christian Origins were not sufficient for the questions that continued to emerge as I moved forward in sharing my scholarship. In particular, the Greek and Latin sources, foundational for my dissertation, did not address the full geographical landscape of the early Christian milieu, effectively resulting in a focus on only one side of the story.

This one-sided story of early Christianity, rooted in Greek and Roman sources and heroes, keeps Africans and blacks on the margins—peripheral, supporting characters in a dominant story of Western, orthodox, Mediterranean religions and worldviews. Fortunately, while at Colgate, I had an academic dean who saw the potential impact of my scholarship and supported my goal of remapping the ancient world through an emphasis on classical Ethiopic (Geʿez) and the Aksumite Empire so that the history and sources of Ethiopia can be brought into sharper focus for biblical studies.

Currently, I am continuing with this trajectory of scholarship through an explicit interdisciplinary turn to exploring how Ethiopic manuscript collections throughout the United States, which house biblical, liturgical,

6. New Testament womanist biblical critic Clarice J. Martin offered a course at Union as a visiting faculty.

7. Gay L. Byron, "Holy Man/Holy Community: Howard Thurman, Early Christian Asceticism, and the Black Church Tradition," *Hungryhearts* 12.3 (2003): 7–12; Byron, "Manuscripts, Meanings, and (Re)Membering: Ethiopian Women in Early Christianity," *Journal of Religious Thought* (2006–2007): 83–99.

theological, historical, and various religious (or "magical") manuscripts, can be used as source material for interpreting the New Testament and early Christianity.[8]

So as I reflect on the long trajectory of my experience in three different contexts over nearly three decades (far too many details to include in this brief essay!),[9] I can clearly see how the early seeds of mentoring and encouragement to follow my vision for remapping New Testament studies were shaped in part by Wimbush, his presidential address, and his ongoing work around theorizing Scriptures (that is, "scripturalizing"), which has been at the core of the Institute for Signifying Scriptures.[10] He is now running full steam ahead as an independent scholar, a *runagate* in the spirit of Frederick Douglass who "positioned himself [outside the circle of the enslaved culture and the Great Farm House] to 'read'—and help others read—the world as it had been and might be ordered."[11] Yet I can't help but wonder what would have happened if Wimbush had stayed in the classroom—teaching, mentoring, and modeling what it looks like to be a Black scholar of the Bible? Surely, Wimbush is more than his blackness (just like late antique Ethiopian Moses was more than his color-ful language) and his legacy extends far beyond his provocative 2010 presidential address. He continues to blur disciplinary boundaries, to unravel racialized discursive politics of the Society, and to inspire scholars like myself and new generations of critical interpreters to "run on and see what the end(s) gon' be."[12]

Bibliography

Byron, Gay L. "Holy Man/Holy Community: Howard Thurman, Early Christian Asceticism, and the Black Church Tradition." *Hungryhearts* 12.3 (2003): 7–12.

---

8. Gay L. Byron, "The Invisible Lives of Ethiopic Manuscripts," 2021–2022, https://tinyurl.com/sbl4527h.

9. Colgate Rochester Crozer Divinity School, Howard University School of Divinity, and the John Hope Franklin Humanities Institute at Duke University.

10. www.signifyingscriptures.org.

11. Wimbush, "Interpreters—Enslaving/Enslaved/Runagate," 20.

12. Vincent L. Wimbush, "Tribunals of Jurists and Congresses of Gentlemen: Signifying (on) Biblical Studies as Colonial-Bereaucratic Masquerade," in *Black Scholars Matter: Visions, Struggles, and Hopes in Africana Biblical Studies*, ed. Gay L. Byron and Hugh R. Page Jr., RBS 100 (Atlanta: SBL Press, 2022), 53–71.

———. "The Invisible Lives of Ethiopic Manuscripts." Humanities Unbounded Visiting Faculty Fellowship, Duke University. 2021–2022. https://tinyurl.com/sbl4527h.

———. "Manuscripts, Meanings, and (Re)Membering: Ethiopian Women in Early Christianity." *Journal of Religious Thought* (2006–2007): 83–99.

———. *Symbolic Blackness and Ethnic Difference in Early Christian Literature*. London: Routledge, 2002.

Wimbush, Vincent L. "Ascetic Behavior and Color-ful Language: Stories about Ethiopian Moses." *Semeia* 58 (1992): 81–92.

———. "Interpreters—Enslaving/Enslaved/Runagate." *JBL* 130 (2011): 5–24.

———. "Tribunals of Jurists and Congresses of Gentlemen: Signifying (on) Biblical Studies as Colonial-Bereaucratic Masquerade." Pages 53–71 in *Black Scholars Matter: Visions, Struggles, and Hopes in Africana Biblical Studies*. Edited by Gay L. Byron and Hugh R. Page Jr. RBS 100. Atlanta: SBL Press, 2022.

A Brief Reflection on My Society of Biblical Literature Experience

ANDREW MBUVI

I joined the Society of Biblical Literature/American Academy of Religion while a PhD student in 1999, and the same year I also presented my first academic conference paper on African eschatology and the Bible, with a total of four attendees—two of them my sympathizing PhD classmates. No Africans, or persons of color, were present! The room had emptied after the other papers by white presenters. As a Kenyan in a predominantly white institution, I was hoping to meet other African scholars or scholars of color, but they were scarce. I had to go to American Academy of Religion sessions to find the few in the conference and to participate in non-Western ("minoritized") sessions where, unfortunately, matters of biblical interpretation were rarely, if at all, addressed.[1] So, my meeting at the conference that year with Musa Dube from Botswana, a recent Vanderbilt University PhD (New Testament) graduate, was both invigorating (she would become a close friend and a source of encouragement in my dissertation writing) and demoralizing (her session was well attended, but I do not remember seeing another African in the room).

A decade later, as one still struggling to find my scholarly voice, I would find Vincent Wimbush's 2010 presidential address a bit confounding, not just because of Wimbush's proclivity to sophisticated verbiage or my own ineptitude or failure to connect with Robert Warren's "Pondy Woods" (unfamiliar to me then) at the beginning of the address or even the very crowded and sometimes noisy room, but also because of my unpreparedness for the subversive way the paper engaged with biblical

1. According to Wimbush, the African American Biblical Hermeneutics unit was the first of the minoritized groups in the Society of Biblical Literature.

scholarship.[2] It was not until I read it as a published article in the *Journal of Biblical Litearture* that its profundity hit me. It was an exacting archeological excavation of the history of biblical studies that voiced the juxtaposition of colonialism, enslavement, and origins of biblical studies.[3] The crux for biblical studies as Wimbush saw it:

> Here is the challenge plainly put: there can be no critical interpretation worthy of the name, without coming to terms with the first contact—between the West and the rest, the West and the Others—and its perduring toxic and blinding effects and consequences. The challenge remains for this Society and all collectivities of critical interpreters in general to engage in persistent and protracted struggle, not symbolic or obfuscating games around methods and approaches such as the impact of the colonial project context on the foundersof biblical studies and its unexamined continuing impact.[4]

And just like that, I had found a kindred spirit, and an established scholar in the field, who shared my hermeneutical preoccupations that prioritized postcolonial underpinnings. This shared hermeneutic of suspicion, and a focus on freedom and justice, was a pleasant connection for me.[5] His contribution in *Stony the Road We Trod* and his edited volume *African Americans and the Bible* had already been foundational texts for my courses on biblical interpretation at the HBCU where I taught.[6] Thus, overall, the value of his writings, his presence as an "elder statesman" for Black scholars and scholars of color in the Society of Biblical Literature,

2. Published as Vincent L. Wimbush, "Interpreters—Enslaving/ Enslaved/Runagate," *JBL* 130 (2011): 5–24. See also Wimbush' Signification Project http://www.signifyingscriptures.org/.

3. See, for example, historical anecdotes on the Society in the presidential address that he consider "shocking" (Wimbush, "Interpreters—Enslaving/Enslaved/Runagate," 5)

4. Wimbush, "Interpreters—Enslaving/Enslaved/Runagate," 9.

5. Andrew M. Mbuvi, *African Biblical Studies and the Unmasking of Embedded Racism and Colonialism in Biblical Studies* (London: T&T Bloomsbury, 2022).

6. Vincent L. Wimbush, "The Bible and African Americans: An Outline of an Interpretive History," in *Stony the Road We Trod: African American Biblical Interpretation*, ed. Cain Hope Felder (Minneapolis: Fortress, 1991), 97–114; Wimbush, ed., *African Americans and the Bible: Sacred Texts and Social Texture* (New York: Continuum, 2001).

and his presidency have been valuable connections that have shaped how I envision my place in the Society and the discipline.[7]

Fast forward another ten years, and I was again privileged to participate in the Society's special session for minoritized scholars prompted by the murder of George Floyd and the BLM-led demonstrations in 2020. Here, another of Wimbush's presentations triggered all sorts of reflections for me.[8] It was vital as a younger African biblical scholar to feel a sense of scholarly heritage that I could tap into in an academic field where, not only one's views but also one's presence, as a nonwhite person, occupy a marginalized space.[9] This is what Wimbush, and the generation that was bold enough to step into the void (e.g., Randall Bailey, Renita Weems), did to pave the way for those of us who have followed in their steps.

Wimbush's presidential address coincided with the beginning of my four-year stint as the chair of the Society's African Biblical Hermeneutics unit (2010–2014). I and a South African colleague were handed the reins of the unit as cochairs by those who had been the pioneers (Musa Dube, Gerald West, Dora Mbuwayesango, and the late Justin Ukpong).[10] But soon, I found myself managing the unit alone as my cochair was appointed into an administrative position in her institution and found herself overwhelmed with work. It was important to the pioneers that the unit's leadership be composed of representatives of different genders, with one person resident in the African continent and the other in the diaspora (Europe, America). This structure of leadership in the unit continues today. Yet, as one of the pioneers would later privately confess to me, they were afraid they had handed us/me "a dying horse," with little expectation that the unit would survive much longer because of sputtering attendance, reflecting the apathy that had greeted arrival of minoritized groups in the Society of Biblical Literature. Thankfully, however, the African Biblical Hermeneutics unit has not only survived but continues to thrive under the leadership of a new cadre of African biblical scholars.

---

7. Vincent L. Wimbush, "Reflections from the President," *SBL Society Report* 2010, p. 7.

8. The virtual session of the Society of Biblical Literature's #BlackScholarsMatter Symposium (August 12–13, 2020).

9. Vincent L. Wimbush, *White Men's Magic Scripturalization as Slavery* (Oxford: Oxford University Press, 2012), 1–21.

10. The program unit was set up in 2004.

During my tenure as chair, we emphasized regular joint sessions with other minoritized groups in the Society. The sessions with African American Biblical Hermeneutics, Asian American Biblical Hermeneutics, and Feminist Biblical Interpretation units, among others, provided some robust and well-attended sessions. It allowed for these groups to plumb topics of shared interest and common experiences, providing a critical mass of participants. It is in this period, too, that two major volumes I was involved in were published. The first was *The Africana Bible*, edited by Hugh Page Jr. and with contributions by African, Caribbean, and African American biblical scholars.[11] While Wimbush did not contribute to this volume, he spoke at the dinner launch for the volume about the sense of inspiration he felt in seeing a volume with contributions by Africana scholars of the Bible, something he could not envision when he arrived at the Society in the 1980s, as one of only a handful of people of color in the organization.

The second was a volume titled *Postcolonial Perspective in African Biblical Interpretations*, which I coedited with Musa Dube and Dora Mbuwayesango.[12] This volume primarily brought together a collection of select papers that had been presented at the African Biblical Hermeneutics unit from its inception in 2004 until 2010. In consultation with the Society's editorial and marketing team about the prohibitive cost of scholarly publications for most African scholars, over two dozen free copies of the volume were mailed to African university, seminary, and theological college libraries. The scholarly reception of the two publications may have drawn increased, though still limited, attention to minoritized interpretations in the Society.

The African Biblical Hermeneutics unit also took advantage of the Society's introduction of four international travel stipends a year (open to all minoritized units) for scholars from the Global South to attend the Annual Meetings, securing two of them for African scholars during my tenure as chair. For a fleeting period in 2014, long before COVID-19 was to make virtual meetings the norm, the African Biblical Hermeneutics section also worked with the the Society's office to find a way to pilot the streaming of meeting sessions to select African universities and seminaries in Kenya, South Africa, and Nigeria. While there were challenges (inter-

11. Hugh Page Jr., ed. *The Africana Bible* (Minneapolis: Fortress, 2010).

12. Musa Dube, Andrew Mbuvi, and Dora Mbuwayesango, eds., *Postcolonial Perspectives in African Biblical Interpretations*, GPBS 13 (Atlanta: Society of Biblical Literature, 2012).

net connections on both sides and time differences being major ones), we were able to stream several sessions, enabling more people in Africa to take part. The cost of the equipment and personnel needed to continue with the streaming, however, proved too high.

Logistics did not always run smoothly. One frustrating and frequent reminder of our marginal existence in the Society was how often African Biblical Hermeneutics sessions were assigned hard-to-find meeting rooms and inconvenient time slots. During the launch session of the edited volume, *Postcolonial Perspectives in African Biblical Interpretations*, the assigned room was so difficult to find that some of the panelists arrived late. Others never made it and later informed me they could not find the room. I remember during one of the sessions on Sexuality and Christianity in Africa, the committee and I accepted a paper on the Ugandan president's attacks on homosexuals. A gay New Testament scholar and priest presented the work. I received quite some flak from some of the African scholars in attendance, who raised issues with both the subject matter and the presenter's own sexual orientation, claiming the views were quite "*un*African and *un*Christian." I was forced to defend the committee's decision and the need to be open to the different marginalized communities, much in the same way that the African Biblical Hermeneutics unit itself strives to broaden the landscape of the Society.

But, even with all the positive aspects of my experience at the Society of Biblical Literature, the Society's presidencies of people of African descent (Wimbush, Musa Dube), while indisputably deserved by the individuals, to me remain essentially symbolic tokenism and not a reflection of the guild's transformation. Wimbush reflects on this in his address, asking:

> What might it mean to address in explicit terms the nature and consequences of first contact for the unstable and fragile big tent that is our Society?… It would make it imperative that we talk about discourse and power, slavery and freedom, life and death.[13]

The Society of Biblical Literature remains very much a white-dominated space with all its racial implications, and the concerns highlighted in CUREMP's Twenty-Fifth Anniversary statement in 2016, still resonates as it marks three decades of existence in 2023: "If we recognize that diversity is about both numbers of bodies as well as a substantive intellectual

---

13. Wimbush, "Interpreters—Enslaving/Enslaved/Runagate," 19.

commitment to varying perspectives and approaches, then we do have to think strategically about what makes our Society."[14] Sporadic changes have happened but no structural overhauls yet that address diversity, inclusion, and equality issues. Membership of scholars of African descent remains stubbornly stagnant at about 4 percent in that time period. Wimbush explained that that "the paucity of black membership is due ultimately not to the bad faith and manners of members of the Society in the past but to something more profound—the (unrecognized, unacknowledged) racialized discursive practices and politics that have defined it."[15] Without a structural overhaul of the Society of Biblical Literature, only limited progress and access can be attained for scholars of color, leaving any sense of a full embrace only an elusive mirage.

Bibliography

Dube, Musa, Andrew Mbuvi, and Dora Mbuwayesango, eds. *Postcolonial Perspectives in African Biblical Interpretations*. GPBS 13. Atlanta: Society of Biblical Literature, 2012.

Mbuvi, Andrew M. *African Biblical Studies and the Unmasking of Embedded Racism and Colonialism in Biblical Studies*. London: T&T Bloomsbury, 2022.

Page, Hugh, Jr., ed. *The Africana Bible*. Minneapolis: Fortress, 2010.

Society of Biblical Literature. "2019 SBL Membership Data." https://www.sbl-site.org/assets/pdfs/sblMemberProfile2019.pdf.

Wimbush, Vincent L., ed. *African Americans and the Bible: Sacred Texts and Social Texture*. New York: Continuum, 2001.

———. "The Bible and African Americans: An Outline of an Interpretive History." Pages 97–114 in *Stony the Road We Trod: African American Biblical Interpretation*. Edited by Cain Hope Felder. Minneapolis: Fortress, 1991.

———. "Interpreters—Enslaving/Enslaved/Runagate." *JBL* 130 (2011): 5–24.

———. "Reflections from the President." *SBL Society Report* 2010.

———. *White Men's Magic Scripturalization as Slavery*. Oxford: Oxford University Press, 2012.

---

14. As of 2019, 85 percent of members are European/Caucasian. See Society of Biblical Literature, "2019 SBL Membership Data," https://www.sbl-site.org/assets/pdfs/sblMemberProfile2019.pdf.

15. Wimbush, "Interpreters—Enslaving/Enslaved/Runagate," 5.

Reading between the Words: Learning to Interpret Worlds alongside Runagate Scriptural Studies

Jacqueline M. Hidalgo

I write this response during yet another pandemic winter in western Massachusetts, an ongoing but unpredictable *entretiempo*, a between-time of peril and possibility where ethical demands confront us.[1] In this between-time, feeling both trapped and adrift, I remember witnessing Vincent L. Wimbush's presidential address in 2010 and how it made me want to take flight. I thought Wimbush told us to run away from the constraints of the Society of Biblical Literature.

Reading the address over a decade later, I find its message to be both more and less radical. This address, a unique ritual genre-piece as all society presidential addresses are, described three interpretive circles and thereby opened up an *entretiempo*, a space-time between human social worlds in which to perceive an ethical demand: that biblical scholars actually talk about the things that matter, "about slavery and freedom, about life and death."[2] Expressed differently and with distinct attention, I see this call woven throughout all four presidential addresses in this volume, an imperative for critics to collaborate in addressing "critical times," to disrupt "systemic psychological and professional brutality," and to place interpretive attention on those who have been made invisible at the intersections of various unequal power relations.[3]

1. C. Gilbert Romero, "Amos 5:21–24: Religion, Politics, and the Latino Experience," *The Journal of Hispanic/Latino Theology* 4.4 (1997): 30.

2. Vincent L. Wimbush, "Interpreters—Enslaving/Enslaved/Runagate," *JBL* 130 (2011): 24.

3. Fernando F. Segovia, "Criticism in Critical Times: Reflections on Vision and Task," *JBL* 134 (2015): 6; Brian K. Blount, "The Souls of Biblical Folks and the Potential

In a time of high inequality, viral infection, and death, but also an era of global protests proclaiming that #BlackLivesMatter, Wimbush's address remains timely, vividly taken up in some corners of the guild, even as others shrink further into spaces of narrow temporal constraint, Manichean visions, and "cultivated obliviousness."[4] I respond as a student of the possible other scholarly worlds imagined in this address. I find myself still challenged by Wimbush's call to a runagate study of scriptures, to enact "an-other"[5] biblical studies, a biblical studies that is less interested in the Bible per se and more attentive to the practices and consequences of interpretation itself. In this piece I offer my own contingent map of the spaces between worlds found in Wimbush's essay and where we might follow him in projecting biblical studies as a field of and about interpretation, a contingent field that reads reading, that attends to the worlds around, between, and beyond words.

Interpreters—Enslaving/Enslaved/Runagate: Reading between Three Wor(l)ds

In his address, Wimbush resituates biblical studies as a product of colonizing violence, and he depicts three categories of "knowers or interpreters, produced by the world of first contact."[6] Wimbush does not exegete a biblical text in this address. Instead, Wimbush carefully reads a passage from Frederick Douglass's first autobiography in order to subtly hold a mirror back at our guild. In the selected passage, Douglass reflects on the songs of the enslaved, that they were "seemingly incoherent" to the (white) enslaving inhabitants of "the Great House Farm," that he understood the songs' meanings differently when he was "within the circle" of those enslaved because he "neither saw nor heard as those without might see and hear" but that, writing about them in his autobiography as a runagate interpreter, their "deep meaning(s)" bring him to tears.[7] In focusing on this

for Meaning," *JBL* 138 (2019): 21; Gale A. Yee, "Thinking Intersectionally: Gender, Race, Class, and the Etceteras of Our Discipline," *JBL* 139 (2020): 7–26.

4. Wimbush, "Interpreters—Enslaving/Enslaved/Runagate," 5–6.

5. I draw this notion of "an-other world" from Charles Long, *Significations: Signs, Symbols, and Images in the Interpretation of Religion* (Philadelphia, PA: Fortress, 1986).

6. Wimbush, "Interpreters—Enslaving/Enslaved/Runagate," 10.

7. Frederick Douglass, *Narrative of the Life of Frederick Douglass, An American Slave* (Boston: Anti-Slavery Office, 1845), 13–14.

passage, Wimbush offers a window into the dynamics of interpretation, three circles of interpreters enmeshed within certain structures of violence. Wimbush's live 2010 address was also accompanied by the playing of songs that could not be captured in printed form.

Allow me also to deploy, briefly, some of the tools of close reading and textual criticism I have learned in biblical studies. Douglass quotes and reinterprets the aforementioned passage again in his second autobiography, *My Bondage and My Freedom*, and then he more concisely excerpts and reinterprets it again within his third autobiography, *The Life and Times of Frederick Douglass*.[8] Throughout his own life, Douglass continued to reflect on how meaning gets made under and across dynamics of coercive violence, enslavement, and freedom.

In all three autobiographies, Douglass situates the passage amid a discussion of those times when enslaved representatives traveled to the Great House Farm in order to collect "their monthly allowance of meal and meat."[9] In his middle autobiography, Douglass depicts the enthusiasm that representatives felt for this outing because the journey offered a chance to be "comparatively free," outside the field and "beyond the overseer's eye and lash."[10] Singing amidst this comparative freedom is all the more remarkable because Douglass depicts how much enslaved singing was also a product of coercive violence: "Slaves are generally expected to sing as well as to work. A silent slave is not liked by masters or overseers.... This may account for the almost constant singing heard in the southern states."[11] Given this coercive context of song, Douglass depicts the deep sorrow of these songs, a sorrow that had to be conveyed in ways that fooled any enslaving listeners. In his first two autobiographies, Douglass also underscores how those songs gave him his "first glimmering conceptions of the dehumanizing character of slavery."[12] Both the songs' performance and interpretation among enslaved singers laid out foundational knowledge and opened a space of critique, a space that remained opaque to enslaving interpreters.

8. Frederick Douglass, *My Bondage and My Freedom* (New York: Miller, Orton & Mulligan, 1855), 99; Douglass, *Life and Times of Frederick Douglass*, rev. ed. (Boston: De Wolfe & Fiske, 1892), 62.

9. Douglass, *My Bondage and My Freedom*, 97.

10. Douglass, *My Bondage and My Freedom*, 98; see also Neil Roberts, *Freedom as Marronage* (Chicago: University of Chicago Press, 2015), 53–88.

11. Douglass, *My Bondage and My Freedom*, 97.

12. Douglass, *My Bondage and My Freedom*, 99.

Across all three iterations of this story, Douglass emphasizes the emotional tenor of certain forms of understanding: the songs "filled my heart with ineffable sadness."[13] In Douglass's third autobiography, he ends the excerpt from his first autobiography there. Expressed distinctly in each of the autobiographies, Douglass conveys to his (mostly white) readers a strong and normative claim about how to interpret these songs, even if their fuller meanings may be understood differently in different circles. Douglass reminds us that songs convey ineffable meanings that exceed verbal description, a challenging interpretive lesson for those of us who especially love written words.

Nevertheless, Douglass's autobiographies persistently describe a wrong interpretation. These songs are not happy. A listener can only misinterpret them as happy because of a lack of self-reflexivity, or rather a cultivated obliviousness, about the highly uneven power dynamics shaping the words that are sung. If an interpreter thinks these songs are happy, it is because they fail to recognize the structures of violence and coercion that shape the conditions of enslaved songs.

Wimbush depicts the persistence of enslaving logics past legal emancipation and the ways that too many in our own guild have helped to maintain the Manichaean violence of enslaving logics by providing interpretive cover.[14] Pointedly, Wimbush challenges the centrality of strictly biblical exegesis as the mainstay of our guild: "How can the ever more sophisticated methods and approaches of the operations of its diverse members focused on a single text tradition or, at most, two complexly related text traditions, avoid functioning as apologetics—for the nation or empire and satellite orders?"[15] There are forms of biblical scholarship that not only misunderstand the wor(l)ds they claim to read, they also do so with dire consequences. Interpreting the Bible and the literature most closely associated with it without attention to the highly uneven power dynamics that have shaped the ways we engage with texts functions, at best, as apologetics for dehumanizing violence.

However, Wimbush does not neatly correlate Douglass's three interpretive worlds with our own. Wimbush does not spend much time examining enslaved interpreters, at least not in this address, but he points to the ways enslaved interpreters have been denied "intersubjectivity,"

13. Douglass, *Life and Times of Frederick Douglass*, 62.

14. See Wimbush "Interpreters—Enslaving/Enslaved/Runagate," 12.

15. Wimbush "Interpreters—Enslaving/Enslaved/Runagate," 20.

the opportunity to craft and inhabit a space between worlds in ways they might choose.[16] Instead, Wimbush focuses on the approaches of Douglass as runagate interpreter who reads between and beyond multiple worlds. Douglass here does not represent some new form of detached objectivity, some revivification of that supposedly neutral, "master" reader from older models of biblical studies.[17] Rather, Douglass is self-consciously, and in painful ways, both from one circle but also alien to it.[18]

Although not the same, Douglass's position has resonated with certain Latinx interpreters, such as Gloria Anzaldúa, who describe the subjectivity of those forced to move between the worlds (those who have been compelled into outsider and marginalized positionalities), those who can think between and about multiple worlds. Out of painful necessity, they have cultivated *la facultad*, an ability to read beyond surface structures, and they too have sought "the deep meanings" found beyond and between words and worlds but in ways that are neither neutral nor detached.[19] *La facultad* depends on self-reflexive attachment and feeling to function.

In turning to *la facultad*, I do not analogize myself to a runagate interpreter, as I see myself implicated within and at the boundaries of a host of dynamics of domination and quests for liberation. However, Wimbush's work has always challenged me to use what freedom I have to read more and to read more than just texts. In this essay, Wimbush describes Douglass as already a runagate interpreter even while still enslaved because he had learned to read "past the text to something more or other, a reading of the self—a historicized collective self."[20] Of course, this interpretive strategy is Wimbush's, his study of scriptures. Wimbush's work does not get stuck on the meaning of any particular text, just like Douglass did not draw our attention to the specific words of the songs except to problematize the surface meanings we might think we hear in them. Douglass's autobiographies pushed readers instead to see the work the songs were

16. Wimbush "Interpreters—Enslaving/Enslaved/Runagate," 15.

17. See descriptions in Fernando F. Segovia, "'And They Began to Speak in Other Tongues': Competing Modes of Discourse in Contemporary Biblical Criticism," in *Social Location and Biblical Interpretation in the United States*, vol. 1 of *Reading from This Place*, ed. Fernando F. Segovia and Mary Ann Tolbert (Minneapolis: Fortress, 1995), 1–32.

18. Wimbush "Interpreters—Enslaving/Enslaved/Runagate," 17.

19. Gloria Anzaldúa, *Borderlands/La Frontera: The New Mestiza* (San Francisco: Spinsters/Aunt Lute, 1987), 47–62.

20. Wimbush, "Interpreters—Enslaving/Enslaved/Runagate," 18.

doing, the systems in which they were enmeshed, and the powerful feelings they reflected and provoked.

Similarly, Wimbush "problematize(s) representation and meaning seeking."[21] Wimbush's study of scriptures has foregrounded people rather than texts. He examines "the work we make scriptures do for us."[22] He has redirected our attention to how the "historically enslaved and conquered peoples of the world" signified on and played with meaning.[23] In so doing, he projected an-other biblical studies, where interpreters redirect the critical gaze upon the act of reading itself, toward what we mean by "the Bible," the roles of the "biblical" and of "studies" in creating the wor(l)d(s) we have and who we are as a collective.

Fugitive Interpretation and An-Other Biblical Studies

In order to understand how Wimbush remapped the field, it is not enough to respond to Wimbush's presidential address. He also worked so hard alongside some of the others profiled in this volume to craft an-other biblical studies. In the 1990s, Wimbush was the first chair and among the founding members of Society of Biblical Literature's then Committee on Racial/Ethnic Minorities in the Profession. Notably, three of the four presidents highlighted in this volume were among those founding members, which in 1992 also included Randall C. Bailey, Fernando F. Segovia, Henry T. C. Sun, and Gale A. Yee. These scholars have all worked to diversify the field, supporting both a wide array of approaches and an embodied diversity of scholars. Members from what is now the Committee on Underrepresented Racial/Ethnic Minorities in the Profession have often gone on to serve the Society in other leadership capacities, including two of the recent chairs of Council, Mary F. Foskett (2015–2017) and Efraín Agosto (2018–2020). Notably, the last four chairs of Council have been racially/ethnically minoritized scholars, and the membership of Council has diversified

21. Vincent L. Wimbush, "TEXTureS, Gestures, Power: Orientation to Radical Excavation," in *Theorizing Scriptures: New Critical Orientations to a Cultural Phenomenon*, ed. Vincent L. Wimbush (New Brunswick, NJ: Rutgers University Press, 2008), 13.

22. The tagline on the Institute for Signifying Scriptures website, http://www.signifyingscriptures.org/.

23. Wimbush, "TEXTureS, Gestures, Power," 14.

significantly since the early 2000s.[24] Additionally, in 2023 the Society of Biblical Literature, for the first time in its history, appointed a Black man as executive director, Steed Vernyl Davidson.

Despite these successes, the Society of Biblical Literature's demographics are less impressive. In 2010, the Society did not report racial/ethnic membership data, but the member report that year included a pie chart reporting the membership as 23 percent women and 77 percent men.[25] The first year that I could find racial/ethnic membership data is the 2014 report (representing 2013) data. Of the 2,884 members surveyed that year, 4 percent identified as African descent, 5 percent as Asian descent, 86 percent as European/Caucasian descent, 3 percent as Latin American descent, 1 percent as Native American/Alaskan Native/First Nation descent, and 0.2 percent as Native Hawaiian/Oceanian descent.[26] The 2019 report (representing 2018) data, the most recent available online at the time of writing, seems to sample a different collective with 3,826 responses. The numbers look very much the same if slightly better for those of Latin American and/or Native American/Alaskan Native/First Nations descent and slightly worse for those of Asian descent: 4 percent identified as African descent, 3 percent as Asian descent, 86 percent as European/Caucasian descent, 4 percent as Latin American descent, 3 percent as Native American/Alaskan Native/First Nations descent, and 0.2 percent as Native Hawaiian/Oceanian descent. Women accounted for 25 percent of a larger membership sample of 5,108 responses.[27] Many questions might be asked about the accuracy and utility of this survey data, but it illuminates that, for minoritized critics, field demographics are perhaps very slowly improving, and for some groups field demographics may be worsening.

---

24. I offer my gratitude to Nicole L. Tilford and Christopher Hooker for helping me research the history of CUREMP and Council leadership. Hooker specifically responded with data available in his files (email, 28 January 2022) and pointed me to the data that is publicly available on the Society of Biblical Literature site (https://www.sbl-site.org/aboutus/reports.aspx) and in the Society's digital archives at Emory University's Pitts Theological Library (https://pitts.emory.edu/collections/digitalcollections/programbooks.cfm). There is a bit of a gap in available data for 1999–2002.

25. Society of Biblical Literature, "Society Report, November 2010," https://www.sbl-site.org/assets/pdfs/SR2010.pdf. See p. 28.

26. Society of Biblical Literature, "SBL Member Profile, November 2014," https://www.sbl-site.org/assets/pdfs/memberProfileReport2014.pdf.

27. Society of Biblical Literature, "2019 SBL Membership Data," https://www.sbl-site.org/assets/pdfs/sblMemberProfile2019.pdf.

At the same time, the available jobs advertised within the broader field of religion have plummeted.[28] In 2011, there were 318 tenure-track jobs and 535 total full-time jobs (which includes tenure-track jobs but can also include visiting positions and non-professorial positions) advertised with the American Academy of Religion and the Society of Biblical Literature. In 2019 there were only 211 tenure-track jobs and 403 full-time jobs advertised. In less than a decade, available full-time jobs in the broader field of religion have shrunk by nearly one-fourth. Any discussion of the future of biblical studies, of the opportunities and challenges we face, must reckon seriously with the material realities we confront. To my mind, these material realities—the comparative lack of racial/ethnic and gender diversity of the membership and the comparative dearth of full-time employment—demand we reconfigure the boundaries and orientations of the field and reimagine the spaces in which scholarship happens. Perhaps Wimbush anticipated this situation when he created the Institute for Signifying Scriptures, which was designed to defy the traditional boundaries of the academy.

Even though the numerical demographics of biblical studies have not shifted sufficiently, minoritized critics have pushed the boundaries and perspectives of what we think of as biblical studies. Black women in Africa and the diaspora have especially written about critical issues of life and death.[29] I have been grateful for a marked rise of publications that take an expressly intersectional and/or womanist perspective since 2010.[30] In

28. The data I cite here come from the American Academy of Religion/Society of Biblical Literature Jobs reports, which consider all the jobs advertised with both organizations. The reports I examined can be found at https://www.sbl-site.org/aboutus/reports.aspx.

29. See, for instance, work from Musa W. Dube, *The HIV and AIDS Bible: Selected Essays* (Scranton, PA: The University of Scranton Press, 2008), to Angela N. Parker, *If God Still Breathes, Why Can't I? Black Lives Matter and Biblical Authority* (Grand Rapids, MI: Eerdmans, 2021).

30. See, for instance, Shanell T. Smith, *The Woman Babylon and the Marks of Empire: Reading Revelation with a Postcolonial Womanist Hermeneutics of Ambiveilence* (Minneapolis: Fortress, 2014); Nyasha Junior, *An Introduction to Womanist Biblical Interpretation* (Louisville: Westminster John Knox, 2015); Gay L. Byron and Vanessa Lovelace, eds., *Womanist Interpretations of the Bible: Expanding the Discourse* (Atlanta: SBL Press, 2016); Stephanie Buckhanon Crowder, *When Momma Speaks: The Bible and Motherhood from a Womanist Perspective* (Louisville: Westminster John Knox, 2016); Wilda C. Gafney, *Womanist Midrash: A Reintroduction to the Women*

2019, Gale A. Yee was the first woman of color and the first Asian American president of the Society of Biblical Literature, and her address focused on intersectionality. As a proportion of the field, these numbers remain small—and, as a Latina, I note the comparative absence of US Latina biblical critics authoring intersectionally focused monographs or coedited volumes—but to be able to cite whole published books represents a meaningful shift. In addition, so many of these texts express a specific commitment to particularity (a refusal of false universality or objectivity) and collaboration (to the need to work with and among others).

Perhaps futilely, I have drawn from these scholars and redescribed a form of biblical criticism as contingent criticism.[31] Contingency here has multiple meanings. Partially it is in recognition that the majority of interpretation is undertaken from those who experience occupational contingency, either as contingent faculty or in other professional roles that carry greater precarity. Contingency is also an epistemic emphasis. All scholars should practice a form of knowledge-construction founded on a greater epistemic realism, a hermeneutical humility that recognizes the temporal and spatial limits of one's perspective.[32] Contingent criticism echoes Segovia's call for greater global collaboration and Joseph A. Marchal's imagining of criticism as enabling a transtemporal, transcultural, and transspatial contingent, a community of allies for the moment, a form of interpretation that is both communal and fugitive.[33] It is a commitment to interpret with and alongside others—*de y en conjunto* in the parlance of Latinx theologies.[34] Instead of pretending to be a solitary reader in control of the text and the world, contingent critics know that

of the Torah and the Throne (Louisville, KY: Westminster John Knox, 2017); Mitzi J. Smith, *Womanist Sass and Talk Back: Social (In)Justice, Intersectionality, and Biblical Interpretation* (Eugene, OR: Cascade, 2018); Mitzi J. Smith and Jin Young Choi, eds., *Minoritized Women Reading Race and Ethnicity: Intersectional Approaches to Constructed Identity and Early Christian Texts* (Lanham, MD: Lexington Books, 2020).

31. Jacqueline M. Hidalgo, "No Future for Biblical Studies? Or Still Living with a Contingent Apocalypse as *Biblical Interpretation* Turns Twenty-Five," in *Present and Future of Biblical Studies: Celebrating Twenty-Five Years of Brill's Biblical Interpretation*, ed. Tat-siong Benny Liew (Boston: Brill, 2018), 133–55.

32. Smith, *Womanist Sass and Talk Back.*

33. Segovia, "Criticism in Critical Times"; Joseph A. Marchal, "'Making History' Queerly: Touches across Time through a Biblical Behind," *BibInt* 19 (2011): 373–95.

34. See, for instance, Neomi De Anda, and Néstor Medina, "Convivencias: What Have We Learned? Toward a Latin@ Ecumenical Theology," in *Building Bridges Doing*

they are entangled with others across time and space, and, as we all surely know better in the *entretiempo* of COVID-19, that we face conditions that cannot be individually controlled.

More contingent imaginaries for biblical criticism have found their way into the pages of the Society's flagship journal, the *Journal of Biblical Literature*. Wongi Park's essay on "Multiracial Biblical Studies" in 2021 critiqued the constraints of the narrowly historical as a relic of a monoracial project, one that must change: "Ultimately, what is necessary are a diversity of texts, a diversity of readings, and a diversity of readers."[35] Who reads, how we read, and what we read can no longer be constrained by one people or one narrow set of tools, texts, and times. In introducing a forum on the politics of citations, the journal's general editor Mark G. Brett suggested that the skills to do biblical studies may require a team of researchers working together.[36] Instead of doctoral programs requiring students learn so many languages, maybe students should practice more collaboration with others. We could greatly expand the language tools at our fingertips if we work together. We can also more readily study across time and space and practice a diversity of approaches if we research with others. In the same forum, Willie James Jennings describes that classical vision of the biblical scholar, one who masters a range of ancient languages and dominates access to textual authority, a vision embedded in a masculine, white supremacist delusion of self-sufficient control.[37] Only in open collaborative partnerships can colleagues truly push us to be more self-reflexive about our own pretenses. We make better scholarship by working together, across difference.

Wimbush's work has already pointed to paths for "unthinking mastery,"[38] to particularizing and dismantling controlling/enslaving hermeneutics, to the epistemic limitations of any one circle of interpreters, to the quest for intersubjectivity and self-reflexivity. In drawing attention

Justice: Constructing a Latina/o Ecumenical Theology, ed. Orlando O. Espín (Maryknoll, NY: Orbis Books, 2009), 185–97.

35. Wongi Park, "Multiracial Biblical Studies," *JBL* 140 (2021): 459.

36. Mark G. Brett, "Social Inclusion and the Ethics of Citation: Introduction," *JBL* 140 (2021): 819–25.

37. Willie James Jennings, "Renouncing Completeness: The Rich Ruler and the Possibilities of Biblical Scholarship without White Masculine Self-Sufficiency," *JBL* 140 (2021): 837–42.

38. Juliette Singh, *Unthinking Mastery: Dehumanism and Decolonial Entanglements* (Durham, NC: Duke University Press, 2018).

to a runagate interpreter and in imagining a more fugitive form of study, Wimbush also modeled interpretation that examined something more than text. He has long redirected interpreters toward textures, gestures, and power; his scholarship reads through words to read worlds.[39] It is a runagate project, yet within and beyond the bounds of biblical studies. I myself have struggled to adequately follow the depth of Wimbush's *facultad*, his ability to read between and beyond words, to craft an-other world, an *entretiempo*, a space-time between the social worlds others have sought to narrowly inscribe. To follow his model of runagate interpretation requires that we relinquish the false pretenses of authority that come from merely exegeting words that are entangled in violence and uneven power relations, that we decenter the Bible from biblical studies. Instead, the study of scriptures could prepare us to read human social worlds and to speak into the ineffable boundaries between them, to grapple with slavery and freedom, life and death.

Bibliography

Anzaldúa, Gloria. *Borderlands/La Frontera: The New Mestiza*. San Francisco: Spinsters/Aunt Lute, 1987.

Blount, Brian K. "The Souls of Biblical Folks and the Potential for Meaning." *JBL* 138 (2019): 6–21.

Brett, Mark G. "Social Inclusion and the Ethics of Citation: Introduction." *JBL* 140 (2021): 819–25.

Byron, Gay L., and Vanessa Lovelace, eds. *Womanist Interpretations of the Bible: Expanding the Discourse*. Atlanta: SBL Press, 2016.

Crowder, Stephanie Buckhanon. *When Momma Speaks: The Bible and Motherhood from a Womanist Perspective*. Louisville: Westminster John Knox, 2016.

De Anda, Neomi, and Néstor Medina. "Convivencias: What Have We Learned? Toward a Latin@ Ecumenical Theology." Pages 185–97 in *Building Bridges Doing Justice: Constructing a Latina/o Ecumenical Theology*. Edited by Orlando O. Espín. Maryknoll, NY: Orbis Books, 2009.

Douglass, Frederick. *Life and Times of Frederick Douglass*. Rev. ed. Boston: De Wolfe & Fiske, 1892.

39. Wimbush, "TEXTureS, Gestures, Power."

———. *My Bondage and My Freedom*. New York: Miller, Orton & Mulligan, 1855.

———. *Narrative of the Life of Frederick Douglass, An American Slave*. Boston: Anti-Slavery Office, 1845.

Dube, Musa W. *The HIV and AIDS Bible: Selected Essays*. Scranton, PA: The University of Scranton Press, 2008.

Gafney, Wilda C. *Womanist Midrash: A Reintroduction to the Women of the Torah and the Throne*. Louisville: Westminster John Knox, 2017.

Hidalgo, Jacqueline M. "No Future for Biblical Studies? Or Still Living with a Contingent Apocalypse as *Biblical Interpretation* Turns Twenty-Five." Pages 133–55 in *Present and Future of Biblical Studies: Celebrating Twenty-Five Years of Brill's Biblical Interpretation*. Edited by Tat-siong Benny Liew. Boston: Brill, 2018.

Jennings, Willie James. "Renouncing Completeness: The Rich Ruler and the Possibilities of Biblical Scholarship without White Masculine Self-Sufficiency." *JBL* 140 (2021): 837–42.

Junior, Nyasha. *An Introduction to Womanist Biblical Interpretation*. Louisville: Westminster John Knox, 2015.

Long, Charles. *Significations: Signs, Symbols, and Images in the Interpretation of Religion*. Philadelphia: Fortress, 1986.

Marchal, Joseph A. "'Making History' Queerly: Touches across Time through a Biblical Behind." *BibInt* 19 (2011): 373–95.

Park, Wongi. "Multiracial Biblical Studies." *JBL* 140 (2021): 435–59.

Parker, Angela N. *If God Still Breathes, Why Can't I? Black Lives Matter and Biblical Authority*. Grand Rapids: Eerdmans, 2021.

Roberts, Neil. *Freedom as Marronage*. Chicago: University of Chicago Press, 2015.

Romero, C. Gilbert. "Amos 5:21–24: Religion, Politics, and the Latino Experience." *The Journal of Hispanic/Latino Theology* 4.4 (1997): 21–41.

Segovia, Fernando F. "'And They Began to Speak in Other Tongues': Competing Modes of Discourse in Contemporary Biblical Criticism." Pages 1–32 in *Social Location and Biblical Interpretation in the United States*. Vol. 1 of *Reading from This Place*. Edited by Fernando F. Segovia and Mary Ann Tolbert. Minneapolis: Fortress, 1995.

———. "Criticism in Critical Times: Reflections on Vision and Task." *JBL* 134 (2015): 6–29.

Singh, Juliette. *Unthinking Mastery: Dehumanism and Decolonial Entanglements*. Durham, NC: Duke University Press, 2018.

Society of Biblical Literature. “2019 SBL Membership Data.” https://www.sbl-site.org/assets/pdfs/sblMemberProfile2019.pdf.

———. “SBL Member Profile, November 2014.” https://www.sbl-site.org/assets/pdfs/memberProfileReport2014.pdf.

———. “Society Report, November 2010.” https://www.sbl-site.org/assets/pdfs/SR2010.pdf. See p. 28.

Smith, Mitzi J. *Womanist Sass and Talk Back: Social (In)Justice, Intersectionality, and Biblical Interpretation*. Eugene, OR: Cascade, 2018.

Smith, Mitzi J., and Jin Young Choi, eds. *Minoritized Women Reading Race and Ethnicity: Intersectional Approaches to Constructed Identity and Early Christian Texts*. Lanham, MD: Lexington Books, 2020.

Smith, Shanell T. *The Woman Babylon and the Marks of Empire: Reading Revelation with a Postcolonial Womanist Hermeneutics of Ambiveilence*. Minneapolis: Fortress, 2014.

Wimbush, Vincent L. “Interpreters: Enslaving/Enslaved/Runagate.” *JBL* 130 (2011): 5–24.

———. “TEXTureS, Gestures, Power: Orientation to Radical Excavation.” Pages 1–20 in *Theorizing Scriptures: New Critical Orientations to a Cultural Phenomenon*. Edited by Vincent L. Wimbush. New Brunswick, NJ: Rutgers University Press, 2008.

Yee, Gale A. “Thinking Intersectionally: Gender, Race, Class, and the Etceteras of Our Discipline.” *JBL* 139 (2020): 7–26.

Prophesying by Night: Practices of Runagate Interpreters

VELMA E. LOVE

I listen. I think perhaps the faint voice that I hear is that of an ancient grandmother of dark hue, an African woman, of the Temne Tribe, who lived by the sea in a small village not too far from the land now known as Freetown, Sierra Leone, along the coast of West Africa. I will never know her name, but her spirit resides in my soul. Her capacity to prophesy by night, disrupt, and embrace the luminous darkness is the legacy she bequeathed to me. She was and is a survivor, a runagate.

Following the trajectory mapped out by Vincent Wimbush in his 2010 address to the attendees at the Annual Meeting of the Society for Biblical Literature, I can surmise that her initial contact with the West was somewhere between the fifteenth and eighteenth centuries. A violent contact it was but survival was her destiny. She had a daughter, who had a daughter, who had a daughter, and so on and so on until I was born. How many generations later, I don't know. But I was born in the Southeastern United States, however many generations later, during the time of racial segregation when black lives did not matter and that was the order of the day.

I was always full of questions and never quite understood the God factor in an unjust world. It was that quest for insight and understanding that ultimately led me to my studies with Wimbush at Union Theological Seminary in New York City and later to Claremont Graduate University in Claremont, California. I was captivated by his unconventional approach to the study of scriptures, the way he created space for field research on African American engagements with the biblical text, assigning weekend intensive forays into the streets of Harlem in New York City, the way he taught us to not stay with the text but to venture into the rich domain of culture, expressive arts, artifacts, rituals and other so-called sacred renderings that were also discursive fields reflecting and representing the script(ures) and power dynamics that impacted life and were impacted by lived experience.

When the term *signifying scriptures* emerged and the Institute for Signifying Scriptures was established at Claremont Graduate University, I was there as associate director. Why? What was driving me? I think it was my soul-level lineage. I think it was the will of that ancestral mother from West Africa whose DNA genetic material called forth the runagate interpreter in me. I ran and kept running until I landed outside the tightly circumscribed path of textual interpretation to a wider world, finding "*ofo ashe*" (words of power) in the living scriptures of the Holy Odu and the lives of those who, like me, were drawn to the light that filtered through the veil.

It is from that position that I revisit Wimbush's 2010 presidential address, "Interpreters—Enslaving/ Enslaved/Runagate," to the Society of Biblical Literature.[1] As I gaze intently at the words on paper and recall the ambience of the occasion, I am transported back to the conference center ballroom at a hotel in downtown Atlanta, Georgia, proud to be among my colleagues who had studied with Wimbush. We had struggled together in ways that created a bond like no other, and we sit together as runagate interpreters, forging our way in the world. What a powerful memory.

Now, nearly twelve years later, when I gaze upon the transcript, I am awed by what stares back at me. I see an artfully crafted message that meets all of the criteria of the "public narrative" as defined by Marshall Ganz, community organizer and university professor, who popularized the term. Ganz argues that public narrative is a leadership strategy that includes a story of self, a story of us, and a story of now with the intent of inspiring action.[2] Wimbush begins with his story of self, establishing his location early on.

> My beginnings are not here in this city in the sixth decade of the twentieth century. In respects more profound and disturbing and poignantly ramifying for professional interpreters, my beginnings should be understood to be that more expansive period and fraught situations of the

1. Published as Vincent L. Wimbush, "Interpreters—Enslaving/Enslaved/Runagate," *JBL* 130 (2011): 5–24.

2. Marshall Ganz, "What Is Public Narrative: Self, Us, Now," Working Paper, Harvard University, 2009, https://tinyurl.com/SBL4527e.

> North Atlantic worlds between the fifteenth and nineteenth century, moments in which the "West" and "the rest" were coming into fateful first contact.... "Contact" is of course studied euphony, rhetorical repression meant to veil the violence and hegemony of the West's large-scale triangular Atlantic slave trading in dark places.[3]

I recall assigning this address to a class of seminary students and asking them to watch the You Tube Video recording and come prepared to discuss their reaction. When we were well into the discussion, a middle-aged black woman raised her hand and proudly said, "I don't know exactly what he said, but I know he got them told." This comment evoked peals of laughter in the room. I used the opportunity to push the conversation a bit, asking, "Got who told? Why do you say that?" Her response was, "Well.... I just know there's truth in what he's saying even though I don't have all of those fancy words, but he got the white people told in a very classy way." Other students in the class were in agreement. It seemed important to them to have the opportunity to bring some deep-seated, soul-level resonance into the conversation, and they took every advantage of the opportunity. For them, the address had created an opening, like a crack in the sidewalk, a space for the story of self to bubble up in the study of scripture.

In his insistence on directing attention to the impact of the discursive histories and power dynamics associated with the history of enslavement, Wimbush makes a compelling case for challenging the conventional study of scripture in order to expand the playing field. He positions himself squarely in alignment with the ancestral realm of literary giants, the likes of Frederick Douglass, Zora Neal Hurston, Franz Fanon, W. E. B. DuBois, and others, to draw from their wells of wisdom, pointing to the maroon and runagate practices that gave them psychic space for anchoring and grounding themselves.

He moves with fluid grace from his personal narrative and sociohistorical location to the story of the guild and its failure to recognize the need to see things differently. Like a skillful fighter, he dances about with a jab here and there, landing his punches where they count most. "Not withstanding all the historical and some continuing stumbling blocks in the way, I suggest that the paucity of black membership is due ultimately not to the bad faith and manners of the Society in the past but to something

3. Wimbush, "Interpreters—Enslaving/Enslaved/Runagate," 6.

more profound—the (unrecognized, unacknowledged) racialized discursive practices and politics that have defined it."[4]

Now, completely warmed up and about halfway through his speech, Wimbush is relentless. He acknowledges the contribution of the black pioneers in the field as well as the attempts of some past presidents to make a difference but points out that those efforts were too few, too tepid, and too late. His "story of us" is interwoven with an urgent call to action. "I stand before you this evening with yet another challenge, imploring the Society—and by extension, all critical interpreters—to start and to sustain 'talkin' 'bout something.' Here is the challenge plainly put: there can be no critical interpretation worthy of the name, without coming to terms with the first contact—between the West and the rest."[5]

This statement is like the scratch, the interrupting pause that the DJ makes in the spinning soundtrack of his storied musical presentation to his audience.[6] The scratch grabs our attention. By proclaiming, "there can be no critical interpretation worthy of the name, without coming to terms with the first contact—between the West and the rest," Wimbush not only challenges interpreters but redefines the task. "How can we remain a society only of Biblical Literature and not of comparative scriptures?… How exciting and compelling and renegade would be a Society of Interpreters that excavate all representations of scriptures in terms of discourse and power!"[7]

While twelve years later there is still yet to be a Society of Interpreters excavating scriptures in terms of discourse and power, there are a growing number of renegade interpreters examining alternative scriptural traditions and interrogating what this means for a community of people. Just two years after Wimbush's presidential address, my monograph, *Divining the Self: A Study in Yoruba Scriptures and Human Consciousness*, the first in the Signifying Scriptures Series, was published.[8] In the ensuing years, my work as a runagate interpreter of the Ifa literary corpus has continued. One of my most favorite excavations is the following story about

4. Wimbush, "Interpreters—Enslaving/Enslaved/Runagate," 8.

5. Wimbush, "Interpreters—Enslaving/Enslaved/Runagate," 9.

6. Adam J. Banks, *Digital Griots: African American Rhetoric in a Multimedia Age* (Carbondale: Southern Illinois University Press, 2011), 1–9.

7. Wimbush, "Interpreters—Enslaving/Enslaved/Runagate," 9.

8. Velma E. Love, *Divining the Self: A Study in Yoruba Myth and Human Consciousness* (University Park: Pennsylvania State University Press, 2012).

the divine feminine. This story, "The Furtive Powers of the Mothers," was shared with me by an African American Priest of Ifa. He learned it from another priest, a griot with a vast oral repertoire of wisdom teachings.[9] The story goes like this:

> One time, Orunmila became so enamored with himself as a diviner he forgot about the power of women. People kept telling him, "Orunmila, if you are going to be successful you need to make *ebo* to powerful beings. What powerful beings, you mean Shango," Orunmila said.
>
> They answered "No, not Shango."
>
> "Oh, you mean Ogun."
>
> "No," his friends said.
>
> "Oh, then you must mean Esu/Elegba."
>
> "No, there's someone more powerful than Shango, more powerful than Ogun, more powerful than Esu."
>
> "Then, who could that be?," Orunmila asked.
>
> They answered in unison, "the women!"
>
> Orunmila scoffed, "The women! Ha! The women! They are weaklings, I don't need to make *ebo* to them." So, he didn't.
>
> Orunmila's life started going up and down. He couldn't get any traction. Things would get a little better but then go right back or get even worse. It seemed as if every time he took one step forward, he took two steps backward. Finally, he began to wonder if it really did have something to do with making *ebo* to the powerful beings. So, one night he prepared the *ebo*, just as he was instructed, and placed it by the tree at the crossroads. He hid behind some bushes and watched to see if he could find out who were the powerful Iyaamis that his friends kept talking about. The power was so great, they said, that they would only speak of the mothers in hushed tones. They said the mothers could wink or blow and one's life would turn upside down. However, they were silent about their power, never spoke of it, but it was super, super powerful.
>
> Orunmila waited and watched, waited and watched, finally he saw a woman approaching. He looked closely and saw that it was his neighbor. He crept out from his hiding place as she picked up some of the *ebo*. He said, "What, you? You're the one causing me this trouble?"
>
> She replied, "Yes, me, and if you forget, I'll do it again." Then she went back in the house. Orunmila had a feeling that she wasn't the only one. So, he waited, and after a while he saw someone else approach-

9. As told to me by Stephen Lewis, January 2022, who heard it from Chief Oluwo Obafemi of the Obafemi Institute for the Divine and Universal Study of Ifa (www.obafemi.org).

ing. She knelt down and took some of the *ebo*. He looked closely and realized that it was his neighbor on the other side. "What?!" he gasped, "You mean you are playing a role in all this trouble that's been coming round here?"

"Yes, me," she said, "and if you forget, I'll do it again." Orunmila shook his head and promised not to forget.

"I had no idea," he said. Stunned, Orumila crept back into the shadows and waited again, noticing that there was still *ebo* on the plate. He waited and watched, watched and waited. Just as he was about to call it at night and head for home, he saw the door of his own house open. He waited, not believing his eyes. His own wife came out and went to the *ebo* plate. She knelt down and picked up some of the *ebo*. Orunmila stepped out of the shadows and said, "Not you, my own wife, the love of my life! You mean you had a role to play in the trouble coming my way"?

"Yes me!" she said. "And if you forget, I'll do it again." By this time Orunmila realized the terrible mistake he had made, and he promised that he would always, always honor the powerful beings. As time went on some men remembered and some forgot, but the most successful ones always remember to honor the mothers, the divine feminine in the scheme of all things.

This mythic tale from the Holy Odu, the sacred scriptures of the Ifa tradition originating with the Yoruba people of West Africa but now practiced throughout the world, directs attention to the importance of recognizing divine feminine power. A few years ago, I had the opportunity to witness this cultural mythology in action when traveling to Nigeria for qualitative research and initiation. Before my arrival, a Nigerian diviner had predicted that there would be one female, a quiet but powerful woman amid five men in a group coming from the United States. When we first arrived, I was a little shy about joining the group when I saw the men sitting around talking. I would always ask if it were okay, before pulling up my chair to join in the conversation.

Finally, the Babalawo who was leading the group took me aside and told me what had been divined for the group before our arrival. He told me that he had been instructed to never leave me out, because things would not go well if I were not included. One morning I woke up to the sound of motorcycles pulling up in the front yard of the guest house where we were staying. Before long, I heard a chorus of rhythmical chants coming from outside. I quickly got dressed and walked out on the front porch. Sixteen Babalawo were gathered in a circle, chanting, and seemingly enjoying themselves immensely. They were passing shot glasses of gin and offering prayers.

Mesmerized, I headed for a chair but before I could even sit, they invited me to join the circle, take a swig of gin, and offer a prayer. Totally unprepared to be a ritual participant, I turned to the priest with whom I was traveling with a quizzical look. He whispered, "They are honoring you as the only woman here. They want you to pray for them." I slowly lifted the shot glass and silently prayed for blessings on the gathering and all the initiation rituals that would be performed. At the time, I had no idea of what this meant, but I was later reminded of the divination narrative that was the guiding Odu for our trip. It was, indeed, a moment of signifying scripture in action. There are many stories in the Holy Odu about the importance of never overlooking the power of Oshun. At that moment I became the embodiment of Oshun, personified scripture in action. I study the Holy Odu as a runagate interpreter.

This is only one of many Ifa stories about divine feminine power. Another favorite of what has become my growing repertoire of oral texts is the one about Ogun, Obarisha, and Odu coming to earth. My version of the story is adapted from Awo Falokun Ftunmbi.

> Legend has it that when Ogun, Obarisha, and Odu came from the Heavens to Earth, Ogun was first, followed by Obarisha and then Odu. Ogun was given the power to make war, build bridges and forge new infrastructure. Obarisha was given the power to shape civilization, organize cultures, and shape human beings. Odu thought both of these powers were really quite awesome, and she was afraid that Olodumare had left her out. So she asked Oludomare, "If Ogun is a great warrior and Obarisha is a great organizer, then what is my power? Did you forget about me?"
>
> "No," said Olodumare, "how could we forget about you. You, my sister, have the greatest power of all. You are the womb of creation. You have the power of the word. You hold the world in your hands. Nothing can come into existence without you. Men will follow you for they can do nothing without you. But you must never ever abuse your power."
>
> As time went on Odu became a little bit proud and began to abuse her power. At first, she controlled the *igbodou*, the sacred forest, and stood guardian over all the mysteries of life. She owned the divination tools and people came to her when they needed healing. She was in charge of the Egungun Masquerade, and it was she who choreographed the masquerade dance for ancestral blessings. Odu was asked to make offerings to express gratitude for her blessings, but she refused. She

> became indignant, said offerings had already been made and she would not do it. Tensions grew between her and the male Orisha, so Olodumare dispersed some of her power. Olodumare formed initiations for the men and taught them the mysteries of Odu, the power of the word. Soon they became the Egungun masquerade dancers, and they learned the power of the word. They became the great diviners.
>
> Odu complained to Olodumare about the men taking her power. Olodumare told her not to worry, that she still could do something that men could not do, that men would never be able to carry life. Olodumare told her that she would be called, "Mother," a name above all names, a power above all powers. And from that day to this, the mothers, the Iyaami, still carry the mysterious, divine feminine power of creation. And from that day to this, men and women are constantly negotiating the gender power dynamics.

Even though the Society for the Study of Sacred Texts or Comparative Scriptures does not yet exist, runagate interpreters can be found beneath the radar in the cracks and crevices of culture. While they may have no association with the Society of Biblical Literature, they are the ones who, according to Donella H. Meadows, are thinking in systems, using their creative energies as leverage points for change.[10] I've uncovered a few, just by focusing my gaze. They show up as digital griots, poets, historians, public theologians, diviners, and healers. All are in some way runagate interpreters engaged in discursive practices and the dynamics of power. As Adam Banks points out in his writings of African American rhetorical styles, "The griot has survived the middle passage, slavery, and centuries of American apartheid and has been diffused into many different spaces and figures: storytellers, preachers, poets, standup comics, DJs, and everyday people all carry elements of the griots role in African American culture."[11] Just as Banks notes that the practices of the DJ offer an important metaphor for African American writing, I would also suggest that the metaphor works just as well for the runagate interpreter.

Banks identifies the following practices: shoutout, crate-digging, mixing, remixing, mixtape, sample all as important tools to provide writers access to participate in or run from societal norms.[12] Reverend

10. Donella H. Meadows, *Thinking in Systems: A Primer*, ed. Diana Wright, Sustainability Institute (White River, VT: Chelsea Green Publishing, 2008).

11. Banks, *Digital Griots*, 25.

12. Banks, *Digital Griots*, 26–27.

Dr. Melva Sampson, Digital Griot, Creator and Curator of "Pink Robe Chronicles," a digital hush harbor, is a classic example of such. The host of a weekly Sunday morning gathering on Facebook Live, she demonstrates all of the above practices in grand style, constantly calling out the names of individuals who enter the digital space, crate-digging by continuously researching ancestral as well as contemporary literary archives to identify and feature sacred texts from African American authors and artists, mixing and remixing textual interpretations to shed light on the stories of black life.[13] I was more than a little surprised when I learned that my own book, *Divining the Self*, was recently featured as a sacred text that served as the foundation for her preaching/teaching dispensations for several weeks.[14] She also featured the writings of other black women authors as sacred texts, including the works of Monica Coleman, Renita Weems, bell hooks, Toni Morrison, Chanequa Walker-Barnes, Candice Marie Benbow, and others. By centering black women's writings as sacred texts, Melva Sampson is certainly a runagate interpreter, creating psychic space for other ways of knowing and tools for excavating discourses of power, taking a courageous stance, indeed.

Another runagate interpreter who exemplifies the DJ style of crate-digging, mixing and remixing black discursive traditions is Will Coleman, PhD, author of *Tribal Talk: Black Theology, Hermeneutics, and African American Ways of "Telling the Story."*[15] Coleman's hush harbor, digital space is a Monday evening open source online meetup, "Bible and Meditation," that has featured an array of topics over the past ten years, including: Hebrew Alphabets and Tarot Meditations, The Science of Mind, The Kybalion, The Twelve Powers, Think and Grow Rich, The Book of Enoch, The Preeminence of the Divine Feminine, Tarot Archetypes and Meditation Techniques, Tribal Talk Hoodoo, African and African American Spirituality (especially Vodun and Ifa), and Reading Original Biblical texts in Hebrew, Greek, and Latin.[16] Coleman's open-source community educa-

---

13. www.drmelvasampson.com.

14. Love, *Divining the Self.*

15. Will Coleman, *Tribal Talk: Black Theology, Hermeneutics, and African/American Ways of "Telling the Story"* (University Park: Pennsylvania State University Press, 2000).

16. This abbreviated list of course topics was received from Will Coleman, PhD, as the result of an e-mail inquiry, January 2022.

tion class on Monday evenings is like a series of mixed tapes and smash ups for hush harbor gatherings that serve as brave spaces for signifying and testifying.

Such virtual space gatherings around text, image, and sound are becoming increasingly prevalent, especially for runagate interpreters who choose not to be bound by conventional approaches, colonial mindsets, and limited definitions of the sacred. Since his 2010 presidential address, Wimbush's work as a runagate interpreter has opened new venues for *scripturalizing* discourses. One example of such is the 2021 virtual exhibit and symposium, "Masquerade: Scripturalizing Modernities Through Black Flesh," sponsored by Candler School of Theology's Pitts Theological Library and the Institute for Signifying Scriptures. Curated by Wimbush, emphasis was on the making and use of scriptures through everyday cultural production. As a panel moderator, my closing comments during this two-day symposium highlighted the conversation with a poetic reading from *Black Imagination*, an excerpt from which I now turn to.

> First, I listen. This is hard when my feelings are screaming, when my body, my heart, and the pieces of me are aching.... At these times I feel most acutely the loss of my cultural traditions. We the children of the unchosen diaspora—the progeny of the stolen, the kidnaped, the shackled, the enslaved—are in many ways still lost. Lost to our indigenous practices. We pray to white Jesus, god of colonizers, and wonder why our prayers aren't answered.[17]

Here Regan Jackson's words could be identified as those of a runagate interpreter, expressing the sentiments of one who is keenly aware of the violence that could be done by oppression under the masquerade of scripturalization. So, while Wimbush's call to action in 2010 may have fallen on deaf ears within the slow-to-change system known as the Society for Biblical Literature, there are indeed runagate interpreters all around. We need only expand our gaze and look beyond the cloistered academy to the poets, storytellers, authors, performers, producers, and creatives within the cultures around us. Ultimately, they are the ones who will help us understand ruminations of the sacred in the scriptures we live.

---

17. Natasha Marin, *Black Imagination* (Seattle: McSweeney's, 2020), 97.

Bibliography

Banks, Adam J. *Digital Griots: African American Rhetoric in a Multimedia Age*. Carbondale: Southern Illinois University Press, 2011.

Coleman, Will. *Tribal Talk: Black Theology, Hermeneutics, and African/American Ways of "Telling the Story."* University Park: Pennsylvania State University Press, 2000.

Ganz, Marshall. "What Is Public Narrative: Self, Us, Now." Working Paper. Harvard University, 2009. https://tinyurl.com/SBL4527e.

Love, Velma E. *Divining the Self: A Study in Yoruba Myth and Human Consciousness*. University Park: Pennsylvania State University Press, 2012.

Marin, Natasha. *Black Imagination*. Seattle: McSweeney's, 2020.

Meadows, Donella H. *Thinking in Systems: A Primer.* Edited by Diana Wright. Sustainability Institute. White River, VT: Chelsea Green Publishing, 2008.

Wimbush, Vincent L. "Interpreters—Enslaving/Enslaved/Runagate." *JBL* 130 (2011): 5–24.

Part 2
Fusion of the Critical/Political and Biblical/Geopolitical

Criticism in Critical Times: Reflections on Vision and Task

FERNANDO F. SEGOVIA

Acceptance of the nomination to serve as president of the Society of Biblical Literature in 2014 immediately set off a process of reflection on my part regarding an appropriate topic for the main function of such a charge, the presidential address. With the passage of time, three ideas, all having to do with various social-cultural dimensions of my term, gradually established themselves as primary in my mind. Eventually, they came together, upon much reflection, in the final determination of the topic. I should like to begin by identifying these converging vectors, doing so by way of chronological emergence and appropriation. They involve, respectively, historical, geopolitical, and spatial dimensions of meaning, although all three such dimensions are present in all three vectors. As such, they involve—individually as well as collectively—a critical reading of the global scene, my own location and stance within it, and my identity and role as a biblical critic. In the end, such reflections led me to the question of critical vision and task as a worthy, indeed imperative, topic for my address, for which I have chosen "Criticism in Critical Times: Reflections on Vision and Task" as the title.

The first insight was historical in character, which led to a juxtaposition of critical times involving relations among global powers in the West. I realized that my term would coincide with major anniversaries of global conflicts during the course of the twentieth century: (1) the Great War (1914–1918)—the centenary of the declaration of war in 1914; (2) the Second World War (1939–1945)—the seventy-fifth anniversary of the outbreak of war in 1939 and the seventieth of D-Day in 1944, the beginning of the end for Nazi Germany and the Axis; and (3) the Cold War (1947–1989/91), a confrontation that would engender multiple regional wars and local clashes—the twenty-fifth anniversary of the beginning of the end in 1989, with the collapse of the communist regimes throughout Eastern Europe, symbolically culminating with the fall of the Berlin Wall in November.[1]

I became aware that it had fallen upon me, as the first president from outside the West, to recall and observe such events. I realized that I could do so only as an outsider-insider. The trajectory for me was clear. The Great War marked the beginning of a relentless descent, through sustained advances in warfare technology, into ever more extreme levels of barbarity, carnage, and destruction. Such a path of destruction would engulf not only the old great powers of Europe and the new power of the United States of America but also the rest of the world in its wake. This path has continued beyond the Cold War into our own days, as the North Atlantic Treaty Organization (NATO) has assumed the role of a global patrol force—the First Gulf War (1990–1991), the Second Gulf War (2003–2011), and now in 2014 the war with the Islamic State.[2] This path has brought to a climax the civilizational crisis of the West that began with the Great War, with no sense of what is to come and much less how to manage it. In this existential quandary I find that we are all together—insiders, outsiders, and outsiders-insiders alike.

Subsequently, a geopolitical insight emerged, which brought together critical times having to do with the state of affairs of the Two-Thirds World and its differential relations of power with the One-Third World. My term, I realized, would parallel the sixtieth anniversary of a foundational period in the discursive and material emergence of the Third World (1952–1955): (1) In 1952, the term appeared for the first time, coined by Alfred Sauvy as "*le tiers monde*," in a piece written for the French socialist weekly *L'Observateur*.[3] (2) In 1954, the French Far East Expeditionary Corps in Indochina suffered a decisive defeat at the hands of the Viet Minh forces

1. I say the beginning of the end because what began in 1989 with a wave of revolutions that brought down the communist regimes ended in 1991 with the formal disbanding of the Warsaw Pact on 25 February and the dissolution of the Union of Soviet Socialist Republics on 26 December.

2. On this point, see Immanuel Wallerstein, "NATO: Danger to World Peace," personal page, 15 November 2014, https://tinyurl.com/SBL1130a.

3. Alfred Sauvy, "Trois mondes, une planète," *L'Observateur* 118 (1952), 14. See also Sauvy, "Note sur l'origine de l'expression 'tiers monde' par Alfred Sauvy," *Le Magazine de l'homme moderne*, https://tinyurl.com/SBL1130b.

of Ho Chi Minh at Dien Bien Phu, bringing to a close the First Indochina War (1946–1954) and ushering in, after the Geneva Accord of 1955 and the partition of Vietnam, the Second Indochina War (1955–1975).[4] (3) In 1955, the Bandung (Indonesia) Conference took place, bringing together the newly independent countries of Africa and Asia in a first attempt to chart a middle, independent course between the dialectics of capitalist and socialist modernism.[5]

I became conscious of the fact that I was to be the first president from the Global South, or what was popularly known from the 1950s through the 1970s as the Third World.[6] This was the world of my origins and primary culture. It is to its diaspora in the Global North that I belong, as a first-generation immigrant and an inescapably transnational subject. This was, therefore, the first time that the Society had ventured outside the parameters of the Euro-American world of the North Atlantic. I had thus become a marker of the tectonic demographic changes taking place throughout the world since the 1960s, whose impact began to reach the Society in the late 1970s and early 1980s, as the field of studies expanded into Africa and the Middle East, Asia and the Pacific, Latin America and the Caribbean.

The last insight was spatial in nature, which led to the conjunction of critical times involving borders and migrations, nations and the Other. I realized that my term would coincide with the fiftieth anniversary of a

---

4. Southeast Asia was one of many areas of the Third World where the United States and the Soviet Union engaged in geopolitical struggle for control during the late 1940s and the 1950s. See Robert J. McMahon, *The Cold War: A Very Short Introduction*, Very Short Introductions (Oxford: Oxford University Press, 2003), 64–74, esp. 70–72.

5. On the Bandung Conference, see Robert J. C. Young, *Postcolonialism: An Historical Introduction* (Oxford: Blackwell, 2001), 182–92, esp. 191–92. Young sees the conference, attended by twenty-nine African and Asian countries, as a foundational moment for postcolonialism, given its constitution as a political pressure group reflecting an "independent transcontinental political consciousness in Africa and Asia" (p. 191). Out of it would eventually come the Movement of Non-Aligned Countries in 1961 and the Tricontinental in 1966, which brought together Africa, Asia, and Latin America.

6. On the concept of the Third World, its origins and variations and trajectory, see M. D. Litonjua, "Third World/Global South: From Modernization, to Dependency/Liberation, to Postdevelopment," *Journal of Third World Studies* 29 (2012): 25–56; Marcin Wojciech Solarz, "'Third World': The Sixtieth Anniversary of a Concept That Changed History," *Third World Quarterly* 33.9 (2012): 1561–73.

similarly foundational period in the country and its relations with Latin America and the Caribbean (1963–1965): (1) In 1963, the assassination of President John Fitzgerald Kennedy signified what Jon Margulis has called the "last innocent year" before the sixties.[7] (2) In 1964, the Civil Rights Act was enacted, a landmark of the civil rights struggle, and the progressive government of President João Goulart of Brazil was overthrown, the first of many military coups to follow in Latin America, which would ultimately lead to the establishment of a web of repression across much of the continent, known as Operation Condor.[8] (3) In 1965, the Immigration and Nationality Act abolished the restrictive immigration laws of the 1920s, which had favored western and northern Europeans, paving the way for the massive demographic transformation still under way, in which Latin Americans and Caribbeans have played a leading part.[9]

I became aware that the city of San Diego would serve as the venue for the Annual Meeting of the Society during my term, where only a few miles to the south stands the westernmost end of the long and freighted border between the United States of America and the Estados Unidos Mexicanos. It is a border that serves as the signifier for a deeper discursive-material border with the whole of Latin America and the Caribbean and, ultimately, for a global divide between haves and have-nots. This deeper border I had traversed, across the Florida Straits, in July of 1961, at the height of the Cold War, as an adolescent and a child of political refugees. In so doing, I was following the trek of millions of Latin Americans who had made and would make their way to the north, becoming thereby a member of a minoritized ethnic formation within the nation-state of the United States. I was also joining the path of untold millions of human beings from the South who had searched and would search for refuge in the North.

In pursuing these converging social-cultural dimensions regarding my term, I was struck by how contemporary discussions regarding such

---

7. Jon Margulis, *The Last Innocent Year: America in 1964; The Beginning of the "Sixties"* (New York: Morrow, 1999).

8. On Operation Condor, see J. Patrice McSherry, *Predatory States: Operation Condor and Covert War in Latin America* (Lanham, MD: Rowman & Littlefield, 2005).

9. Indeed, a decisive signifier of such ongoing transformation is the new policy on immigration, with Latinos/as foremost in mind, announced by President Barack Obama just prior to the beginning of this Annual Meeting; see Michael D. Sheer, "Obama, Daring Congress, Acts to Overhaul Immigration," *New York Times*, 20 November 2014, https://tinyurl.com/SBL1130c.

vectors of meaning, surrounding major anniversaries of landmark events, approached these critical times of the past as having direct significance and relevance for the present, drawing upon them to shed light on the critical times of today.

Thus, analysis of the Great War and its ramifications reached into the present and future not only of Europe but also of the globe.[10] It turned for counsel and direction to the uncertain situation involving the great powers at the beginning of the twentieth century, highly charged and precarious, in dealing with the equally shifting and uncertain situation of the great powers at the beginning of the twenty-first century, no less charged and precarious. Similarly, scrutiny of the Global South turned to the concept of the Third World in the second half of the twentieth century. It looked for enlightenment and guidance to the problematic of the Third World in the dialectical world order of industrial capitalism in coming to terms with the fate of the Global South within the neoliberal world order of global capitalism.[11] Further, analysis of the border with Mexico and the phenomenon of Latino/a immigration, and of borders and migration in general, reached back to the decade of the 1960s. It sought wisdom and insight, from within a context of paranoic fear of the Other and massive projects of national security involving militarization and snooping, in the discourse of civil rights, the liberal attitude toward immigration, and the trajectory of relations with Latin America.[12]

Given such emphasis on significance and relevance for the present, I came to see that this convergence of vectors of meaning and association of events

---

10. Such comparisons have continued. See, e.g., Margaret MacMillan, "The Rhyme of History: Lessons of the Great War," The Brookings Essay, 14 December 2013, https://tinyurl.com/SBL1130d; Dominique Moïsi, "The Return of the Sleepwalkers," Project Syndicate, 25 June 2014, https://tinyurl.com/SBL1130e.

11. See, e.g., Arif Dirlik, "Global South: Predicament and Promise," *Global South* 1 (2007): 12–23.

12. See, e.g., Antonia Darder and Rodolfo D. Torres, "Latinos and Society: Culture, Politics, and Class," in *The Latino Studies Reader: Culture, Economy and Society*, ed. Antonia Darder and Rodolfo D. Torres (Malden, MA: Blackwell, 1998), 3–26; and, in the same volume, Edna Acosta-Belén and Carlos E. Santiago, "Merging Borders: The Remapping of America," 29–42, and Rosaura Sánchez, "Mapping the Spanish Language along a Multiethnic and Multilingual Border," 101–25. See also Ramón Grosfoguel, Nelson Maldonado-Torres, and José David Saldívar, eds., *Latinos/as in the World System: Decolonization Struggles in the Twenty-First Century U.S. Empire*, Political Economy of the World-Systems Annual (Boulder, CO: Paradigm, 2006).

regarding my term deserved, even demanded, a response on my part as a biblical critic. What should I as a critic do in the face of our critical times? How should I conduct my métier? This I saw as a daunting task, but imperative nonetheless. I shall attempt to formulate an initial response to this question.

1. Presidential Preoccupations in Critical Times of Yesteryear

I begin my response by tracing the topics pursued by former presidents in their addresses to the Society of Biblical Literature during the critical times in question.[13] Such a sense of rhetorical choice will serve as a telling signifier for the wider problematic regarding the function of criticism with respect to social-cultural context. Presidential addresses in general, as Patrick Gray has noted in his study of the genre, have gone in two directions: speaking either to the few or to the many, that is, taking up a specific question within a specialized area of research or turning to a general question touching upon the field of studies as a whole.[14] I shall focus here on the years of the First World War. What were the concerns of choice on the part of former presidents of the Society as Europe and the world plunged ever deeper into an abyss of unparalleled violence and utter inhumanity?

In 1914, the president was Nathaniel Schmidt (1862–1939), a native of Sweden who had immigrated to the United States in 1884. He was Professor of Semitic Languages and Literature at Cornell University (1896–1932). His topic was "The Story of the Flood and the Growth of the Pentateuch."[15] Charles Cutler Torrey (1863–1956) became president in 1915, speaking on "The Need of a New Edition of the Hebrew Bible." He served at the time as Professor of Semitic Philosophy and Comparative Grammar at

---

13. The information on presidents and presidential addresses has been gathered from a variety of sources, among which the following are salient: Ernest W. Saunders, *Searching the Scriptures: A History of the Society of Biblical Literature, 1880–1980*, BSNA 8 (Chico, CA: Scholars Press, 1982); John H. Hayes, ed., *Dictionary of Biblical Interpretation*, 2 vols. (Nashville: Abingdon, 1999).

14. Patrick Gray, "Presidential Addresses," *JBL* 125 (2006): 167–77. This distinction I do not see as a binomial, since addresses dealing with particular areas of research do mention from time to time the ramifications of the positions advanced for the field in general.

15. The address was not published in the *Journal of Biblical Literature*, and, to the best of my knowledge, it was not published elsewhere. Before coming to Cornell, Schmidt had been Professor of Semitic Languages and Literature at Colgate University (1888–1896).

Yale University (1900–1932).[16] Morris Jastrow Jr. (1861–1922) followed in 1916, a native of Poland and son of a prominent rabbi and scholar; Jastrow had immigrated as a young child with his family in 1866. A professor of Semitics at the University of Pennsylvania (1884–1919), he spoke on "Constructive Elements in the Critical Study of the Old Testament."[17] Warren J. Moulton (1865–1947) became president in 1917, speaking on "The Dating of the Synoptic Gospels." For many years he was associated with Bangor Theological Seminary, where he served as Hayes Professor of the New Testament Language and Literature (1905–33) and as president (1921–33).[18] In 1918, the president was James A. Montgomery (1866–1949), Professor of Hebrew and Aramaic at the University of Pennsylvania and the Philadelphia School of Divinity (1909–38). His topic was "Present Tasks of American Biblical Scholarship."[19]

These were all learned scholars. Their topics entertained major disputed questions of their time. With one exception, however, none made reference to the war and the global state of affairs in their presentations. The one voice to do so was that of Montgomery. Shortly after the signing of the Armistice (11 November), he invoked the Great War in crafting a vision for American scholarship, analyzing its present moorings[20] and envisioning its future paths[21] (26 December). His reflections are worth examining, given their incisive and unusual, yet ultimately contradictory, character.

16. The address was not published in the *Journal of Biblical Literature*, and, again, to the best of my knowledge, it was not published elsewhere. Before his appointment at Yale, Torrey had been Professor of Semitic Languages at Andover Theological Seminary (1892–1900).

17. Morris Jastrow Jr., "Constructive Elements in the Critical Study of the Old Testament," *JBL* 36 (1917): 1–20.

18. Warren J. Moulton, "The Dating of the Synoptic Gospels," *JBL* 37 (1918): 1–19. Before Bangor, he taught for a few years in the Semitic and Biblical Department at Yale University (1888–1902). See the *In Memoriam* notices by Charles C. Torrey, Millar Burrows, and William F. Albright, "In Memoriam Warren Joseph Moulton, 1865–1947," *BASOR* 107 (1947): 1, 5–7.

19. James A. Montgomery, "Present Tasks of American Biblical Scholarship," *JBL* 38 (1919): 1–14. See also "James Alan Montgomery (1866–1949)," Penn Biographies, https://tinyurl.com/SBL1130f.

20. The context is sharply drawn: (a) a rejection of all things German, including German scholarship; (b) a denunciation of biblical scholarship for its failure to play any role in the war; (c) a critique of American scholarship for the narrowness of its focus; and (d) an exposition of the weaknesses of such scholarship.

21. The vision is, in principle, expansive. (A) Montgomery calls for a turn to

For Montgomery, the global framework functions as the context for rather than object of discourse. The crisis provides the grounds for a twofold call. On the one hand, in a biting critique of his fellow scholars, whom he chides for having had nothing to say about or contribute to the war effort, he calls for a committed study of the Bible as a document that is quintessentially religious in character, that has much to say regarding the human condition, and that stands for the values of Western civilization at its best and hence of the victorious Allies in particular. On the other hand, in a sharp challenge to his assembled colleagues, whom he upbraids for their constricted focus on philology and science, he calls for a most expansive agenda of historical research (philological, historiographical, archaeological) alongside a finely tuned program of public dissemination. In the end, the two parts of the vision fail to come together. The first call, grounded in a mixture of unabashed liberal humanism and outright religious (Protestant) sentiment, remains totally undeveloped, while the second, grounded in a vigorous sense of American leadership, is amply outlined. As a result, what is meant as an imperative corrective to the previous, overriding focus on science in the field loses its impact, vanishing anew under a renewed emphasis on research without any theoretical integration of the religious, human, and civilizational values upheld. Historicism emerges thereby as the key to the future.

French and British scholarship, whose countries are described as "racially, politically and intellectually our nearest neighbors, bound to us now by a brotherhood knit in blood." One finds throughout, it should be noted, a strong essentialist strain of racial-ethnic discourse, including a reference to "uncivilized races," apparently meaning those outside the fold of Europe ("Present Tasks," 8, 4). (B) He asks scholars to see themselves "first as citizens of the human polity" and to take up the call of the world upon all "to pool their interests and capitals," such as "the science of the Bible," in the pursuit of causes that have "worth-value, spiritual or material" (pp. 1, 2). (C) He outlines such a cause for scholarship by returning to the reason for the study of the Bible: "its assumed value to humanity" (p. 2). Thus, technical expertise must be at the service of the "philosophy of the Bible," which stands "for just those things for which we and our Allies have fought and triumphed"—challenging all human idolatry, "every human thing which would set itself in the seat of God," and providing ideals for the kingdom of God, "right and peace," "natural humanity and sane democracy," "idealism" in contrast to "realities" (pp. 4–5). (D) Montgomery calls for American scholarship to intensify the historical study of the Bible along any number of lines and to sharpen the communication of the results of such study outside academic circles. In the end, the vision is, in practice, limited: it is by far this last point that prevails.

This set of addresses is no different from those delivered during the critical times to follow: the Second World War and the Cold War, whether at the beginning, during the rise of the Third World (1952–1955), or at its height, the eruption of the sixties (1963–1965). They all reveal a sharp disconnect, in sustained and systematic fashion, between what was going on in the academic-scholarly world of the Society and what was taking place in the social-cultural world of national/international affairs. Most were devoted to specialized questions, with no consideration whatever of the wider context of criticism, local or global. Those that opted for a broader optic of the field did not have their respective critical times in mind at all or did so only in passing and by way of material background. Only Montgomery reflected seriously on the global state of affairs and its discursive ramifications for the field. Even here, however, there was no proper theorization or incorporation of the urgent recommendations proposed. In sum, in critical times presidents have kept the world of criticism and the world of politics quite apart from each other.

2. The Function of Criticism as Problematic

In this second part of the response, I turn to the problematic regarding critical vision and task as such, approaching it from a variety of discursive frameworks other than biblical criticism: intellectual, historical, and literary studies. My aim is to situate the rhetorical choice followed by presidential addresses within a comprehensive spectrum of opinion regarding the pursuit of critical inquiry. In effect, former presidents have unreflectively assumed a position within a spectrum of opinion regarding the task of criticism—its nature and role in society and culture. It is imperative, therefore, to examine the design and parameters of any such spectrum—its structural principles and defining boundaries. Here I foreground the category of the intellectual.

The task of the intellectual in the analysis of society and culture is neither self-evident nor determinate. Although it was advanced more than twenty years ago now, I find no better point of entry into this question than Edward W. Said's BBC Reith Lectures of 1993, "Representations of the Intellectual."[22] This was a reflection on the intelligentsia and thus on criti-

22. Edward W. Said, *Representations of the Intellectual: The 1993 Reith Lectures* (repr., New York: Vintage Books, 1996). Said (1935–2003), University Professor at Columbia University at the time, was a foremost cultural critic, at home in any

cism writ most large in the modern world. Toward the end of the twentieth century, Said undertook a genealogy of the intellectual beginning with the early part of the century. In so doing, he engaged in dialogue with a wide number of figures, positions, and writings through the century, not only in Europe and the West but also in the Third World.

The genealogy yields a spectrum of opinion ranging from the numerous-collaborationist to the selective-oppositional, with a key theory as representative of each pole—Antonio Gramsci and Julien Benda, respectively.[23] At the populist pole, Gramsci allowed for a wide variety of intellectuals, with a distinction between traditional and organic. The former, encompassing functionaries associated with traditional institutions (teachers, priests, administrators), stayed at a distance from society, carrying out their task in routinarian fashion through the years. The latter, involving functionaries in modern institutions (technicians, experts, organizers), were actively involved in society, seeking ever greater influence and power. At the restricted pole, Benda portrayed intellectuals as members of a small, heroic circle, pursuing truth and justice rather than their gain, advancement, or favor with power. Such pursuit entailed not retreat from the world but rather resolute engagement with it, in opposition to corruption, oppression, authoritarianism throughout.

This genealogy Said updates to his own times, the modern world of the late twentieth century. The world of intellectuals, he argues, has turned out largely along the lines predicted by Gramsci. With the growth of the knowledge industry and the proliferation of new professions, there are engaged intellectuals to be found in the production and distribution of knowledge throughout a host of institutions. They work as professionals who, assigned a specific function within such institutions, work for

---

number of discursive frameworks. In the introduction (pp. ix–xix) he provides a sharp analysis of the Lectures as a cultural phenomenon.

23. For Gramsci (1891–1937), Said relies on his *Quaderni del carcere* or *Prison Notebooks*, written from 1929 to 1935, while in prison under the Fascist regime in Italy. They were not published until the 1950s in the original and the 1970s in English translation: *Selections from the Prison Notebooks of Antonio Gramsci*, ed. and trans. Quintin Hoare and Geoffrey Nowell-Smith (New York: International, 1971). For Benda (1867–1956), he relies on *La trahison des clercs*, originally published in 1927 and updated in 1946. It was first translated into English in 1928: *The Treason of the Intellectuals*, trans. Richard Aldington (New York: Morrow, 1928); it was published in 1955 as *The Betrayal of the Intellectuals*, trans. Richard Aldington, introduction by Herbert Read (Boston: Beacon, 1955).

the benefit of the institutions. In such a world the contrarian, moral ideal of Benda has by and large vanished. Indeed, rather than speaking to the world at large in terms of what is true and just, intellectuals today speak to one another within their respective institutions by way of an abstruse and exclusionary language.

Within this general mapping and contemporary scenario, Said opts for Benda's ideal, although in revised fashion. The intellectual, he argues, must be "an individual with a specific public role in society that cannot be reduced simply to being a faceless professional, a competent member of a class just going about her/his business."[24] The intellectual task, therefore, is defined as representing a message to and for a public. Such representation has a sharp, double edge to it: first, to question, expose, challenge any type of settled doctrine or attitude on the part of the status quo, local or global; second, to do so on behalf of what is excluded or marginalized, whether issues or persons. Such representation further entails a distinctive, twofold way of acting: first, it must be contextual and personal in mode, bringing together the private and public spheres at all times; second, it must be cosmopolitan and moral in scope, appealing to universal principles regarding humanity as espoused by the global community.[25]

It is in the matter of praxis that Benda is reconceptualized and reformulated. On the one hand, Benda remained resolutely, unconsciously European in his position—Europe as the center of and for the world. After mid-century, such an assumption was no longer possible: with the rise of the Third World, such factors as ethnicity, nationality, and continent had to be taken into account in representation. On the other hand, Benda never expanded on the concepts of justice and truth, their origins or meaning—such principles remained abstract. After mid-century, such a vision was no longer tenable: with the emergence of the United Nations, a series of accords

24. Said, *Representations of the Intellectual*, 11.

25. Said summarizes such principles: "that all human beings are entitled to expect decent standards of behavior concerning freedom and justice from worldly powers or nations, and that deliberate or inadvertent violations of these standards need to be testified and fought against courageously" (*Representations of the Intellectual*, 11–12). It is a position that he sees as reasserting a "grand narrative of emancipation and enlightenment" in the face of postmodernism and its emphasis on "local situations and language games": "For in fact governments still manifestly oppress people, grave miscarriages of justice still occur, the co-optation and inclusion of intellectuals by power can still effectively quieten their voices, and the deviation of intellectuals from their vocation is still very often the case" (18).

and treaties giving flesh to such principles had to be assumed in representation, such as the United Nations Declaration on Human Rights of 1948.

In the end, for Said, the world is political to the core, full of beckoning representations, and it proves impossible for the intellectual to escape from politics, whether it be "into the realms of pure art and thought or, for that matter, into the realms of disinterested objectivity or transcendental theory."[26] Intellectuals inevitably adopt a position in representation, no matter where they stand in the spectrum. This position can oscillate between the professional-accommodationist, entrenched within the apparatus and horizon of an organization, and the amateur-protesting, opening up to a world in conflict and siding with truth and justice at all times.

This spectrum of the intellectual life is very similar, mutatis mutandis, to those offered in historiography by Gabrielle Spiegel in her 2009 presidential address to the American Historical Association, "The Task of the Historian,"[27] and in literary criticism by both Terry Eagleton in his 1996 overview of literary theory, "Political Criticism," and Vincent Leitch in his recently published essay on "The Tasks of Critical Reading."[28] What are the consequences of such a spectrum across a variety of discursive frameworks for my response? In largely pursuing pressing questions of the discipline while bypassing pressing questions of the world, as they overwhelmingly did in critical times, presidential addresses assumed a political stance of abstraction from the realm of global affairs into the realm of scholarship.

---

26. Said, *Representations of the Intellectual*, 21.

27. Gabrielle M. Spiegel, "The Task of the Historian," *AHR* 114 (2009): 1–15. At the time, Spiegel was the Krieger-Eisenhower University Professor of History at the Johns Hopkins University. A medievalist by training, Spiegel has multiple interests, among which lies a concern with theory and practice in historiography; on this, see her edited volume, *Practicing History: New Directions in Historical Writing after the Linguistic Turn*, Rewriting Histories (New York: Routledge, 2005), esp. her "Introduction" (pp. 1–31). See also Spiegel, *The Past as Text: The Theory and Practice of Medieval Historiography*, Parallax (Baltimore: Johns Hopkins University Press, 1997), esp. part 1, "Theory."

28. Terry Eagleton, *Literary Theory: An Introduction*, 2nd ed. (Minneapolis: University of Minnesota Press, 1996), 169–89. See also his historical trajectory of criticism, *The Function of Criticism: From the Spectator to Post-Structuralism* (London: Verso, 1984), and his exposition of Marxist literary criticism, *Marxism and Literary Criticism* (Berkeley: University of California Press, 1976), esp. 37–58 (ch. 3, "The Writer and Commitment"). Vincent Leitch, *Literary Criticism in the Twenty-First Century: Theory Renaissance* (London: Bloomsbury, 2014), 33–49 (ch. 3, "The Tasks of Critical Reading").

In so doing, they ensconced themselves in the dynamics and mechanics of a discipline devoted to the construction of biblical antiquity and deploying historiographical principles of objectivity and impartiality. The point to keep in mind is that any spectrum of opinion allows for a gamut of other positions and that any position must be acknowledged and theorized. In other words, things need not have been, and need not be, this way, as, alas, James Montgomery grasped all too well in 1918.

3. Critical Analysis of the Global State of Affairs

The third part of my response calls for critical analysis of our own times. If critics are to adopt an activist position within the spectrum on critical task, to address their social-cultural context, and to marshal the resources of their field in this endeavor, then it is indispensable to secure a firm grasp on the global state of affairs today. That our times are perceived as critical, and universally so, should go without saying. Wherever one looks, such is the verdict. Such is certainly the case with respect to any area of society and culture. It is also the case in terms of their overall conjunction as a world system. Indeed, it is not at all unusual to portray our times as uniquely critical, beyond all critical times of the twentieth century, severe as these were.

What are "our times"? Where does the contemporary global state of affairs begin? If the Cold War marked the course of an era, extending over the second half of the century, its end signifies the beginning of a new epoch. The dialectical struggle unto death between East and West, the two superpowers and their corresponding blocs of nations, came to an end with the collapse of the East in 1989/91. We find ourselves, therefore, in a state of affairs best described for now in postist terms—the era of the post–Cold War.

Here a twofold development should be kept in mind. There ensued at first a period of vibrant optimism, bordering on the utopian, if not the millennial. The work of Francis Fukuyama stands as a perfect signifier of this moment. Writing in 1989, he argues that the march of liberal democracy, politically and economically, has proved triumphant, signaling perhaps the "End of History."[29] Peace and progress would now prevail

29. Francis Fukuyama, "The End of History," *National Interest* (Summer 1989). At the time, Fukuyama, a former analyst at the RAND Corporation, was deputy director

for all, given no competing vision in sight. This initial effervescence would not last long. In time, a period of grave pessimism began to emerge, ultimately entrenching itself in global consciousness. The work of Fukuyama again serves as an ideal indicator of the times. Writing twenty-five years later, and with the anniversary in mind, he offers a chastened assessment of the End of History, still optimistic but only in the long range and with the right corrective measures.[30] Other voices, writing on the anniversary, prove far more dismissive of such claims and far more somber regarding future prospects.[31] The reason for such a shift within the post–Cold War era is not hard to ascertain.

During this past quarter of a century, crisis has followed upon crisis, fueling an ever-widening and ever-deepening sense of dis-order. Such disease has involved any number of interlinked developments across society and culture, local and global alike: geopolitical multipolarity and multijousting; political paralysis or breakdown at the level of the nation-state; global economic meltdown and inequality; radical ecological transformation; seismic population trends and reactions; explosion of violence at all levels. One could go on. The result has been a pervasive sense of disorientation, powerlessness, uncertainty. Such has been the consensus across the ideological spectrum, in terms of both critique and construction: on the left, much reinvigorated, pressing for substantial structural changes; on the right, thoroughly dismayed, advocating the strong assertion of structural power; and in the center, straddling the fence, pressing for corrective structural reforms.

This sense of fragility and threat I have sought to capture by way of three particular discourses and critiques: global economics, climatological projections, and worldwide migration. I highlight global economics here. For this

---

of the State Department's policy planning staff. This theory was expanded in a later volume, *The End of History and the Last Man* (New York: Free Press, 1992).

30. Francis Fukuyama, "At the 'End of History' Still Stands Democracy," *Wall Street Journal*, 7–8 June 2014, http://online.wsj.com/articles/at-the-end-of-history-still-stands-democracy-1402080661. At the time of this address, Fukuyama is a senior fellow at the Freeman Spogli Institute for International Studies at Stanford University. See further his *Political Order and Political Decay: From the Industrial Revolution to the Globalization of Democracy* (New York: Farrar, Straus & Giroux, 2014).

31. See, e.g., Timothy Stanley and Alexander Leesep, "It's Still Not the End of History," *The Atlantic*, 1 September 2014, https://tinyurl.com/SBL1130g; and Mario Vargas Llosa, "Las guerras del fin del mundo," *El País*, 7 September 2014, http://elpais.com/elpais/2014/09/04/opinion/1409856348_817996.html.

I turn to a highly incisive and programmatic piece by Alfred J. López, "The (Post) Global South."[32] It advances, on the one hand, a critical account of globalization as a process involving three stages: construction, deconstruction, alternatives (possibilities for a different future, both already at work and yet to come).[33] What emerges as a result is a vision of the Global South as a postglobal reality and signifier of subalternity across boundaries, material and discursive alike. The piece calls, on the other hand, for a broadly based analysis of this reality: the development of a postglobal discourse that draws upon the full spectrum of fields of studies in the academy.

Globalization, López argues, emerged in the 1980s and accelerated through the 1990s as the global master narrative. It is thus, in effect, the hegemonic discourse of the post–Cold War era. The narrative presents the process of globalization, as generated and sustained by the economic policies of neoliberalism, as yielding such growth as to lift the entire world in its wake, from the very rich to the very poor. Such growth requires the development of an integrated world economy, based on free trade and free markets and governed by the laws of exchange. Such growth not only would benefit those individuals directly engaged in the process but also would solve all social ills and thus resolve social contradictions.[34]

The reality behind this narrative, López continues, proved quite different, leading to a counter-narrative that exposes the downside of the project. This narrative points to a series of financial crises that have called into question any dream of an integrated world economy ruled solely in terms of the market and capital.[35] Here one should keep in mind that López is writing

32. Alfred J. López, "The (Post) Global South," *Global South* 1 (2007): 1–11. López is professor of English at Purdue University and a scholar with interests in postcolonial, Caribbean, and globalization studies. See also his *Posts and Pasts: A Theory of Postcolonialism*, Explorations in Postcolonial Studies (Albany: State University of New York Press, 2001); and his edited volume, *Postcolonial Whiteness: A Critical Reader on Race and Empire* (Albany: State University of New York Press, 2005).

33. These stages are at once sequential and simultaneous, given the speed that marks the project of globalization.

34. Among its proponents stand prominent voices, such as Anthony Giddens (*Runaway World: How Globalization Is Reshaping Our Lives* [London: Profile Books, 1999]) and Joseph Stieglitz (*Globalization and Its Discontents* [New York: Norton, 2003]; and Stieglitz, *Making Globalization Work* [New York: Norton, 2006]). Both believe that globalization can be rescued and made to work for all.

35. The list is worth reproducing: "These setbacks include the Asian, Russian, and Brazilian economic crises of 1997–8; the end of the U.S. market boom in 2000; the

prior to the Great Recession of 2008. The narrative also foregrounds the differential consequences of neoliberal policies, which have only served to heighten social ills and accentuate social contradictions. Thus, while the interests of the elite have been protected and furthered, a series of setbacks for the working and middle classes has resulted: lower wages and fewer benefits, an increase in unemployment alongside a decrease in job security, a reduction of social services for the working poor.[36] Indeed, as many economists now argue, it has been the poor, the disadvantaged, and the marginalized who have paid the price of the project, among whom minorities and immigrants are the greatest number by far.[37]

For López, therefore, the Global South of yesteryear, the South of colonial discourse and postcolonial studies, has become the Post–Global South of today, the South of subalterns throughout the world, who are keenly aware that the project of globalization has failed utterly and that they embody the margins of "the brave new liberal world of globalization." This Post–Global South thus moves beyond the North–South divide of yore, insofar as such subalterns are to be found, as immigrants and minorities, throughout the global cities of the geographical North as well. They have been dis-placed from the geographical South and find themselves dis-jointed in the geographical North, at once put to use and set at a distance, despite a host discourse of "multiculturalism, rights, and tolerance of social difference." Immigrants—broadly understood as including descendants—become thereby both "avatar and pariah—simultaneously a product of globalization and a scapegoat for its many failures."[38]

---

attack on the World Trade Center on September 11, 2001; the exposed multibillion-dollar scams of Enron and other major corporations, culminating in their collapse; the Argentine fiscal crisis; and the current crises and infrastructural meltdowns in Iraq and New Orleans" (López, "[Post] Global South," 4).

36. Here López has recourse to the work of David Harvey, *A Brief History of Neoliberalism* (Oxford: Oxford University Press, 2005).

37. Among the poor, the disadvantaged, and the marginalized, López points out, lie also the white working poor and shrinking middle class, who see globalization as a threat to the nation—politically, economically, and culturally. What emerges out of such anxiety is often an extreme form of nationalism that leads to racism, signified by discrimination and violence against immigrants and minorities. "As they so often do in our literal wars," he remarks, "the immigrant and the working-class white native thus become the unacknowledged and largely unwitting foot soldiers of globalization" ("[Post] Global South, 3).

38. López, "(Post) Global South," 3–4.

From an academic-scholarly point of view, therefore, the task is to explore the subjectivity and agency of subalterns—those who live in the débris of global capitalism, without access to its benefits—through the development of a postglobal discourse. For López, globalization calls forth—as rapidly as it unfolds—opposition. The reason is clear. On the one hand, its wreckage is unquestionable: "widespread poverty, displacement and diaspora, environmental degradation, human and civil rights abuses, war, hunger, disease"—present in a Post-Global South that includes not only the geographical South but also the metaphorical South present in the geographical North. On the other hand, the struggle for survival is equally undeniable: the emergence of subaltern cultures and economies by way of ethnic, religious, or national identity construction—a spectrum of transnational groups working out of the same logic of opposition. Postglobal discourse is to take up, therefore, in inter- and multidisciplinary fashion, the "condition" of such groups: the who—the question of identity, local or global; the why—the logic of globalization; and the how—the cultures of opposition. Its aim in so doing is to search for a "glimpse" of the future—the potential for "a postglobal politics and economics of inclusion and enfranchisement."[39]

Very similar accounts of our sense of fragility and menace in the post–Cold War era emerge in the discourses and critiques regarding climatological projections and international migration, as drawn, respectively, by Dipesh Chakrabarty in "The Climate of History: Four Theses"[40] and Khalid Koser in his volume entitled *International Migration*.[41] The result is

---

39. López, "(Post) Global South," 7.

40. Dipesh Chakrabarty, "The Climate of History: Four Theses," *Critical Inquiry* 35 (2009): 197–222. Chakrabarty is the Lawrence A. Kimpton Distinguished Service Professor of History, South Asian Languages and Civilizations and the College at the University of Chicago. He is a scholar of wide-ranging interests, with a particular concern for matters of method and theory in the areas of modern South Asia studies, subaltern studies, and postcolonial studies.

41. Khalid Koser, *International Migration: A Very Short Introduction*, Very Short Introductions (Oxford: Oxford University Press, 2007). Koser, deputy director and academic dean at the Geneva Centre for Security Policy, is an expert in the subject of migration with a long trajectory of publications and an extensive record of administrative positions. Among such positions, the following should be noted: chair of the UK Advisory Panel on Country Information, editor of the *Journal of Refugee Studies*, and vice-chair of the World Economic Forum Global Council on Migration. In 2014 he was named Member of the Order of the British Empire (MBE) in recognition of his

an analytic description of the times in postist fashion. What López characterizes as the postglobal, from the perspective of economics, Chakrabarty describes as the posthuman, from the perspective of climate change, and Khoser as the postnational, from the perspective of world migration. These studies expose but three of the major problematics affecting the global state of affairs. There are many others, as previously mentioned, all accompanied by similar analytical accounts of peril and tenuousness. Further, as all such studies variously indicate, these problematics are closely interdependent and mutually reinforcing. The result is precisely that prevailing sense of the times as uniquely critical, best described perhaps as a crisis of the world system.

What ramifications do such assessments of individual crises and overall assertion of an interlocking global crisis bear for my response? These accounts point, without exception, to the impact of such problematics, both singly and jointly, on the academic-scholarly realm, not only with respect to individual fields of study but also with regard to the full gamut of fields of study—the duty to integrate and respond in some way. That such a verdict applies to religious studies in general and biblical studies in particular should go without question.[42] If critics are to pursue the pressing questions of the world and assume a political stance of engagement in the world, pointed knowledge of the global state of affairs is of the essence. To begin with, there is need for thorough acquaintance with the crises at hand, as conceptualized and formulated, discussed and debated, in their respective discursive and critical trajectories. Beyond that, there is need for a theoretical framework capable of dealing with the intersecting nature of a crisis of the world system. Such impact, I should point out, James Montgomery grasped, within the terms of his own modernist context, perfectly well in 1918.

---

work with refugees and asylum seekers in the United Kingdom. Khalid also holds a professorship in Conflict, Peace and Security at the United Nations University–Maastricht Economic and Social Research Institute on Innovation and Technology and its School of Governance (UNU-MERIT) in the Netherlands.

42. Here the 2012 presidential address of Otto Maduro to the American Academy of Religion is very much to the point, "Migrants' Religions under Imperial Duress: Reflections on Epistemology, Ethics & Politics in the Study of the Religious 'Stranger,'" *JAAR* 82 (2014): 35–46. Maduro addresses the ramifications of the migration crisis, through the lens of migration from Latin America to the United States, for the social study of religion as an academic-scholarly field, since such study lies itself embedded in this context of global crisis. Such ramifications, Maduro argues, scholars can ignore altogether or address directly.

4. A Theoretical Framework for Engaging Our Times

In the fourth part of my response, I turn to the demand for a proper theoretical framework for engaging our times. Given the global state of affairs in the post–Cold War era, a critical framework is needed that can properly embrace and address—beyond focalized problematics and responses—the conjunction of so many crises and challenges, so many corresponding discourses and critiques, in intersectional fashion, in order to keep the system as such in mind at all times. A crisis of the world system demands the adoption of a world theory and hence a dialogue with global studies. Only then can a critic successfully construct an activist position within the field, pointedly engage the social and cultural context, and profitably bring to bear the resources of the field on such an undertaking.

There are two lines of thought that I find crucial in this regard. One has to do with developments in social theory in the Global North that theorize the global nature of the contemporary world scene. Here I draw upon Steven Seidman's ongoing overview of social theory.[43] Three "revisions and revolts" vis-à-vis the classical tradition are outlined, the third and most recent of which is assigned the title of "Theories of World Order."[44] The other involves a strand of social theory in the Global South, with representation in the Global North as well, that approaches the global nature of the world today through the optic of the South. Here I foreground the work on "epistemologies of the South" by Boaventura de Sousa Santos."[45]

---

43. Steven Seidman, *Contested Knowledge: Social Theory Today*, 5th ed. (Chichester: Wiley-Blackwell, 2013). Seidman, professor of sociology at the State University of New York at Albany, is a distinguished social theorist, with expertise in a number of areas. This overview of social theory has been going on for two decades, the first edition of the volume having been published in 1994.

44. Seidman, *Contested Knowledge*, 267–301 (part 6, "Revisions and Revolts: Theories of World Order"). The other two movements include "The Postmodern Turn" and "Identity Politics and Theory" (parts 4 and 5, respectively).

45. Boaventura de Sousa Santos, "Introducción: Las epistemologías del Sur," in *Formas-Otras: Saber, nombrar, narrar, hacer*, ed. Alvise Vianello and Bet Mañe, Colección Monografías (Barcelona: CIDOB, 2011), 9–22. De Sousa Santos is professor emeritus of sociology at the University of Coimbra, where he is also the director of the Center for Social Studies. A renowned social theorist, his research encompasses a broad variety of fields of study. See also his *Epistemologies of the South: Justice against Epistemicide* (Boulder, CO: Paradigm, 2014); and *Una epistemología del sur:*

In the classical tradition, from Auguste Comte to Max Weber, Seidman argues, the nation-state—a state with a common identity based on common descent and culture—was viewed as the basic unit of modern social life and analysis, and change in nation-states was explained in terms of internal factors. In recent times, a number of theorists have pointed to a relative decline in the primacy of the nation-state and a corresponding change in the global order. The reason adduced for such a change of fortune is external: the growth of a transnational order with dynamics and mechanics that go beyond the boundaries of nationalism. Globalization emerges thereby as the primary element of present-day social life and analysis. How this new global order is evaluated differs considerably. There is, to be sure, the highly positive view of neoliberalism, centered on economics. At the same time, Seidman points to three analytical traditions highly critical of this hegemonic approach.

The first tradition, associated with the London School of Economics, is represented by David Held and Mary Kaldor.[46] Globalization is seen as a mixture of economic, social, and political dimensions. It is potentially positive, provided that the social and political dimensions are activated. The vision is one of a global civil society and democratic order—with chaos as the alternative. Immanuel Wallerstein and Manuel Castells stand as the voices of the second tradition, linked to the theory of world systems. [47] Globalization emerges as a junction of politics and economics,

---

La reinvención del conocimiento y la emancipación social, Siglo XXI Editores (Buenos Aires: CLACSO, 2009).

46. David Held is presently master of University College and professor of politics and international relations at Durham University in the United Kingdom. Previously, he had been the Graham Wallas Professor of Political Science at the London School of Economics. His publications on globalization are extensive. The following are among the most recent: *Gridlock: Why Global Cooperation Is Failing* (London: Polity, 2013); and *Cosmopolitanism: Ideals and Realities* (London: Polity, 2010). Mary Kaldor is professor of global governance in the Department of International Development and director of the Civil Society and Human Security Research Unit at the London School of Economics and Political Science. Among her many works on globalization are *Global Civil Society: An Answer to War* (Cambridge, UK: Polity, 2003); and *New and Old Wars: Organised Violence in a Global Era*, 3rd rev. and updated ed. (Stanford, CA: Stanford University Press, 2012).

47. At present, Immanuel Wallerstein is senior research scholar at Yale University. After appointments at Columbia University (1958–1971) and McGill University (1971–1976), Wallerstein joined Binghampton University, State University of New York, as Distinguished Professor of Sociology and director of the Fernand Braudel

the present stage of the world economy of capitalism, within the world system of modernity. It is altogether negative, with inequality at the core, and in profound crisis since the 1960s. The vision is one of utter transformation—in the face of collapse or dystopia. The third tradition, associated with empire and imperialism, brings together Michael Hardt and Antonio Negri, Michael Mann, and David Harvey.[48] Globalization is regarded as a mixture of economics and geopolitics, involving either an international, transnational Empire (Hardt and Negri) or a national, statist empire anchored by the United States (Mann; Helder). It is potentially positive, though decidedly more visionary than realistic, along the lines of a Coun-

---

Center for the Study of Economies, Historical Systems, and Civilizations. His theory of world systems, which has now seen four volumes and remains unfinished, is summarized in *World-Systems Analysis: An Introduction*, A John Hope Franklin Center Book (Durham, NC: Duke University Press, 2004). After appointments at the University of Paris (1967–1979) and the University of California, Berkeley (1979–2003), Manuel Castells joined the University of Southern California as University Professor and the Wallis Annenberg Chair Professor of Communication Technology and Society at the Annenberg School of Communication. He is also professor of sociology and director of the Internet Interdisciplinary Institute at the Open University of Catalonia (UOC) in Barcelona. His major work is *The Information Age: Economy, Society, and Culture*, 3 vols. (Oxford: Blackwell, 1996–1998).

48. Michael Hardt, a literary critic and political philosopher, is professor of literature and Italian at Duke University and professor of philosophy and politics at the European Graduate School (Saas-Fee, Canton Wallis, Switzerland). Antonio Negri, a political activist and philosopher, taught first at the University of Padua and then, while in exile in France, at the Université de Paris VIII and the Collège Internationale de Philosophie (1983–1997). Together, Hardt and Negri have written a series on empire today: *Empire* (Cambridge: Harvard University Press, 2001); *Multitude: War and Democracy in the Age of Empire* (New York: Penguin Books, 2004); and *Commonwealth* (Cambridge: Belknap Press of Harvard University Press, 2009). Michael Mann is professor of sociology at the University of California at Los Angeles, where he has taught since 1987, after appointments at the University of Essex (1971–1977) and the London School of Economics and Political Science (197719–87). He is well known for the multivolume work *The Sources of Social Power*, 4 vols. (New York: Cambridge University Press, 1986, 1993, 2012, 2013). This theoretical framework on power he brings to bear on the United States in *Incoherent Empire* (London: Verso, 2003). David Harvey, an expert in geography and critical social theory, became Distinguished Professor of Anthropology at the City University of New York in 2001 (2001–), after appointments at various institutions, including John Hopkins University (1969–1987, 1993–2001) and Oxford University (1987–1993). For his work on imperialism, in relation to postmodernity and globalization, see *The New Imperialism* (Oxford: Oxford University Press, 2003); and *Brief History of Neoliberalism*.

ter-Empire of Resistance (Hardt and Negri) or the utter transformation of the United States (Mann; Helder)—with dystopia as the alternative.

For de Sousa Santos, the theories of the North, be they hegemonic or critical, prove woefully inadequate. It is to the epistemologies of the South, in their struggle for a better world, that one must look. These have as point of departure a form of injustice that grounds and contaminates all others, at work since the inception of modern capitalism—cognitive injustice. This revolves around the belief that there is but one valid form of knowing, modern science, which is advanced as perfect knowledge and is largely the product of the Global North. In the face of such epistemic exclusivism, the epistemologies of the South clamor for new modes of production, new valorization of valid knowledges, and new relations among different forms of knowing. This they do from the perspective of social groups and classes that have suffered systematic destruction, oppression, and discrimination at the hands of capitalism, colonialism, and resultant unequal formations of power.[49]

The premises of the epistemologies of the South are radically different. First of all, they view the understanding of the world as much broader, by far, than that of the West. As such, the social transformation of the world can take place in ways, modes, and methods beyond the imagination of the West. Second, they affirm that the diversity of the world is boundless, along any number of lines.[50] In the face of hegemonic knowledge, such diversity remains invisible. Lastly, they take such diversity as defying any sort of general theory. Rather, its activation and transformation, theoretical as well as empirical, demand a plurality of knowledges and, ultimately, a general theory that accounts for the impossibility of a general theory. Only through such a plurality of knowledges, grounded in their own historical trajectories and not the universal history of the West, can a vision of utopia arise for the future of the world.

---

49. These are worth citing: market exchange, individual property, the sacrifice of the land, racism, sexism, individualism, the placement of the material over the spiritual, and all other *monocultivos* ("monocultures") of mind and society that seek to block a liberating imagination and sacrifice the alternatives. See de Sousa Santos, "Las epistemologías del Sur," 16.

50. These include different ways of thinking, feeling, and acting; different types of relations among human beings and between human beings and nature; different conceptions of time, of viewing the past, present, and future; and different forms of collective life as well as of the distribution of goods and resources.

What are the consequences of such a panoply of world theories for my response? These accounts bring out, against a common specter of impending chaos, the broad diversity of approaches to the world system and the crisis at hand. If critics are to deal with the intersecting nature of the crisis in the world system, they have no option but to examine and address such a crisis from a variety of perspectives, theorizing in the process their own locations in and perception of the world. They must engage the angles of vision of the Global North, its hegemonic as well as critical discourses. They must eschew cognitive injustice and embrace diversity in understanding and transforming the world. They must, therefore, engage the angles of vision of the Global South, its array of epistemologies and histories. Throughout, they must develop a utopian vision of the future that has a better world for all in mind, especially those who have been and continue to be the most deprived and the most excluded. Ultimately, they must imagine new projects of interpretation that embody such ideals. The need for such a type of project James Montgomery sensed ever so well in 1918, again within the modernist and eurocentric boundaries of his context; yet he failed to find or develop a proper theoretical framework for its execution.

5. Imagining an Interpretive Project for Our Times

I should like to conclude by imagining one such project of interpretation that would be in keeping with the various elements of my response to the question of critical vision and task. Such a project requires the disposition of a new grand model of interpretation. For some time now, I have approached the critical trajectory and repertoire of the field in terms of a set of six paradigms—historical, literary, sociocultural, ideological, cultural, and religious-theological.[51] I have described them as closely related to other fields of study in the academy and thus, to one degree or another,

---

51. Such umbrella models I have described as follows. First, as paradigms, these movements encompass a variety of approaches within their angles of vision: the approaches possess a number of discursive features in common, although each has its own method and theory as well. Second, they emerge in the field in largely, although not entirely, sequential fashion: the process of development reveals a theoretical logic at work as well as impinging material factors. Third, these movements, while distinctive and competing, are not necessarily mutually exclusive: the discursive boundaries are often porous and interactive.

as interdisciplinary in character.[52] The proposed paradigm is no exception. A proper designation for it I do not find easy to capture, but I would offer, as a working suggestion, that of global-systemic.[53] Its objective, scope, and lens could be described as follows.

The objective is ambitious: to bring the field to bear upon the major crises of our post–Cold War times, in both individual and converging fashion. Such conjunction would entail two analytical dimensions. First, it would require interaction with by now well-established discourses regarding each crisis. Second, it would demand interchange with discourses addressing the convergence of crises, the global state of affairs, by way of world theories from the North and alternative theories from the South. The scope is expansive: the world of production (composition, dissemination, interchange) as well as the world of consumption (reception, circulation, discussion). It would thus encompass the following foci of attention: (1) the texts and contexts of antiquity; (2) the interpretation of these texts and contexts, and the contexts of such interpretations, in the various traditions of reading the Bible, with a focus on modernity and postmodernity; and (3) the interpreters behind such interpretations, and their corresponding contexts.[54] The lens is wide-angled: interaction with the other grand models of interpretation as imperative, determined at any one time by the specific focus of the inquiry in question, since all such angles of inquiry are applicable—in one way or another, to one degree or another—to the analysis of the individual crises as well as the global crisis.

---

52. With the passage of time, the interdisciplinary character of criticism has multiplied and intensified. To begin with, critical dialogue with corresponding fields and discourses outside biblical criticism has become ever more explicit, extensive, and sophisticated. At the same time, to be sure, all such fields and discourses have become quite diverse in their own right. In addition, critical dialogue across grand models of interpretation in biblical criticism has become more common and pronounced as well. Lastly, the problematic of critical dialogue with a range or even the totality of fields of study or grand models of interpretation has become more pressing, in an effort to move away from atomization and toward intersectionality.

53. As the first part of the hyphenated designation, "global" names the terrain or sphere of action—the material context; the second part, "systemic," points to the mode or angle of pursuit—the discursive context.

54. Epistemically, these foci may be approached not as independent but as interdependent realms: the representations of the texts and contexts of antiquity as representations of antiquity in modernity and postmodernity on the part of situated and interested interpreters.

In effect, just as historical, literary, sociocultural, ideological, cultural, and religious dimensions crisscross the global-systemic, so does the global-systemic impact upon and intersect with all such dimensions.

Needless to say, this is a tall order. The proposed undertaking demands a critical movement: a joint effort on the part of critics who regard such preoccupations as very much a part of the critical task and stand ready to integrate them into their academic and professional lives and work. Such a movement, moreover, needs to be as diverse as possible, so that the effort proves equal to the problematic and task. I would highlight two kinds of diversity. On the one hand, religious-theological diversity: the view of the Bible and its corresponding mode of reading. No one stance need serve as the driving force behind this undertaking; rather, the entire of spectrum of opinion on this matter can take part. On the other hand, geographical-spatial dimension: the global parameters and perspectives of the field of studies today. No one area of the world should set the pace and tone of the undertaking by itself.

For such a critical movement to prosper, a number of measures would prove helpful. Some would be material in nature. Perhaps a network of digital communication and publishing ventures on the part of interested critics could be established. Perhaps a major academic-scholarly center in each area of the world would be willing to serve as a nerve center in this regard. Perhaps the Society itself could serve as an overall coordinating center, given its extensive network of connections and publications. Others would be discursive. Perhaps such an undertaking could begin with a focus on one crisis in particular. Perhaps it could devise a model for carrying out the proposed conjunction with global studies.

Perhaps I am just dreaming. However, I find that various efforts and ventures along these lines are already under way, showing that concern and interest do exist and establishing a discursive trajectory in the process. Dreaming or not, I find that I have no choice but to follow in this path—as an outsider-insider in the West, as a child of the Global South, and as an international migrant. I should like to conclude by recalling two further anniversaries taking place this year, which I find very much to the point in this regard.

The first is partly fictive and partly real. I am referring to a key dystopic novel of the twentieth century: George Orwell's *Nineteen Eighty-Four*, published in 1949. This year represents the sixty-fifth anniversary of its publication and the thirtieth of its narrative setting. Its elements of Big Brother, doublethink, and newspeak—among many others—have been more than surpassed in our days. In fact, their counterparts today constitute yet another of our crises, the total loss of privacy through total multioptical surveillance.

In the year 1946, between the conclusion of the Second World War and the appearance of the novel, Orwell wrote a piece entitled "Why I Write."[55] There are various reasons why authors write, he states, and they are all to one degree or another present in their work.[56] For him, it was political purpose that predominated after 1936–1937—the Spanish Civil War (1936–1939).[57] From that point on, he declares, "Every line of serious work that I have written … has been written, directly or indirectly, *against* totalitarianism and *for* democratic socialism, as I understand it."[58] In so doing, he adds, he has sought to make "political writing into an art"—a fusion of the political and the esthetic.[59] His last novel, *Nineteen Eighty-Four*, emerges as a climax of such resolve.

The second is altogether real. I have in mind a landmark volume of poetry by the Chilean poet Pablo Neruda—*Canción de gesta* (*Epic Song*), which, though published in 1960, took a different turn in composition during 1959 as a result of the triumph of the Cuban Revolution.[60] This year

55. George Orwell, "Why I Write," in *Collected Essays* (London: Mercury Books, 1961), 435–42. The essay was originally published in the last issue of a short-lived English literary magazine, *Gangrel* 4 (Summer 1946).

56. These are sheer egoism, aesthetic enthusiasm, historical impulse, and political purpose. These, he states, "exist in different degrees in every writer, and in any one writer the proportions will vary from time to time, according to the atmosphere in which he is living" (Orwell, "Why I Write," 437).

57. The political purpose is described as follows: "Desire to push the world in a certain direction, to alter other people's idea of the kind of society that they should strive after" (Orwell, "Why I Write," 438.)

58. Orwell, "Why I Write," 440.

59. Orwell, "Why I Write." The conclusion to the essay is pointed: "And looking back through my work, I see that it is invariably where I lacked a *political* purpose that I wrote lifeless books and was betrayed into purple passages, sentences without meaning, decorative adjectives and humbug generally."

60. The first edition of the volume—minus its final poem—was published in Cuba: Pablo Neruda, *Canción de gesta* (Havana: Imprenta Nacional de Cuba, 1960). As the preface to the first edition indicates, and as outlined by Ferro González ("Isla en el canto de un poeta," *A contra corriente: Una revista de historia social y literatura de América Latina* 8.1 [2010]: 321–31), the volume, consisting of forty-two poems, was written in three stages: (a) its initial focus was on the status and struggle of Puerto Rico (1958)—written in Chile, at Neruda's home in Isla Negra; (b) then it turns to

is the fifty-fifth anniversary of both the Revolution and Neruda's paean to Cuba as the future for all of Latin America. Neruda had written politically engaged poetry before and would do so afterwards as well,[61] but *Canción de gesta* marks an important shift in his life and work.[62] Its emphasis on solidarity calls to mind yet another crisis of our days, the loss of human values and pathos through untrammeled self-interest and competition.[63]

Following upon the 20th Congress of the Communist Party of the Soviet Union in 1956, in which Nikita Khrushchev (1894–1971) denounced the policies of Josef Stalin (1878–1953), Neruda underwent a personal and political crisis. It was with the hope of the Cuban Revolution that he began to forge a new political cosmovision of marxist humanism, away from real socialism and toward democratic socialism. In this work he takes on the role of epic troubadour, as described in the preface: "For my part I here assume yet again, and with pride, my duties as a poet of public service, that is, a pure poet."[64] This poetic voice involving historical

---

Cuba and the Caribbean in general (1959)—undertaken while Neruda was residing in Venezuela and during the first year of the Cuban Revolution; and (c) finally, the volume was completed in 1960 (April 12) aboard the mail steamer *Louis Lumière* en route to Europe. The volume is dedicated as follows: to the liberators of Cuba, Fidel Castro and his companions, and the people of Cuba; to all those in Puerto Rico and the Caribbean who struggle for freedom and truth under constant threat from the "United States of America of the North."

61. Prior to *Canción de gesta* one finds, for example: *España en el corazón: Himno a las glorias del pueblo en la guerra* (1937) and *Tercera residencia, 1935–1945* (1947). Following upon it, for example, is *Incitación al Nixoncidio y alabanza a la Revolución Chilena* (1972) and, posthumously, *Elegía* (1974).

62. On context, literary as well as political, see the study by Greg Dawes, "*Canción de gesta* y la 'Paz Furiosa' de Neruda," *Gramma* 21.47 (2010): 128–62.

63. See Paul Verhaeghe, *What About Me? The Struggle for Identity in a Market-Based Society* (Melbourne: Scribe, 2014). See also George Mombiot, "Sick of This Market-Driven World? You Should Be," *Guardian,* 5 August 2014, https://tinyurl.com/SBL1130h.

64. "Por mi parte aquí asumo una vez más, y con orgullo, mis deberes de poeta de utilidad pública, es decir de puro poeta." The volume, he writes, represents "a direct and directed weapon, a fundamental and fraternal aid that I give to our brother peoples for each day of their struggles" ("Este libro no es un lamento de solitario ni una emanación de la oscuridad, sino un arma directa y dirigida, una ayuda elemental y fraternal que entrego a los pueblos hermanos para cada día de sus luchas"). The edition I use is the following: *Canción de gesta: Las piedras de Chile,* ed. Hernán Loyola, De Bolsillo, Biblioteca - Contemporánea (Barcelona: Random House Mondadori, 2010). All translations are mine; for an English translation, see *Song of Protest,* trans.

witness and political engagement is explained in the poems: a "pure poet" is one who brings poetry and politics together, form and content, beauty and commitment.[65] This fusion he describes in the poem "Ask Me Not" as follows: "I have a pact of love with beauty / I have a pact of blood with my people." Its task he sets forth as follows: "we must do something on this earth / because in this planet we were birthed / and one must see to the affairs of human beings / because we are neither birds nor dogs."[66]

In the light of contemporary events, both writers, one in the Global North and the other in the Global South, found that they had to pursue their craft as they did, that they could not do otherwise. I see no reason why, in the face of our own contemporary times, we biblical critics should not aim for a similar conjunction of the scholarly and the political. The goal is not a displacement of the other paradigms of interpretation: Who would want to lose such wisdom and knowledge? Who would want to abandon such important problematics and discussions? The goal, rather, is the construction of a new paradigm in conversation with all others. One that would bring closely together biblical criticism and the global scene. One that would foreground sustained theorization of critical vision and task as well as the global state of affairs. A paradigm, in sum, from and for the unique, indeed unprecedented, critical times in which we find ourselves.

As a field of studies and as a learned organization, we owe global society and culture no less. In 1918 James Montgomery, a voice from the Global North, argued precisely the same point: critics should see themselves first as "citizens of the human polity" and answer the call of the world. Today, ninety-five years after its publication in 1919, I, a voice from the Global South, would reiterate that call. I find no better way to do so than by invoking Neruda. If I may be allowed to paraphrase the great Neruda: We have

---

and introduction by Miguel Algarín (New York: Morrow, 1976). Algarín, it should be noted, is one of the poets comprising the Nuyorican Poets.

65. See esp. Poem 15, "Vengo del Sur" (I Come from the South); Poem 22, "Así es mi vida" (Thus Is My Life); Poem 29, "No me lo pidan" (Ask Me Not); and Poem 43, "Meditación sobre la Sierra Maestra" (Meditation on the Sierra Maestra).

66. The title of the poem, "Ask Me Not," has in mind critics who would want him to write poetry of a different nature, without reference to the politics of the day. The lines cited form part of his response and rejection: "debemos hacer algo en esta tierra / porque en este planeta nos parieron / y hay que arreglar las cosas de los hombres / porque no somos pájaros ni perros." He ends by saying "tengo un pacto de amor con la hermosura: / tengo un pacto de sangre con mi pueblo."

all made a pact of love with criticism; let us now make a pact of blood with the world.

Bibliography

Acosta-Belén, Edna, and Carlos E. Santiago. "Merging Borders: The Remapping of America." Pages 29–42 in *The Latino Studies Reader: Culture, Economy and Society*. Edited by Antonia Darder and Rodolfo D. Torres. Malden, MA: Blackwell, 1998.

Benda, Julien. *The Treason of the Intellectuals*. Translated by Richard Aldington. New York: Morrow, 1928.

Castells, Manuel. *The Information Age: Economy, Society, and Culture*. 3 vols. Oxford: Blackwell, 1996–1998.

Chakrabarty, Dipesh. "The Climate of History: Four Theses." *Critical Inquiry* 35 (2009): 197–222.

Darder, Antonia, and Rodolfo D. Torres. "Latinos and Society: Culture, Politics, and Class." Pages 3–26 in *The Latino Studies Reader: Culture, Economy and Society*. Edited by Antonia Darder and Rodolfo D. Torres. Malden, MA: Blackwell, 1998.

Dawes, Greg. "Canción de gesta y la 'Paz Furiosa' de Neruda." *Gramma* 21.47 (2010): 128–62.

Dirlik, Arif. "Global South: Predicament and Promise." *Global South* 1 (2007): 12–23.

Eagleton, Terry. *The Function of Criticism: From the Spectator to Post-Structuralism*. London: Verso, 1984.

———. *Literary Theory: An Introduction*. 2nd ed. Minneapolis: University of Minnesota Press, 1996.

———. *Marxism and Literary Criticism*. Berkeley: University of California Press, 1976.

Fukuyama, Francis. "At the 'End of History' Still Stands Democracy." *Wall Street Journal*. 7–8 June 2014. http://online.wsj.com/articles/at-the-end-of-history-still-stands-democracy-1402080661.

———. "The End of History." *National Interest* (Summer 1989).

———. *The End of History and the Last Man*. New York: Free Press, 1992.

———. *Political Order and Political Decay: From the Industrial Revolution to the Globalization of Democracy*. New York: Farrar, Straus & Giroux, 2014.

Giddens, Anthony. *Runaway World: How Globalization Is Reshaping Our Lives*. London: Profile Books, 1999.

González, Ferr. "Isla en el canto de un poeta." *A contra corriente: Una revista de historia social y literatura de América Latina* 8.1 (2010): 321–31.

Gramsci, Antonio. *The Betrayal of the Intellectuals*. Translated by Richard Aldington. Introduction by Herbert Read. Boston: Beacon, 1955.

———. *Selections from the Prison Notebooks of Antonio Gramsci*. Edited and Translated by Quintin Hoare and Geoffrey Nowell-Smith. New York: International, 1971.

Gray, Patrick. "Presidential Addresses." *JBL* 125 (2006): 167–77.

Grosfoguel, Ramón, Nelson Maldonado-Torres, and José David Saldívar, eds. *Latinos/as in the World System: Decolonization Struggles in the Twenty-First Century U.S. Empire*. Political Economy of the World-Systems Annual. Boulder, CO: Paradigm, 2006.

Hardt, Michael, and Antonio Negri. *Commonwealth*. Cambridge: Belknap Press of Harvard University Press, 2009.

———. *Empire*. Cambridge: Harvard University Press, 2001.

———. *Multitude: War and Democracy in the Age of Empire*. New York: Penguin Books, 2004.

Harvey, David. *A Brief History of Neoliberalism*. Oxford: Oxford University Press, 2005.

———. *The New Imperialism*. Oxford: Oxford University Press, 2003.

Hayes, John H., ed. *Dictionary of Biblical Interpretation*. 2 vols. Nashville: Abingdon, 1999.

Held, David. *Cosmopolitanism: Ideals and Realities*. London: Polity, 2010.

———.*Gridlock: Why Global Cooperation Is Failing*. London: Polity, 2013.

"James Alan Montgomery (1866–1949)." Penn Biographies. https://tinyurl.com/SBL1130f.

Jastrow, Morris, Jr. "Constructive Elements in the Critical Study of the Old Testament." *JBL* 36 (1917): 1–20.

Kaldor, Mary. *Global Civil Society: An Answer to War*. Cambridge, UK: Polity, 2003.

———. *New and Old Wars: Organised Violence in a Global Era*. 3rd rev. and updated ed. Stanford, CA: Stanford University Press, 2012.

Koser, Khalid. *International Migration: A Very Short Introduction*. Very Short Introductions. Oxford: Oxford University Press, 2007.

Leitch, Vincent. *Literary Criticism in the Twenty-First Century: Theory Renaissance*. London: Bloomsbury, 2014.

Litonjua, M. D. "Third World/Global South: From Modernization, to Dependency/Liberation, to Postdevelopment." *Journal of Third World Studies* 29 (2012): 25–56.

López, Alfred J. "The (Post) Global South." *Global South* 1 (2007): 1–11.

———. *Postcolonial Whiteness: A Critical Reader on Race and Empire.* Albany: State University of New York Press, 2005.

———. *Posts and Pasts: A Theory of Postcolonialism.* Explorations in Postcolonial Studies. Albany: State University of New York Press, 2001.

MacMillan, Margaret. "The Rhyme of History: Lessons of the Great War." The Brookings Essay. 14 December 2013. https://tinyurl.com/SBL1130d.

Maduro, Otto. "Migrants' Religions under Imperial Duress: Reflections on Epistemology, Ethics & Politics in the Study of the Religious 'Stranger.'" *JAAR* 82 (2014): 35–46.

Mann, Michael. *Incoherent Empire.* London: Verso, 2003.

———. *The Sources of Social Power.* 4 vols. New York: Cambridge University Press, 1986, 1993, 2012, 2013.

Margulis, Jon. *The Last Innocent Year: America in 1964; The Beginning of the "Sixties."* New York: Morrow, 1999.

McMahon, Robert J. *The Cold War: A Very Short Introduction.* Very Short Introductions. Oxford: Oxford University Press, 2003.

McSherry, J. Patrice. *Predatory States: Operation Condor and Covert War in Latin America.* Lanham, MD: Rowman & Littlefield, 2005.

Moïsi, Dominique. "The Return of the Sleepwalkers." Project Syndicate. 25 June 2014. https://tinyurl.com/SBL1130e.

Mombiot, George. "Sick of This Market-Driven World? You Should Be." *Guardian.* 5 August 2014. https://tinyurl.com/SBL1130h.

Montgomery, James A. "Present Tasks of American Biblical Scholarship." *JBL* 38 (1919): 1–14.

Moulton, Warren J. "The Dating of the Synoptic Gospels." *JBL* 37 (1918): 1–19.

Neruda, Pablo. *Canción de gesta.* Havana: Imprenta Nacional de Cuba, 1960.

———. *Canción de gesta: Las piedras de Chile.* Edited by Hernán Loyola. De Bolsillo, Biblioteca - Contemporánea. Barcelona: Random House Mondadori, 2010.

———. *Song of Protest.* Translation and introduction by Miguel Algarín. New York: Morrow, 1976.

Orwell, George. "Why I Write." Pages 435–42 in *Collected Essays.* London: Mercury Books, 1961.

Said, Edward W. *Representations of the Intellectual: The 1993 Reith Lectures.* Repr., New York: Vintage Books, 1996.

Sánchez, Rosaura. "Mapping the Spanish Language along a Multiethnic and Multilingual Border." Pages 101–25 in *The Latino Studies Reader: Culture, Economy* and *Society*. Edited by Antonia Darder and Rodolfo D. Torres. Malden, MA: Blackwell, 1998.

Saunders, Ernest W. *Searching the Scriptures: A History of the Society of Biblical Literature, 1880–1980*. BSNA 8. Chico, CA: Scholars Press, 1982.

Sauvy, Alfred. "Note sur l'origine de l'expression 'tiers monde' par Alfred Sauvy." *Le Magazine de l'homme modern*. https://tinyurl.com/SBL1130b.

———. "Trois mondes, une planète." *L'Observateur* 118 (1952).

Seidman, Steven. *Contested Knowledge: Social Theory Today*. 5th ed. Chichester: Wiley-Blackwell, 2013.

Sheer, Michael D. "Obama, Daring Congress, Acts to Overhaul Immigration." *New York Times*. 20 November 2014. https://tinyurl.com/SBL1130c.

Sousa Santos, Boaventura de. *Una epistemología del sur: La reinvención del conocimiento y la emancipación social*. Siglo XXI Editores. Buenos Aires: CLACSO, 2009.

———. *Epistemologies of the South: Justice against Epistemicide*. Boulder, CO: Paradigm, 2014.

———. "Introducción: Las epistemologías del Sur." Pages 9–22 in *Formas-Otras: Saber, nombrar, narrar, hacer*. Edited by Alvise Vianello and Bet Mañe, Colección Monografías. Barcelona: CIDOB, 2011.

Spiegel, Gabrielle M. *The Past as Text: The Theory and Practice of Medieval Historiography*. Parallax. Baltimore: Johns Hopkins University Press, 1997.

———. *Practicing History: New Directions in Historical Writing after the Linguistic Turn*. Rewriting Histories. New York: Routledge, 2005.

———. "The Task of the Historian." *AHR* 114 (2009): 1–15.

Stanley, Timothy, and Alexander Leesep. "It's Still Not the End of History." *The Atlantic*. 1 September 2014. https://tinyurl.com/SBL1130g.

Stieglitz, Joseph. *Globalization and Its Discontents*. New York: Norton, 2003.

———. *Making Globalization Work*. New York: Norton, 2006.

Torrey, Charles C., Millar Burrows, and William F. Albright. "In Memoriam Warren Joseph Moulton, 1865–1947." *BASOR* 107 (1947): 1, 5–7.

Vargas Llosa, Mario. "Las guerras del fin del mundo." El País. 7 September 2014. http://elpais.com/elpais/2014/09/04/opinion/1409856348_817996.html.

Verhaeghe, Paul. *What About Me? The Struggle for Identity in a Market-Based Society*. Melbourne: Scribe, 2014.

Wallerstein, Immanuel. "NATO: Danger to World Peace." Personal page. 15 November 2014. https://tinyurl.com/SBL1130a.

———. *World-Systems Analysis: An Introduction. A John Hope Franklin Center Book*. Durham, NC: Duke University Press, 2004.

Young, Robert J. C. *Postcolonialism: An Historical Introduction*. Oxford: Blackwell, 2001.

Wojciech Solarz, Marcin. "'Third World': The Sixtieth Anniversary of a Concept That Changed History." *Third World Quarterly* 33.9 (2012): 1561–73.

Presidential Reflection

FERNANDO F. SEGOVIA

Several years ago, in 2014, I used the forum provided by the presidential address to the Society of Biblical Literature to reflect on a topic that had long hovered over my work as a critic and that had been singularly underaddressed in the field. This was the issue of critical posture—the vision and the mission of criticism. This topic I pursued, in line with my principles as a critic, in contextualist and perspectival fashion: a situated and ideological undertaking shaped by and targeted at the times in question. These I characterized as critical, given what I perceived as a set of major crises bearing down upon the world, individually as well as collectively, and bringing about a crisis in the world-system as such.

These crises I implicitly classified in terms of gravity: while I regarded all as major, a number of these I viewed as grave, and one in particular I looked upon as pivotal. At the time, I identified a trio of grave crises: global economics, climate change, and worldwide migration. I also mentioned, in passing, a number of other major crises: geopolitical competition, political breakdown, and the explosion of violence. I further foregrounded the crisis of economics as pivotal: the global meltdown or Great Recession of 2008 was still of recent memory, and its damaging effects were still very much in evidence around the globe. The global scenario constituted by this set of crises I described as "uniquely critical, beyond all critical times of the twentieth century, severe as these were." Consequently, I argued, any crafting of a critical posture in and for such times called for expansive interdisciplinary engagement with the fields of study in question and the use of informed theoretical models from such fields.

Since that time, a host of intervening developments have led me to a thorough revision of this initial assessment regarding our times. Indeed, what has transpired in the space of but a few years I find remarkable, forcing a marked reconfiguration of the global scenario alongside a vision of the present juncture as more critical still. To begin with, I have had to expand significantly the number of major crises coming together at once. In addition, I have been compelled to make two additions to the set of grave crises: human welfare and populist nationalism, given the outbreak of a viral pandemic and the irruption of far-right supremacy, respectively. Lastly, I have had to foreground climate change as the pivotal crisis. In the process, my sense of gravity regarding the times has witnessed intense heightening: the global juncture has taken on an aura of end times. In this regard, the year 2021 marked for me a decisive point of inflection, in the light of various extraordinary developments.

Foremost among these stands the series of extreme weather events experienced throughout the world. To be sure, the crisis of climate change has been anticipated for quite some time, and signs of its presence have already been detected for years in no uncertain ways. Now, however, it has arrived in full force, much earlier than expected, making itself felt in widespread and terrifying ways in 2021. There can be no doubt at this point that the long-feared threshold in the Anthropocene epoch, the point of no return, has been reached. All that remains now, it would seem, is containment, for prevention has been rendered out of the question. I posit this crisis as pivotal because it lays open a future of radical uncertainty, marked by wide devastation for the world and looming peril for humanity.

Keenly foreboding as well is the crisis of human welfare unleashed by the outbreak of the Coronavirus disease of 2019. Having emerged in the People's Republic of China in the winter of 2019–2020, it spread rapidly around the globe through 2020, evolving in 2021 into two highly aggressive and contagious variants, delta and omicron. This is certainly not the first pandemic that has afflicted the human species, nor will it be the last. It has, however, been the most extensive in over a hundred years, since the Great Influenza of 1918, and has wreaked much havoc throughout. It is also clear that it is here to stay, in one way or another. I regard this crisis as grave because, over and beyond its medical dimension, it has surfaced and intensified—with trenchant clarity—the many differential chasms that cut across society and culture everywhere. As a result, it has further enhanced that sense of radical uncertainty surrounding the future that hovers over the whole of humanity.

No less unsettling is the crisis of populist nationalism that has emerged from the far right across the West, particularly in the United States. This phenomenon involves a panoply of distinctive features: white in ethnic-racial identity; supremacist in social-cultural constitution; nativist in attitude toward and treatment of the Other; and messianic in religious-theological orientation. This is nothing new for the West of empires and colonies, but it had lain rather dormant for some time. In recent years, however, it has surfaced again in sustained and escalating fashion, as a result of repeated waves of migration from the Global South and the economic detritus left behind by the economic recession of 2008. Nowhere more so, certainly, than during 2017–2021 with the rise of Donald Trump and the crusade of Make America Great Again. In 2021, following the electoral defeat of the leader-savior, it reached a turning point when the movement mounted an open insurrection against the state, seeking a violent interruption of the electoral process, while invoking a narrative of a stolen election by a deep state. I see this crisis as grave because, despite its ready dismantlement, it has exposed and emboldened—at the core of global power—its far-reaching roots, its considerable power, and its will to triumph. Consequently, it has heightened further the feeling of radical uncertainty regarding the future awaiting all of humanity.

All three developments—climate extremes, pandemic waves, supremacist crusades—have affected the Global North and the Global South alike. Yet, as is always the case, these crises—and all others beside them—bear far more grievous consequences for both the Global South and minoritized ethnic-racial groups in the Global North. Such, then, are the times that I now perceive, several years after my presidential address of 2014 and especially in the aftermath of 2021, as our context, from which a critical posture is to be fashioned for criticism in general and minoritized ethnic-racial criticism in particular. These are end times in the face of which a pointed sense of critical vision and mission is imperative—a criticism from, in, and for end times.

Learning with the Times

TAT-SIONG BENNY LIEW

Starting with a retrospective list of various major world events since the twentieth century, Fernando Segovia's presidential address made me think back to my time as a doctoral student at Vanderbilt University. If memory does not fail me, I believe it was the spring of 1991 (the second semester of my coursework) when I was taking a class on the social world of early Christianity with Segovia. I cannot remember if it was before class began or during a break, but he showed me a book and said that I might be interested in reading it. It was *The Empire Writes Back: Theory and Practice in Post-colonial Literatures* by Bill Ashcroft, Gareth Griffiths, and Helen Tiffin.[1] At the time, I had not heard of postcolonial studies, Edward Said, or Gayatri Chakravorty Spivak. In many ways, that brief book recommendation from Segovia could be understood as a launching pad for my career's research trajectory, which includes, among others, postcolonial studies, literary theory, and Asian American literature.

Segovia describes himself as "an outsider-insider in the West, as a child of the Global South, and as an international migrant" as well as a "transnational subject."[2] I can identify with many of these descriptions, except—being born and raised in Hong Kong, which used to be a British colony but now a "Special Administrative Region" (SAR) of the People's Republic of China—I would say I am also an outsider-insider in both the Global North and the Global South. In fact, I think outsider-insider might be a good way to describe my own feelings as I reflect on my journey as a New Testament scholar. I still remember someone, mainly because I

1. Ashcroft, Bill, Gareth Griffiths, and Helen Tiffin, *The Empire Writes Back: Theory and Practice in Post-colonial Literatures* (London: Routledge, 1989).

2. Fernando F. Segovia, "Criticism in Critical Times: Reflections on Vision and Task," *JBL* 134 (2015): 23, 4.

have served many years as a faculty mentor for the FTE (formerly Fund for Theological Education and now Fund for Theological Exploration), expressing honest surprise upon learning that I had never received any FTE fellowships throughout my doctoral studies. I would never presume a successful application, but I never applied because I did not even know during those years that FTE existed. Just as I used to know nothing about postcolonial studies, I didn't know what FTE was or what FTE did. Entering the educational system of the United States as an undergraduate student from Hong Kong and then leaving my rather conservative denomination shortly after I started my study at Vanderbilt, I did not have a support network, and I was unfamiliar with the ins and outs of graduate education of my (then) adopted country.[3] I was also too preoccupied with my academic studies and my various part-time employments to find information about external funding support. Perhaps that is why I rarely if ever turn down opportunities to mentor, especially those who are from racial/ethnic minoritized communities or from outside the United States. I know about the opportunity gap that keeps many persons from advancing in their education and their careers.[4]

I do not know if Segovia shares this feeling about the academic guild of biblical studies, but I often still do feel like an outsider-insider in it despite finishing my doctorate in the field and having been a guild member since the 1990s. This may have to do with my own investment in pursuing biblical studies through a transdisciplinary path. Or it may have to do with the competitive and egoistic ethos of the academy, geopolitical power differential, or racial/ethnic difference—or even all of the above. I want to be clear that I am not saying this to complain because I consider myself rather lucky in my career as a scholar and a faculty member. I am saying

3. I became a resident alien with a green card by the time I started my work at Vanderbilt.

4. Sociologists differentiate *opportunity gap* from *ability gap*. The latter refers to a difference in abilities, but the former refers to a difference in opportunities. Because of their backgrounds, many persons do not have the knowledge, privilege, or simply the opportunity to develop or demonstrate their abilities. See, for example, Paul C. Gorski, *Reaching and Teaching Students in Poverty: Strategies for Erasing the Opportunity Gap* (New York: Teachers College, 2013); Vijay Pendakur, ed., *Closing the Opportunity Gap: Identity-Conscious Strategies for Retention and Student Success* (Sterling: Stylus Publishing, 2016); Osly J. Flores, "(Re)constructing the Language of the Achievement Gap to an Opportunity Gap: The Counternarrative of Three African American Women School Leaders," *Journal of School Leadership* 28 (2018): 344–73.

this to underscore the importance of CUREMP and other pockets within the Society of Biblical Literature and the wider guild where I and many Others have been able to find some sense of belonging. An African American colleague once shared with me his experience of working with some white colleagues in the field. He said—and I am paraphrasing here—"They see you and they immediately talk about work. They don't ask how you are doing. They don't want to know about your family." I do not know how representative his experience with white colleagues is, but I know many racial/ethnic minoritized colleagues do not insert a distance into their engagements like the white colleagues he described. Perhaps it is because we do talk about family with one another that we give each other a sense of home in a still white-dominated guild. Segovia is actually an exemplar in this regard. Just about six months ago, a Latinx colleague mentioned how Segovia would always ask about her partner when they interacted, particularly how Segovia would express care if something concerning was happening in her partner's country of origin in the so-called Middle East. As this same colleague pointed out to me, that is because Segovia pays attention to what is going on around the world.

It is no wonder, then, that Segovia advocates for a "global-systemic" paradigm for biblical criticism to address the many crises of today's world. Almost a year after hearing Segovia's presidential address in 2014, I picked up a book by Gary Y. Okihiro. Seeking to "unbind" the writing of United States history by bestowing "historical significance to oceans and islands" rather than to continents (which have often, like whites and men, been given priority because of their sheer size), Okihiro refuses the traditional but narrow understanding of what is "national" or "continental" and retells United States history from "the fringes of the national consciousness," not only through the presence and resistance of Asian Americans, Native Hawai'ians, and Pacific Islanders but also through the incorporation of various Asian countries into an "expanding capitalist world-system" that started inducing labor migrations from Asia and Africa long before the founding of the United States of America.[5] Segovia's and Okihiro's calls to widen the interpretive frame by "provincializing" the traditional center in their respective fields confirms for me the central claim of feminist standpoint theory: namely, those who are marginalized and minoritized often

5. Gary Y. Okihiro, *American History Unbound: Asian and Pacific Islanders* (Berkeley: University of California Press, 2015), 20, 18, 50.

know more and they are more likely to question existing social orders than those who occupy the top rungs of a social ladder.[6]

To widen my own interpretive frame, I have tried my best to be in conversation with scholars of other racial/ethnic minoritized communities by working with Segovia, Randall C. Bailey, and many other colleagues associated with CUREMP through publication projects and a Society of Biblical Literature program unit on minoritized biblical criticism.[7] Since I now live and work in the United States, I know I must also be intentional in unbinding my perspectives from those of the United States and in learning about those of the Global South. This has led me to help found the Society of Asian Biblical Studies (SABS). At the same time, I am keenly aware of the colonial and exploitative tendencies of many Global North scholars, however unintended they may be, when they enter spaces of the Global South. The network and exchange that I have experienced through the biennial meetings of SABS in the last fifteen years have kept me energized, and I hope I have engaged my Global South colleagues there with humility and accountability. It is good that the Society of Biblical Literature has both CUREMP and the International Cooperative Initiative (ICI) Committee, and I am glad to see that some nonwhite colleagues from outside the United States have started joining the CUREMP gathering at the Annual Meeting. However, I think it is important that we do not confuse or collapse ICI with CUREMP, since many nonwhite colleagues are not minoritized on the basis of race/ethnicity in their countries.

The more I learn, the more I know I need to learn. Segovia specifies "global economics, climatological projections, and worldwide migration" as the context of his presidential address in 2014, but he does so with "a focus on global economics" in this age of neoliberal capitalism.[8] Looking back, I wish I had done more to learn about economics or at least about how to approach and read biblical texts with economic sense and sensibil-

6. See, e.g., Sandra Harding, "Rethinking Standpoint Epistemology: What Is Strong Objectivity?," *The Centennial Review* 36 (1992): 437–70. For *provincializing*, see Dipesh Chakrabarty, *Provincializing Europe: Postcolonial Thought and Historical Difference* (Princeton: Princeton University Press, 2000).

7. Randall C. Bailey, Tat-siong Benny Liew, and Fernando F. Segovia, eds., *They Were All Together in One Place? Toward Minority Biblical Criticism*, SemeiaSt 57 (Atlanta: SBL Press, 2009); Tat-siong Benny Liew and Fernando F. Segovia, eds., *Reading Biblical Texts Together: Pursuing Minoritized Biblical Criticism*, SemeiaSt 98 (Atlanta: SBL Press, 2022).

8. Segovia, "Criticism in Critical Times," 18, 6.

ity. If "the (class)room is appropriately named, for it is indeed a room of class,"[9] then class readings should impress upon students the importance of reading class. I regret that this is not often the case in many biblical studies classrooms in the United States, even or especially when racism and classism often work together here in mutually reinforcing ways. I need to learn to read class with and alongside my students.

I also need to keep on learning because, as Segovia's address shows, times change. In addition to updating my education, I must not lose sight of the sociopolitical realities of our time when I pursue my research and scholarship. As I reread Segovia's call to biblical critics in these critical times to "make a pact of blood with the world," I am reminded of the provocative question raised by the legendary interracial activist couple, James Boggs (an African American) and Grace Lee Boggs (an Asian American): "What time is it in the world clock?"[10] Because times change, I must not become so settled with and in my ideas that I stop learning and connecting. The Boggs also write, "We never know how our small activities will affect others through the invisible fabric of our connectedness. In this exquisitely connected world, it's never a question of 'critical mass.' It's always about critical connections."[11] I am grateful for the connections that I have made and maintained not only with Segovia but also with colleagues of CUREMP and of the Global South.

Bibliography

Ashcroft, Bill, Gareth Griffiths, and Helen Tiffin. *The Empire Writes Back: Theory and Practice in Post-colonial Literatures.* London: Routledge, 1989.

Bailey, Randall C., Tat-siong Benny Liew, and Fernando F. Segovia, eds. *They Were All Together in One Place? Toward Minority Biblical Criticism.* SemeiaSt 57. Atlanta: SBL Press, 2009.

Boggs, James, and Grace Lee Boggs. *Revolution and Evolution in the Twentieth Century.* New York: Monthly Review, 1974.

9. Miguel A. De La Torre, "Salsa Dancing with Blount," *The Bible & Critical Theory* 17.1 (2021): 33.

10. Segovia "Criticism in Critical Times," 29; James Boggs and Grace Lee Boggs, *Revolution and Evolution in the Twentieth Century* (New York: Monthly Review, 1974), 168.

11. Boggs and Lee Boggs, *Revolution and Evolution in the Twentieth Century*, 44.

Chakrabarty, Dipesh. *Provincializing Europe: Postcolonial Thought and Historical Difference.* Princeton: Princeton University Press, 2000.

De La Torre, Miguel A. "Salsa Dancing with Blount." *The Bible & Critical Theory* 17.1 (2021): 27–35.

Flores, Osly J. "(Re)constructing the Language of the Achievement Gap to an Opportunity Gap: The Counternarrative of Three African American Women School Leaders." *Journal of School Leadership* 28 (2018): 344–73.

Gorski, Paul C. *Reaching and Teaching Students in Poverty: Strategies for Erasing the Opportunity Gap.* New York: Teachers College, 2013.

Harding, Sandra. "Rethinking Standpoint Epistemology: What Is Strong Objectivity?" *The Centennial Review* 36 (1992): 437–70.

Liew, Tat-siong Benny, and Fernando F. Segovia, eds. *Reading Biblical Texts Together: Pursuing Minoritized Biblical Criticism.* SemeiaSt 98. Atlanta: SBL Press, 2022.

Okihiro, Gary Y. *American History Unbound: Asian and Pacific Islanders.* Berkeley: University of California Press, 2015.

Pendakur, Vijay, ed. *Closing the Opportunity Gap: Identity-Conscious Strategies for Retention and Student Success.* Sterling: Stylus Publishing, 2016.

Segovia, Fernando F. "Criticism in Critical Times: Reflections on Vision and Task." *JBL* 134 (2015): 6–29.

"The Times They Are A-Changin"

YAK-HWEE TAN

When I first enrolled as a doctoral student of the Graduate Department of Religion at Vanderbilt University, I remembered many students asked me this question, "Who are you planning to study with while you are here?" In all honesty, I did not know that the department's New Testament professors were renowned in their fields of expertise; I just wanted to learn. My goal was to study with all the New Testament professors, and so there was no prior notion as to with whom I ought to study. I was first in the family to go overseas to study, and it was indeed commendable in the eyes of my family and friends to be able to get into the doctoral program in an established university in the United States. I made my family beam with pride. Because I was a woman, I was also a source of envy for my male church colleagues.

At Vanderbilt, I had the opportunity to study with all the New Testament professors, and one of them was Fernando F. Segovia, who, I came to understand, was a renowned Johannine scholar. I was advised that I should take Segovia's "Method and Theory Course in Biblical Criticism." I was glad that I did because I learned about the shifting paradigms in biblical criticism, from historical criticism to cultural studies.[1] Flesh-and-blood reader! It was the first time I heard of this term. Segovia had advocated for the important role of the real, flesh-and-blood reader in the reading of the biblical text. The real, flesh-and-blood reader is conditioned by his or

---

The title of this essay is drawn from Bob Dylan's Song, "The Times They Are A-Changin."

1. Fernando F. Segovia, "'And They Began to Speak in Other Tongues': Competing Modes of Discourse in Contemporary Biblical Criticism," in *Social Location and Biblical Interpretation in the United States*, vol. 1 of *Reading from This Place*, ed. Fernando F. Segovia and Mary Ann Talbot (Minneapolis: Augsburg Fortress, 1995), 1–32.

her social location.[2] I remembered feeling a sense of liberation because it meant that I could have the liberty to engage the biblical text from my own perspective. In short, I found my personal voice in engaging the text. In an article titled "My Personal Voice," Segovia articulated a similar personal journey as a biblical critic: first using historical criticism until he reached his current status as a postcolonial critic.[3]

While I have found my voice, I realized that my voice is not univocal. I have many voices because of my multifaceted and shifting social locations, which affects my reading of the biblical texts. On the one hand, the literary voice is to be found as I investigate the biblical text from a particular perspective; however, accompanying that literary voice is the physical voice, which I express in my lectures and presentations in academia. Though I have these voices, it was and still is challenging for me as a woman lecturer teaching in theological colleges in Asia, where the faculty is male-dominated, hierarchical and patriarchal. It was and still is expected for a woman scholar to pursue and specialize in a practical aspect of Christian ministry, such as Christian education or children ministry, but not in the area of theology and Bible. These two disciplines are seen as hard sciences in which men are able to wrestle with the tough questions and issues but not the women. Nonetheless, I celebrate that I have a physical voice even though I was viewed with much suspicion by the leadership in the church and seminaries.

An example to show how someone, especially a woman, can have both literary voice and physical voice is to examine the character of the slave girl Rhoda in Acts 12:12–27. I have used a socioliterary approach to look at slaves, especially female slaves during the Greco-Roman time, and to uncover the point of view of Rhoda, one who is incapacitated. The *uncovering* of Rhoda is the first step of feminist analysis and leads to the next, that is, to *re-cover* Rhoda.[4] Unlike the members of the household, Rhoda need not see the physical Peter in order to recognize him. In the face of being called hysterical and crazy, Rhoda did not succumb to ridicule but

2. Segovia, "And They Began to Speak," 30–31.

3. Fernando F. Segovia, "My Personal Voice: The Making of a Postcolonial Critic," in *The Personal Voice in Biblical Interpretation*, ed. Ingrid Rosa Kitzberger (London: Routledge, 1999), 25–37.

4. Tan Yak-hwee, "Rhoda (Acts 12:12–17) 'Un-covering' and 'Re-covering' Rhoda: A Feminist Perspective," in *What Is New about Reading the Bible with New Eyes?*, ed. Huang Po Ho (Tainan, Taiwan: Grace Foundation, 2020), 139–53.

persisted in truth. From my social location as a woman biblical scholar, I seek to give a literary voice to Rhoda in the pericope in Acts but also to use my physical voice as I investigate the text in the seminary where I teach.

In addition, my social location gives me opportunities to express multiple voices because social location is also about locality where relations and power structures are challenged and negotiated. Location, or place, is a multifaceted notion where identities are fluid and subject to various interpretations. This brings me to my participation in the Society of Biblical Literature as a biblical critic from Asia. I like to distinguish myself from Asian American identities because I am not an American, nor have I resided in the United States except for my time as a graduate student. I am an Asian Asian who engages biblical criticism in Asia where the context is different from the United States. Whenever I attend the Annual Meeting of the Society of Biblical Literature, I found myself in a state of *dis-ease* in a predominantly white academy whose primary language of communication is English and whose participants are possibly economically able. For an Asian Asian to participate at such a meeting, the factors of language, identity, and finance are to be considered.

My identity marker as an Asian woman makes that visibility apparent and allows me to be *here* at the academy, but that identity marker, ironically, is also under suspicion in my participation in sessions that are not Asian or Asian-America focused. In other words, I was and still am identified with a certain category by which to understand the biblical texts. As an Asian woman scholar, I am placed in a contentious relationship with other female scholars who are not Asian, primarily because of my race and ethnicity. Moreover, there are important nuances to my identity as an Asian Asian vis-à-vis Asian American. The nuances are ethnicities, history, culture, and economics, and they are translated into different concerns and agenda. We are same, same but different. And the world and its state of affairs are in some ways, same same but different.

In his presidential address in 2014, Segovia challenged the academy to examine the global state of affairs and their impact upon biblical criticism.[5] The global state of affairs that have to be taken into consideration include, for example, the impact of global economics upon ecology and migration. With the COVID-19 global pandemic in 2020, the global state

5. Fernando F. Segovia, "Criticism in Critical Times: Reflections on Vision and Task," *JBL* 134 (2015): 6–29.

of affairs has evolved since 2014 into the politics of vaccines. The global pandemic brought people of all nations together regardless of their economic status. However, nations with rich economies were able to afford medical attention for their own citizens but not for citizens from countries with poor economies. Moreover, the closure of borders restricted the migration of workers to work, affecting the economies locally and globally. In short, the particulars of the local are always connected politically and economically to the global. As such, it avoids the homogenizing one or the other—essentialism of the local or the global. In the light of biblical criticism, I am reminded of the *glocal* nature of doing biblical criticism, where "the local and global are co-complicit, each implicated in the other."[6] Not only is the social location of the biblical critic conditioned by his or her particular location, the global also impinges upon him/her in ways s/he must consider in his/her investigation of the biblical text. The social location is an exciting but also a complex category for doing biblical criticism, especially in our current state of global affairs, which are ever changing and evolving and impacting the lives of people everywhere.

Bibliography

Friedman, Susan Stanford. "Locational Feminism: Gender, Cultural Geographies, and Geopolitical Literacy." Pages 13–32 in *Feminist Locations: Global and Local, Theory and Practice*. Edited by Marianne Dekoven. New Brunswick, NJ: Rutgers University Press, 2001.

Segovia, Fernando F. "'And They Began to Speak in Other Tongues': Competing Modes of Discourse in Contemporary Biblical Criticism." Pages 1–32 in *Social Location and Biblical Interpretation in the United States*. Vol. 1. of *Reading from This Place:* Edited by Fernando F. Segovia and Mary Ann Talbot. Minneapolis: Augsburg Fortress, 1995.

———. "Criticism in Critical Times: Reflections on Vision and Task." *JBL* 134 (2015): 6–29.

———. "My Personal Voice: The Making of a Postcolonial Critic." Pages 25–37 in *The Personal Voice in Biblical Interpretation*. Edited by Ingrid Rosa Kitzberger. London: Routledge, 1999.

6. Susan Stanford Friedman, "Locational Feminism: Gender, Cultural Geographies, and Geopolitical Literacy," in *Feminist Locations: Global and Local, Theory and Practice*, ed. Marianne Dekoven (New Brunswick, NJ: Rutgers University Press, 2001), 31.

Tan, Yak-hwee. "Rhoda (Acts 12:12–17) 'Un-covering' and 'Re-covering' Rhoda: A Feminist Perspective." Pages 139–53 in *What Is New about Reading the Bible with New Eyes?* Edited by Huang Po Ho. Tainan, Taiwan: Grace Foundation, 2020.

Decolonizing Acts: Violence and the Politics of Knowledge in the Discipline of Biblical Studies

ABRAHAM SMITH

> A decolonizing reader strives to arrest the violence of an imperializing text by exposing its effect and seeking ways of perceiving and promoting difference.
>
> —Musa W. Dube, "Readings of Semoya"

Introduction

Few serious scholars today would fail to acknowledge the historic harms and lasting legacy of the colonial project of empires, that is, each empire's projection of its will and power to control the lands, extract the wealth, disrupt the languages, and even invent the social identities of the subject populations of other continents. Commenting on the predatory nature of the European empire's colonial project, for example, J. C. Young has noted that "by the early twentieth century, nine-tenths of the entire land surface of the globe was controlled by European or European derived power."[1] Offering a more robust account of the predatory acts of Europeans (who deemed themselves as the center) on the subjects of distant lands (whom Europe deemed as the periphery), Andrew M. Mbuvi adds

> From the "center" would come weapons, militaries, administrators, explorers, and missionaries, and from the "periphery" would come natural resources (slaves, gold, ivory, timber; cash crops like cotton, spices, palm oil, coffee, cocoa, tea; sugar, etc.) and all the things that the center

1. J. C. Young, *Postcolonialism: A Very Short Introduction* (Oxford: Oxford University Press, 2003), 2.

> craved but did not have at home. The Empire would plunder and pilfer the periphery to feed the insatiable greed of the imperial economy.[2]

This essay acknowledges the massive scale of the grand larceny of empires—a violence that continues today in what may be called late imperialism. Thus, after two preceding modes of imperialism—early imperialism (a mercantilist phase that lasted roughly from the sixteenth through the eighteenth centuries) and high imperialism (a monopoly capitalism phase that lasted from the nineteenth to the mid-twentieth century)—the plunder mode of empires still operates in late imperialism, a neoimperial and neocolonial phase of capitalism that has extended from the mid-twentieth century until now. As I have stated elsewhere

> Late imperialism now also supports neo-liberalism (or global capitalism), a set of policies ideologically presupposing an unlimited faith in the market, materially favoring free trade in a globally integrated economy, and politically ceding control over a nation-state's economy and labor force to transnational corporations … despite their excessive production demands, exploitative workplace conditions, and horrendous environmental abuses.[3]

Given the history of plunder and the violence that has continued since the beginning of the colonial project, what are the tasks of engaged biblical critics in our own critical times? This is a question that Fernando F. Segovia took up in his 2014 Society of Biblical Literature presidential address, "Criticism in Critical Times: Reflections on Vision and Task."[4] In this essay, I wish to join Segovia in configuring a set of tasks (or acts) that engaged biblical critics might do *specifically* to stem the tide of the very violent times in which we live. To do so, though, I suggest that we follow Segovia's lead in developing an understanding of violence that includes what Segovia calls "cognitive injustice" or harms caused by the failure to

---

2. Andrew M. Mbuvi, *African Biblical Studies: Unmasking Embedded Racism and Colonialism in Biblical Studies* (London: Bloomsbury: T&T Clark, 2023), 21.

3. Abraham Smith, "Taking Spaces Seriously: The Politics of Space and the Future of Western Biblical Studies," in *Transforming Graduate Biblical Education: Ethos and Discipline*, ed. Elisabeth Schüssler Fiorenza and Kent Harold Richards, GPBS 10 (Atlanta: Society of Biblical Literature, 2010), 72.

4. Fernando F. Segovia, "Criticism in Critical Times: Reflections on Vision and Task," *JBL* 134 (2015): 6–29.

recognize the value of other epistemologies or other ways of knowing.[5] Thus, after offering a brief review of the salient emphases in Segovia's address, I will theorize on the broad nature of violence, especially as violence may manifest itself in what some scholars would call epistemicide. Next, I will note some examples of cognitive injustice or epistemic hegemony in biblical studies.[6] Finally, in examining African biblical studies generally and the scholarship of Musa W. Dube specifically, I will highlight how some Global South scholars seek to arrest epistemic violence through their decolonizing acts within the discipline of biblical studies.

The Call to Avoid Cognitive Injustice in Segovia's Presidential Address

Segovia's presidential address befittingly assessed the times in which we live, appraised a theoretical framework that biblical critics might take up as instructive for our intellectual work, and commensurately adumbrated a set of tasks for an informed, engaged, and creative deployment of our discipline. Along the way, Segovia also summoned the Society of Biblical Literature to avoid creating cultural productions that reinforce "cognitive injustice."[7] Thus, on the one hand, Segovia recognized that his role as president of the Society of Biblical Literature in 2014 may be viewed as "a marker of the tectonic demographic changes taking place throughout the world since the 1960s, whose impact began to reach the Society in the late 1970s and early 1980s, as the field of studies expanded into Africa and the Middle East, Asia and the Pacific, Latin America and the Caribbean."[8] On the other hand, as one fully aware of his outsider-insider status, Segovia soberingly noted that theoretical frameworks for intellectual projects historically and in more contemporary times have typically operated with a politics of exclusion that rendered what is now deemed the Global South invisible.[9]

5. Segovia, "Criticism in Critical Times," 24.

6. On the term *epistemic hegemony*, see Sabelo J. Ndlovu-Gatsheni, "Introduction: Seek Ye Epistemic Freedom First," in *Epistemic Freedom in Africa: Deprovincialization and Decolonization*, ed. Sabelo J. Ndlovu-Gatsheni (New York: Routledge, 2018), 8.

7. Segovia, "Criticism in Critical Times," 24.

8. Segovia, "Criticism in Critical Times," 8.

9. Segovia, "Criticism in Critical Times," 7, 27.

Violence and the Politics of Knowledge

Segovia's call for members of the Society of Biblical Literature to avoid cognitive injustice may be seen as a part of a growing wave of scholarship that has tried to theorize on the wider frames by which violence should be understood. In sociology, for example, Norwegian philosopher Johann Galtung brings structural violence and cultural violence into focus,[10] and ecocritic and writer Rob Nixon distinctively articulates how violence may be hidden when we fail to consider its work over extended periods of time.[11] Nixon, being very much aware of our tendency to focus both on immediate and spectacular harms, foregrounds a type of structural violence that works gradually and unspectacularly, with violent and disastrous consequences that over time are decoupled from their primary catalysts.[12] Those who wish to treat such *slow violence* must "engage directly with our contemporary politics of speed."[13]

More to Segovia's point, though, various scholars now also speak about a type of violence known as epistemic violence, that is, broadly speaking, the failure to count select knowers and their alternative bodies of knowledge as epistemically valid. Theorizing on the politics of representation deployed in the archival records of the postconquest settlement of the kingdom of Sirmaur by the British East India Company, for example, the subaltern theorist Gayatri Chakravorty Spivak initially coined the term epistemic violence to demonstrate the connection between "worlding" (a literary representation of already inhabited land as if it were *terra nullius* [empty land]) and colonialism.[14] Then, presupposing Michel Foucault's concept of "subjugated knowledge," Spivak parses the term *epistemic violence* geopolitically as "the remotely orchestrated, far-flung, and heterogeneous project to constitute the colonial subject Other."[15] Epistemic

---

10. See, for example, Johan Galtung, "Violence, Peace, and Peace Research," *Journal of Peace Research* 6 (1969): 167–91. Also, see Galtung, "Cultural Violence," *Journal of Peace Research* 27 (1990): 291–305.

11. Rob Nixon, *Slow Violence and the Environmentalism of the Poor* (Cambridge: Harvard University Press, 2011), 27.

12. Nixon, *Slow Violence*, 28.

13. Nixon, *Slow Violence*, 11.

14. See Gayatri Chakravorty Spivak, "The Rani of Sirmur: An Essay in Reading the Archives," *History and Theory* 24 (1985): 263.

15. Gayatri Chakravorty Spivak, "Can the Subaltern Speak?," in *Marxism and the Interpretation of Culture*, ed. Cary Nelson and Lawrence Grossberg (Urbana: University of Illinois Press, 1988), 280.

violence occurs when the voices of subaltern subjects, especially marginalized women, are silenced through representations of them from others, not from what the marginalized know about themselves.

Segovia's term *cognitive injustice* hails from the scholarship of Bonaventura de Sousa Santos, a Portuguese social scientist and legal scholar who has written extensively about epistemologies from the South.[16] In an effort to overcome what he calls epistemicide or the slighting, if not the dismissal and invisibilizing altogether of non-Western forms of knowledge, Santos argues that (1) modern science cannot possibly capture the diversity of the entire world; (2) the tendency to slight or disregard altogether alternative forms of knowledge is a case of cognitive injustice or epistemicide, and (3) the path forward toward cognitive justice must begin with the recognition that modern (Western) science is a provincial form of knowledge. The ultimate objective for Santos, though, is not to dismiss science, but to provincialize any form of knowledge that poses as universal and to develop what may be called an ecology of knowledges, with all types of knowledge being included and respected.

These broader theoretical perspectives on violence thus show that beyond physical assaults and even the social harms worked out through policies and programs, it is possible to do harm through the means whereby other types of violence are justified *and* through the failure to recognize the right of others as knowers and producers of knowledge. Engaged biblical scholars who seek to decolonize the bible and biblical studies then must be aware of the multiple ways in which violence is perpetuated.

Epistemic Hegemony in the Discipline of Biblical Studies

As the discipline of biblical studies operates today, biblical scholars must acknowledge how epistemic violence or cognitive injustice has been and currently is deeply embedded in a variety of our professional productions, protocols, and practices—through the geopolitical biases of our leading journals, the use of English as a lingua franca, the exoticization of the contributions from authors who are not Anglo-American.[17] Given the for-

---

16. Bonaventura de Sousa Santos, *Epistemologies of the South: Justice against Epistemicide* (New York: Routledge, 2016), viii–211.

17. For this set of indices by which epistemic violence may be assessed, see Lily Kong and Junxi Qian, "Knowledge Circulation in Urban Geography/Urban Studies, 1990–2010: Testing the Discourse of Anglo-American Hegemony through Publica-

mation of the Society of Biblical Literature in the United States in 1880 and given that the Society began under the auspices of forty-five members all of whom were white, Protestant males in the United States,[18] for example, it is little wonder that most of the contributors to the Society's flagship journal, the *Journal of Biblical Literature*, have been Western contributors, especially from Anglophone spheres.

Also, for many in the Society, English is the lingua franca (or at least the primary language if other select European languages are included). Thus, for the knowledge productions of persons from the Global South to be heard, such productions must often be published in English, or their contributions may not be read by a wide audience of interlocutors. Furthermore, conveying concepts or theoretical frames that were initially developed in languages other than English, French, and German may often require an extra step for persons whose knowledge base represents non-Western communities.

Worse yet is the danger that one's non-Western scholarship may be exoticized, commodified, and made into a display within what Stanley Fish would call "boutique multiculturalism."[19] In the case of publishing firms, the goal may not be truly to hear the voices of the Global South but—in alignment with market dynamics—to sell their voices on the market, as long as such voices represent the flavor of the times. When select voices are not selling, the market simply turns to a new set to use. The goal of the market, in any case, is not that the book buyers learn new or different knowledge but that these firms turn a profit. Crudely but truthfully stated, whether or not there is really a groundswell of people who now believe Black Lives Matter, for example, the Western publishing world knows that

---

tion and Citation Patterns," *Urban Studies* 56 (2019): 47. On the geopolitics of knowledge in general, see Walter D. Mignolo, "The Geopolitics of Knowledge and the Colonial Difference," *South Atlantic Quarterly* 101 (2002): 57–96; and Ramón Grosfoguel, "The Structure of Knowledge in Westernized Universities: Epistemic Racism/Sexism and the Four Genocides/Epistemicides of the Long Sixteenth Century," *Human Architecture* 9 (2013): 73–90.

18. The numbers given by scholars for the early membership of the Society of Biblical Literature vary. The numbers presented here follow Ernest Saunders, *Searching the Scriptures: A History of the Society of Biblical Literature, 1880–1980*, BSNA 8 (Atlanta: Scholars Press, 1997).

19. Stanley F. Fish, "Boutique Multiculturalism: Or, Why Liberals Are Incapable of Thinking about Hate Speech," *Critical Inquiry* 23 (1997): 378–95.

the sale of books about black and other marginalized lives matters (at least, until something else does)!

Moving the Center: Decolonizing Acts from the Global South in African Biblical Studies

If engaged biblical scholars seek what may be called an "epistemic break" or a rupture from the kind of violence that slights epistemologies from the Global South, then what is to be done?[20] To paraphrase the words of Ngugi wa Thiong'o, what must be done is to move the center, that is, to denounce epistemic hegemony in any form. This, Ngugi wa Thiong'o states, will "contribute to the freeing of the world of cultures from the restrictive walls of nationalism, class, race and gender."[21] Thus, in two ways, this essay assays now to highlight with candor and without an exoticizing ulterior motive the knowledge productions of those who hail from the South: (1) by describing *generally* one kind of scholarship from the South, namely, African biblical studies; and (2) by highlighting *specifically* decolonizing acts taken up in the scholarship of the postcolonial feminist Musa Dube, the current president of the Society of Biblical Literature (2023).

With respect to African biblical studies, what is it and what does it seek to do? Although African biblical studies is not consensually defined, it may be viewed as a theoretical-political project with a distinctive orientation, a broad range of practitioners, a plurality of methodologies, and an interventionist agenda. The orientation, which focuses more on the contemporary present than solely on the ancient past, makes African realities "the subject of interpretation."[22] While the scope of the field includes Africa-wide

---

20. Sabelo J. Ndlovu-Gatsheni, "Decoloniality as the Future of Africa," *History Compass* 13.10 (2015): 485.

21. Ngugi wa Thiong'o, *Moving the Centre: The Struggle for Cultural Freedoms* (Oxford: Currey, 1993), xvii.

22. Justin S. Ukpong defined his own method, inculturation hermeneutics, as one in which "the African context forms the subject of interpretation of the Bible." See Justin S. Ukpong, "Developments in Biblical Interpretation in Modern Africa," *Missionalia* 27 (1999): 325. Also, see David T. Adamo, preface in *Navigating African Biblical Hermeneutics: Trends and Themes from Pots and Calabashes*, ed. Madipoane Masenya (Ngwan'a Mphahlele) and Kenneth N. Ngwa (Newcastle: Cambridge Scholars, 2018), xi. As noted by Mbuvi, African biblical studies "refuses to deal with the Bible simply as an ancient text and demands that it be engaged to deal with present concerns, addressing issues that resonate with African (and world) realities." See Andrew M.

professional analysts from the biblical studies field, religious studies, and other academic disciplines, it also includes clergy, laity, and a wide range of everyday readers.[23] Furthermore, African biblical studies may deploy a variety of methodologies or reading approaches—from older methods such as inculturation hermeneutics, black liberation hermeneutics, and a variety of gender-based studies to newer studies informed by postcolonial studies, translation studies, sexuality studies, and health-concerns.[24] Such a variety of methods is necessary to expose the provinciality and limitations of Western scholarship that falsely deems itself as universal. The agenda of African biblical studies, moreover, is decidedly interventionist because the goal is to summon or deconstruct scriptural texts, sometimes with a *hermeneutics of trust* and sometimes with a *hermeneutics of suspicion*, but consistently with a *hermeneutics from the underside*, for both "personal and social transformation."[25]

With respect to Dube, what are the decolonizing acts in her scholarship? At least three acts are visible, and all three in essence challenge the idea of a universal epistemology: (1) decolonizing readers and readings; (2) decolonizing history; and (3) decolonizing translation studies.

Decolonizing Readers and Readings

For the purpose of avoiding the circular argumentation implicit in the historical reconstruction of ancient biblical readers (or auditors), scholars influenced by audience-oriented criticism have deployed the term *implied reader* (audience) and various offshoots such *as ideal reader* or *competent*

Mbuvi, "African Biblical Studies: An Introduction to an Emerging Discipline," *CurBR* 15 (2017): 154.

23. Madipoane Masenya (Ngwan'a Mphahlele) and Kenneth N. Ngwa, "Introduction: What Comes Out of the African Pots and Calabashes?," in *Navigating African Biblical Hermeneutics: Trends and Themes from Pots and Calabashes*, ed. Madipoane Masenya (Ngwan'a Mphahlele) and Kenneth N. Ngwa (Newcastle: Cambridge Scholars, 2018), 3.

24. Masenya (Ngwan'a Mphahlele) and Ngwa, "Introduction," 2.

25. On the quoted material, see Ukpong, "Developments in Biblical Interpretation," 325. Also, on a hermeneutics of suspicion and a hermeneutics of trust in African biblical studies, see Gerald O. West, "African Biblical Scholarship as Post-colonial, Tri-polar, and a Site of Struggle," in *Present and Future of Biblical Studies Celebrating Twenty-Five Years of Brill's Biblical Interpretation* (Leiden: Brill, 2018), 250, 254.

reader.[26] Scholars deploying such constructions sought to allow the literary features of a text to serve as the center of attention. Such static expressions invariably led, however, to a generalizing of readers (or auditors) that all too often implied by default a disinterest in the historical circumstances and the distinctive struggles of real flesh-and-blood readers.

Dube decolonizes readers by dehomogenizing readers, whether an aggregate of readers includes varying women subjects, varying African subjects, or various persons reading the Bible with each other to address the on-the-ground realities of everyday people. The effect is to show the provincial posture of any class of knowers who seem to speak for all and thus who by such speaking deny both the complex plurality of voices and the unequal configurations of power among those voices within the aggregate.

Drawing on the work of Chandra Talpade Mohanty and Laura Donaldson, for example, Dube critiques the idea of woman that she finds in select feminist discourse. With Mohanty, Dube critiques the use of the category of woman, which amounts to a "universally homogenous entity."[27] Such a category has the potential both to elevate white women categorically as ideal and to relegate non-Western women categorically as victims (as in the case of Mary Daly's *Gyn/Ecology*, in which "Daly portrayed all African women as victims of genital mutilation").[28] With Donaldson, moreover, Dube critiques any analysis that focuses so exclusively on gender that it cannot incorporate other, intersecting factors through which imperializing logic also works.[29] In her book *Postcolonial Feminist Interpretations of the Bible*, Dube thus constructs a methodology that seriously considers how imperial literary texts, from ancient to modern times, deploy gender as a colonizing literary strategy.[30]

Dube also dehomogenizes African subjects.[31] She notes the rich diversity of the African continent: its multiple religious traditions such

26. See Stephen Mailloux, *Interpretive Conventions: The Reader in the Study of American Fiction* (Ithaca, NY: Cornell University Press, 1982), 19.

27. Musa W. Dube, *Postcolonial Feminist Interpretation* (Saint Louis: Chalice, 2000), 24.

28. Dube, *Postcolonial Feminist Interpretation*, 25.

29. Laura E. Donaldson, *Decolonizing Feminisms: Race, Gender & Empire-Building* (Chapel Hill: University of North Carolina Press, 1992), 33.

30. Dube, *Postcolonial Feminist Interpretation*, 57–95.

31. Note, for example, her remarks on her use of Africa: "I do not consent to the use of 'Africa' insofar as it implies a uniform people. My reading is representative of neither Africa nor of Botswana, my country. Africa is too large and diverse to be

as African indigenous religions, Christianity, and Islam; its rich complexity of languages; and its varying regions of contributions to Christianity, whether from North Africa in the earliest inflections of Christianity or from sub-Saharan Christianity, where Christianity thrives today.[32] Furthermore, in addition to questioning the notion of disinterested readings and in addition to sanctioning a variety of biblical readings from the Global South, Dube also adumbrates twelve types of scholarly and everyday readings performed by African interpreters.[33]

Decolonizing History

Despite the limits of historical criticism, biblical studies has profited much from historical criticism, especially its wresting of sole or primary authority over the interpretation of scriptural texts away from sacerdotal powers.[34] Much of the doubt raised about history has come from the wider historical field itself, as historians outside of biblical studies have

represented by one person's view. I am using this category insofar as I find it heavily imposed on me by the First World and because it has come to be representative of our common oppression." See Musa W. Dube, "Toward a Post-colonial Feminist Interpretation of the Bible," *Semeia* 78 (1997): 11–23.

32. For example, Dube speaks about a variety of Bantu languages such as Kalanga and Shona. See Musa W. Dube, "Introduction (The Scramble for Africa as the Biblical Scramble for African: Postcolonial Perspectives)," in *Postcolonial Perspectives in African Biblical Interpretations*, ed. Musa Dube, Andrew M. Mbuvi, and Dora Mbuwayesango, GPBS 13 (Atlanta: Society of Biblical Literature, 2012), 1–26.

33. See Musa Dube, "African Biblical Interpretation," in *The Oxford Encyclopedia of Biblical Interpretation*, ed. Musa Dube (Oxford: Oxford Biblical Studies Online, 2009), 1–8. That Dube deconstructs the idea of disinterested readings altogether is clear in her article "Intercultural Biblical Interpretations," *Swedish Missiological Themes* 98 (2010): 361–88. Drawing on the work of Segovia, Dube shows how this quest for disinterested readings is simply "a colonizing ideology that in fact imposed western constructed meanings on the rest and universalized them" (372). See Fernando F. Segovia, "'And They Began to Speak in Other Tongues': Competing Modes of Discourse in Contemporary Biblical Criticism," in *Social Location and Biblical Interpretation in the United States*, vol. 1 of *Reading from the Place*, ed. Fernando F. Segovia and Mary Ann Tolbert (Minneapolis: Fortress, 1995), 1–32. On Dube's sanctioning of various readings from the Global South, see Dube, "Intercultural Biblical Interpretations," 378–82.

34. For a critique of historical criticism within biblical studies (that is, a critique of the grand narratives that underwrote historical criticism's notion of objectivity), see Wayne A. Meeks, "Why Study the New Testament?," *NTS* 51 (2005): 155–70.

critiqued the notion of objectivity and the inherent politics of exclusion that often operates either in the selection of the subject matter of history or in the orienting frames by which the details of history have been placed into larger narrative wholes. Furthermore, given the narrow temporal and spatial frames by which many histories are constructed, historians themselves, again apart from biblical criticism, have raised such questions as: "What if time in select cultures is not measured in centuries?" and "What if cartological frames in select traditions operate with a different set of mapping traditions? What if such traditions construe space, for example, "through cosmological mandalas (as in Hindu cultures), songlines (as among Australian aborigines), and charcoal sketches (as among Koreans and the Japanese)"?[35]

How then do we decolonize history? Aware of the past prominence of historical criticism in biblical studies, Dube once wrote, "Historical criticism, the then-dominant method of reading in ways to bring out the 'objective,' 'neutral' and intended authorial meaning, was a colonially informed approach that insisted on there being one meaning of the text and one universal way of reading—thereby suppressing heterogeneity."[36] Also, being informed by Ella Shohat and Robert Stam's *Unthinking Eurocentrism*, Dube argues the need for a robust, interdisciplinary biblical studies that "interrogates the boundaries of academic scholarship and its curriculum."[37] What is needed is not less history but more—not rendering ancient history obsolescent but interrogating its Eurocentric biases toward "Greece as the center of all knowledge."[38] In effect, what is needed is to recognize the provincial nature of focusing on the European part of the biblical world without considering the role of African parts of that world (e.g., in Egypt or in the land mass that was known as Kush in the ancient world).

Also, what is needed is not to eliminate the history of interpretations altogether but to interrogate such history for how and why "colonial bibli-

35. Smith, "Taking *Spaces* Seriously," 87.

36. Musa W. Dube, "Border-Crossing in Diasporic Academic Space," in *The Bible, Centres and Margins: Dialogues between Postcolonial African and British Biblical Scholars*, ed. Musa W. Dube and Johanna Stiebert (London: T&T Clark, 2018), 10.

37. Musa W. Dube, "Journeys of a Postcolonial Feminist in Biblical Studies," in *Breaking the Master's S.H.I.T. Holes: Doing Theology in the Context of Global Migration*, ed. Musa W. Dube and Paul L. Leshota (Leipzig: Evangelische Verlagsanstalt, 2020), 103.

38. Dube, "Journeys of a Postcolonial Feminist," 101.

cal readers [missionaries] translated indigenous cultures, religious spaces, gender."[39] That is, an examination of the practices of the colonizers reveals the attribution of objectivity onto the colonizers' culture-specific methods and research tools while designating other readings as eisegesis whenever they departed from the regimen and prescriptions of the so-called universal methods.[40] For Dube, then, such culture-specific methods and research tools must be provincialized.

Decolonizing Translation Studies

In her 2014 article "Translating *Ngaka*," Dube names the salient shift in translation studies from the 1980s to the middle of the second decade in the twenty-first century. While translation studies once presupposed that translations were attempts to find a correct rendering of a source text into a target language, the objective in the 1980s and beyond was to discover the power relations and the contextual functions of translations.[41]

Accordingly, in her work "Consuming the Colonial Cultural Bomb," Dube acknowledges that translations are not innocent representations of some original truth but always involve power dynamics. She notes that in the Setswana Bible translation, the colonial missionaries used the word *Badimo* (originally a *neuter* word for ancestral intermediaries) to translate the Greek word for "demons," thus both changing the gender of the expression and viewing *Badimo* in a pejorative manner.[42]

Extending her translation studies beyond the translation of biblical texts, moreover, Dube has also argued that the term *Ngaka* (meaning an indigenous healer or promoter of public health among the Batswana [the people of Botswana]) was negatively translated as a sorcerer in Robert Moffatt's *Missionary Labours and Scenes in Southern Africa* (1842). Given that the *Dingaka* (the plural form of *ngaka*) were Moffatt's rivals and persons who resisted the introduction of Christianity, Moffatt rewrote the term *Ngaka*

39. Dube, "Journeys of a Postcolonial Feminist," 102.

40. Musa W. Dube, "Post-colonial Biblical Interpretations," in *Dictionary of Biblical Interpretation*, ed. John H. Hayes (Nashville, TN: Abingdon, 1999), 299–300.

41. Musa W. Dube, "Translating *Ngaka*: Robert Moffat Rewriting an Indigenous Healer," *Studia Historiae Ecclesiasticae* 40 (2014): 157–58.

42. Musa W. Dube, "Consuming the Colonial Cultural Bomb: Translating Badimo into Demons in the Setswana Bible (Matt. 8:28–34; 15:22; 10:8)," *JSNT* 73 (1999): 33–59.

as an evil person in league with Satan.[43] In acts of resistance, though, the Batswana people also rewrote both Moffatt and Jesus (the latter as depicted in the Gospel of Luke, for example) as healer-doctors.[44] Reflecting on the whole archive of colonial projections of terms such as "heathens" and "savages" from a "dark" and "evil" continent, Dube sees Moffatt's rewriting of the term *Ngaka* as yet another instance of a cultural bomb, a weapon intended to alienate African cultures away from their own beliefs and traditions.[45] In exposing such cultural bombs, African biblical scholars are thus demonstrating the provincial epistemology of the colonial missionaries.

Conclusion

To inspire members of the Society of Biblical Literature in 2014, Segovia concluded his presidential address with two artistic exemplars: one from the Global North (the novelist George Orwell) and one from the Global South (the poet Pablo Neruda), both of whom revealed their motivations for writing. Orwell wrote to fuse the aesthetic with the political in the hope of changing minds. Neruda wrote to bring the two together because of a pact he had with the blood of his people. Thus, in paraphrasing Neruda, Segovia concluded: "We have all made a pact of love with criticism; let us now make a pact of blood with the world."[46]

At a time when several scholars from the Society of Biblical Literature collectively are celebrating the work of the Committee on Underrepresented Racial and Ethnic Minorities in the Profession on the occasion of that committee's thirtieth anniversary, I, too, would like to conclude with some words of inspiration from Ngugi wa Thiong'o, who revealed his motivation for writing despite the physical, structural, and epistemic violence that he and other Africans continued to face even after Kenya had won the hard-earned political struggle for independence from Britain in 1963. Sixty years ago, he wrote:

> But within our field as artists, writers, and intellectuals, let our Pen, Brushes and Voices articulate the dreams of all the children of Southern Africa for a world in which their integrated survival and development is

43. Dube, "Translating *Ngaka*," 166.
44. Dube, "Translating *Ngaka*," 168–69.
45. Dube, "Translating *Ngaka*," 170.
46. Segovia, "Criticism in Critical Times," 27–29.

ensured. Let us sing songs of the possibility of a new tomorrow, a new world. A luta continua![47]

Bibliography

Adamo, David T. Preface in *Navigating African Biblical Hermeneutics: Trends and Themes from Pots and Calabashes*. Edited by Madipoane Masenya (Ngwan'a Mphahlele) and Kenneth N. Ngwa. Newcastle: Cambridge Scholars, 2018.

Donaldson, Laura E. *Decolonizing Feminisms: Race, Gender & Empire-Building*. Chapel Hill: University of North Carolina Press, 1992.

Dube, Musa W. "African Biblical Interpretation." Pages 1–8 in *The Oxford Encyclopedia of Biblical Interpretation*. Edited by Musa Dube. Oxford: Oxford Biblical Studies Online, 2009.

———. "Border-Crossing in Diasporic Academic Space." Pages 7–14 in *The Bible, Centres and Margins: Dialogues between Postcolonial African and British Biblical Scholars*. Edited by Musa W. Dube and Johanna Stiebert London: T&T Clark, 2018.

———. "Consuming the Colonial Cultural Bomb: Translating Badimo into Demons in the Setswana Bible (Matt. 8:28–34; 15:22; 10:8)." *JSNT* 73 (1999): 33–59.

———. "Intercultural Biblical Interpretations." *Swedish Missiological Themes* 98 (2010): 361–88.

———. "Introduction (The Scramble for Africa as the Biblical Scramble for African: Postcolonial Perspectives)." Pages 1–26 in *Postcolonial Perspectives in African Biblical Interpretations*. Edited by Musa W. Dube, Andrew M. Mbuvi, and Dora Mbuwayesango. GPBS 13. Atlanta: Society of Biblical Literature, 2012.

———. "Journeys of a Postcolonial Feminist in Biblical Studies." Pages 95–111 in *Breaking the Master's S.H.I.T. Holes: Doing Theology in the Context of Global Migration*. Edited by Musa W. Dube and Paul L. Leshota. Leipzig: Evangelische Verlagsanstalt, 2020.

———. "Post-colonial Biblical Interpretations." Pages 299–303 in *Dictionary of Biblical Interpretation*. Edited by John H. Hayes. Nashville, TN: Abingdon, 1999.

———. *Postcolonial Feminist Interpretation*. Saint Louis: Chalice, 2000.

47. Ngugi wa Thiong'o, *Moving the Centre*, 81.

———. "Readings of Semoya: Batswana Women's Interpretation of Matt 15: 21–28." *Semeia* 73 (1996): 111–29.

———. "Translating *Ngaka*: Robert Moffat Rewriting an Indigenous Healer." *Studia Historiae Ecclesiasticae* 40 (2014): 157–72.

———. "Toward a Post-colonial Feminist Interpretation of the Bible." *Semeia* 78 (1997): 11–23.

Fish, Stanley F. "Boutique Multiculturalism: Or, Why Liberals Are Incapable of Thinking about Hate Speech." *Critical Inquiry* 23 (1997): 378–95.

Galtung, Johan. "Cultural Violence." *Journal of Peace Research* 27 (1990): 291–305.

———. "Violence, Peace, and Peace Research." *Journal of Peace Research* 6 (1969): 167–91.

Grosfoguel, Ramón. "The Structure of Knowledge in Westernized Universities: Epistemic Racism/Sexism and the Four Genocides/Epistemicides of the Long Sixteenth Century." *Human Architecture* 9 (2013): 73–90.

Kong, Lily, and Junxi Qian. "Knowledge Circulation in Urban Geography/Urban Studies, 1990–2010: Testing the Discourse of Anglo-American Hegemony through publication and Citation Patterns." *Urban Studies* 56 (2019): 44–80.

Mailloux, Stephen. *Interpretive Conventions: The Reader in the Study of American Fiction.* Ithaca, NY: Cornell University Press, 1982.

Masenya, Madipoane (Ngwan'a Mphahlele), and Kenneth N. Ngwa. "Introduction: What Comes Out of the African Pots and Calabashes?" Pages 1–18 in *Navigating African Biblical Hermeneutics: Trends and Themes from Pots and Calabashes.* Edited by Madipoane Masenya (Ngwan'a Mphahlele) and Kenneth N. Ngwa. Newcastle: Cambridge Scholars, 2018.

Mbuvi, Andrew M. "African Biblical Studies: An Introduction to an Emerging Discipline." *CurBR* 15 (2017): 149–78.

———. *African Biblical Studies: Unmasking Embedded Racism and Colonialism in Biblical Studies.* London: Bloomsbury: T&T Clark, 2023.

Meeks, Wayne A. "Why Study the New Testament?" *NTS* 51 (2005): 155–70.

Mignolo, Walter D. "The Geopolitics of Knowledge and the Colonial Difference." *South Atlantic Quarterly* 101 (2002): 57–96.

Ndlovu-Gatsheni, Sabelo J. "Decoloniality as the Future of Africa." *History Compass* 13 (2015): 485–96.

———. "Introduction: Seek Ye Epistemic Freedom First." Pages 1–41 in

Epistemic Freedom in Africa: Deprovincialization and Decolonization. Edited by Sabelo J. Ndlovu-Gatsheni. New York: Routledge, 2018.
Ngugi wa Thiong'o. *Moving the Centre: The Struggle for Cultural Freedoms.* Oxford: Currey, 1993.
Nixon, Rob. *Slow Violence and the Environmentalism of the Poor.* Cambridge: Harvard University Press, 2011.
Santos, Bonaventura de Sousa. *Epistemologies of the South: Justice against Epistemicide.* New York: Routledge, 2016.
Saunders, Ernest. *Searching the Scriptures: A History of the Society of Biblical Litearture, 1880–1980.* BSNA 8. Atlanta: Scholars Press, 1997.
Segovia, Fernando F. "'And They Began to Speak in Other Tongues': Competing Modes of Discourse in Contemporary Biblical Criticism." Pages 1–32 in *Social Location and Biblical Interpretation in the United States.* Vol. 1 of *Reading from the Place.* Edited by Fernando F. Segovia and Mary Ann Tolbert. Minneapolis: Fortress, 1995.
———. "Criticism in Critical Times: Reflections on Vision and Task." *JBL* 134 (2015): 6–9.
Smith, Abraham. "Taking Spaces Seriously: The Politics of Space and the Future of Western Biblical Studies." Pages 59–92 in *Transforming Graduate Biblical Education: Ethos and Discipline.* Edited by Elisabeth Schüssler Fiorenza and Kent Harold Richards. GPBS 10. Atlanta: Society of Biblical Literature, 2010.
Spivak, Gayatri Chakravorty. "Can the Subaltern Speak?" Pages 271–313 in *Marxism and the Interpretation of Culture.* Edited by Cary Nelson and Lawrence Grossberg. Urbana: University of Illinois Press, 1988.
———. "The Rani of Sirmur: An Essay in Reading the Archives." *History and Theory* 24 (1985): 247–72.
Ukpong, Justin S. "Developments in Biblical Interpretation in Modern Africa." *Missionalia* 27 (1999): 313–29.
West, Gerald O. "African Biblical Scholarship as Post-colonial, Tri-polar, and a Site of Struggle." Pages 240–73 in *Present and Future of Biblical Studies Celebrating Twenty-Five Years of Brill's Biblical Interpretation.* Leiden: Brill, 2018.
Wittman, Emily O. "Literary Narrative Prose and Translation Studies." Pages 438–50 in *The Routledge Book of Translation Studies.* Edited by Carmen Millán and Francesca Bartrina. New York: Routledge, 2103.
Young, J. C. *Postcolonialism: A Very Short Introduction.* Oxford: Oxford University Press, 2003.

Integrative and Responsible Biblical Scholarship

EKAPUTRA TUPAMAHU

Representation matters. When Fernando Segovia was elected president of the Society of Biblical Literature in 2013, I was in my second year of doctoral studies at Vanderbilt University working directly under his supervision. As a graduate student who grew up in the Global South, far from the elite network of biblical scholarship, I had been wrestling with my identity as a scholar. Who am I? What kind of scholar am I? I had been trained for many years to think like a white person, to ask white questions, to wrestle with questions that are far from myself and what I care about. Why? Because at that time such questions were markers of good scholarship. Yet in thinking like this, and in asking such questions, I almost lost sight of who I am and my sense of identity in pursuing my scholarship. I didn't see my experience, my story, as being important to my work as a biblical scholar. Under the guidance of Segovia, however, that changed significantly. Taking his classes, discussing many things with him, and reading his works gave me a new perspective. I began to realize that my particular story, my particular identity, and my particular concerns do matter in doing scholarship. I don't have to be someone I am not in order to be a biblical scholar. For all those reasons, watching, listening to, and reading Segovia's presidential address in San Diego was truly a moment of pride for me. He was indeed "the first president from the Global South."[1] I felt seen.

That year, I attended a session at the Society of Biblical Literature dedicated to honoring Segovia and his works. In the question-and-answer

1. Fernando F. Segovia, "Criticism in Critical Times: Reflections on Vision and Task," *JBL* 134 (2015): 7.

session, I asked the panelists: Can we say that, through the election of Segovia as the president of the Society of Biblical Literature, the landscape of biblical scholarship has shifted from one in which the European mode of scholarship dominated to one in which the Global South takes over? No. Biblical scholarship remains a white-dominant space. While this is true, Segovia's presidency nonetheless gives me profound hope that the wind of change is still blowing through biblical scholarship. The voices of scholars from the Global South are now louder. Yet we still have significant work to do.

The Need for Scholarly Engagement in Global Affairs

In the past three centuries, the dominance of the white European historical paradigm in biblical scholarship has been almost unshakable. In this paradigm, to be a biblical scholar is technically to be a historian. It is a past-oriented enterprise grounded mainly in the world behind the text that holds its power to this day. Scholars do not really engage with world struggles, as Segovia showed us in his critical analysis of past presidential addresses. Neither has the rise of the narrative paradigm in the twentieth century brought attention to the struggles and crises in the world. As it mainly focuses on the world within the text (plot, character, setting, etc.), practitioners of narrative criticism mostly do not engage with the world around them. Segovia's presidential address challenged this well-established tendency.

A word that keeps coming to my mind when I think of Segovia's presidential address is *beyond*. He invites biblical scholars to move beyond their usual business. Biblical scholarship should not only engage with the past history around the text nor only with the story within the text: it should also engage with global crises today. Scholars have to attune to, respond to, and reflect on the "the contemporary global state of affairs," states Segovia.[2] Such sensibility and attention to the social, political, and economic crises at the global level is no surprise to me because Segovia is himself an immigrant. He knows how global politics can affect one's life. Reflecting on the crisis at the border near San Diego, the humanitarian issues in Latin America and in other parts of the Global South, and particularly his own social location as an immigrant to the United States, Segovia writes:

2. Segovia, "Criticism in Critical Times," 17.

> Given such emphasis on the significance and relevance for the present, I came to see that this convergence of vectors of meaning and association of events regarding my term deserved, even demanded, a response on my part as a biblical critic. What should I as a critic do in the face of our critical times? How should I conduct my métier? This I saw as a daunting task, but imperative nonetheless.[3]

For Segovia, biblical scholars should not sit on the sidelines working on their Greek or Hebrew words merely watching the world struggling with various crises. We biblical scholars must go *beyond* such business as usual because we are tasked with responding to the issues that the world is facing. This *beyond* should not be either some side interest or extra work, but the work itself. To borrow Segovia's words, we have a duty "to integrate and respond in some way" to the global issues.[4]

This project is clearly "ambitious," as Segovia points out, because it aims at "bring(ing) the field [of biblical scholarship] to bear upon the major crises of our post-Cold War times, in both individual and converging fashion."[5] Such a duty of "engaging our times" demands an open dialogue with other disciplinary areas.[6] Biblical scholars, in other words, have to listen to those discourses regarding the global crises and to integrate theories from both the North and the South.

Segovia offers quite a broad theoretical framework to do this kind of work in section 4 of his address. He argues that biblical scholars need to be in conversation with global studies. Segovia attends to theories from both the North and the South. On the one hand, the theories from North cover specific aspects of the world system, such as world order, globalization, and empire. From the Global South, on the other hand, Segovia argues that the work of scholars such as Boaventura de Sousa Santos proves to be helpful.[7] De Sousa Santos argues for "the epistemologies of the South" characterized by (1) a broader understanding of the world,

---

3. Segovia, "Criticism in Critical Times," 13.

4. Segovia, "Criticism in Critical Times," 21.

5. Segovia, "Criticism in Critical Times," 26.

6. Segovia, "Criticism in Critical Times," 21.

7. It is worth noting that Boaventura de Sousa Santon was accused of sexual harassment and suspended from his professorship position at the Portuguese University of Coimbra. See "Due to Allegations of Sexual Harassment, Boaventura de Sousa Santos Is Suspended from University," Euro ES Euro, 15 April 2023, https://tinyurl.com/SBL4527g; Mariama Correia, "Brazilian State Deputy Says She Was Sexu-

(2) acknowledgment of the diversity of the world, and (3) incorporating the diversity of the world into a general system.[8] Segovia suggests that scholars need to engage all these theories in order to imagine not only a "utopian vision of the future," but also "new projects of interpretation that embody such ideals."[9]

About six years after Segovia gave his presidential address in San Diego, the world was rocked by the multiple effects of the COVID-19 virus. In March 2020, the world was on almost complete lock down. The fear, the terror, the grief were real. Social distancing became the new normal while the death toll skyrocketed. Hospitals were overcrowded. Schools were closed. Businesses were shuttered and struggled to survive everywhere in the world. Governments issued travel bans as they scrambled for solutions. The word that was often used to describe the global situation was *unprecedented.*

Indeed, the COVID-19 pandemic posed a serious challenge to the world. It demanded a response from biblical scholars. So how did we do?

The Coronavirus Pandemic

In 2020, the *Journal of Biblical Literature* published a forum entitled "Biblical Studies in a Pandemic." This was an important move from the editorial board of the journal to respond to this crisis. Mark Brett and Susan Hylen wrote an editorial introduction stating that the pandemic is a serious crisis that requires biblical scholars to respond. They said:

> The virus has brought planetary questions to the forefront in ways that cannot be avoided. Where do the disciplines of biblical study sit within the current tragedies? The question needs to be addressed from many different perspectives. Beyond the narrow specializations of our fields, we also need to think more broadly about systemic forces that shape our experiences as scholars, the lives of our students, and the world we inhabit.[10]

---

ally Assaulted by Boaventura de Sousa Santos," *Agência Pública*, 14 April 2023, https://tinyurl.com/SBL4527i.

8. See Segovia's discussion of this in Segovia, "Criticism in Critical Times," 24–25.

9. Segovia, "Criticism in Critical Times," 25.

10. Mark G. Brett and Susan E. Hylen, "The JBL Forum, an Occasional Exchange: Biblical Studies in a Pandemic," *JBL* 139 (2020): 597–99.

Knowing the struggle that the world was going through at that time, this call was and remains extremely important. Just as Segovia did in his 2014 presidential address, so too Brett and Hylen challenged biblical scholars to "think more broadly about systemic forces that shape our experiences." In this forum, the editors brought seven biblical scholars from various backgrounds and scholarly expertise to write about this topic. Roger Nam wrote on the economic aspect of the pandemic.[11] Ying Zhang reflected on the suffering and existential questions in the Job in light of the global COVID-19 pandemic.[12] Annette Weissenrieder wrote on embodied vulnerability during the pandemic.[13] Monica Melanchthon and Mothy Varkey dealt with the issue of biblical studies pedagogy, especially in the context of India.[14] And Jacqueline Hidalgo focused on the pandemic as a racialized crisis. Interestingly, Hidalgo was the only scholar who quoted Segovia's presidential address, reminding biblical scholars "to follow [his] recommendations" to deal with global crises. All these essays are indeed doing what Segovia was trying to say in 2014, long before the pandemic arrived.

The irony of this publication, however, is that the forum was published in the same issue with eight other peer-reviewed research articles, none of which discussed the pandemic. They talked about the imperial cults in Thessalonica, the Judean community in Elephantine, the iconography in the book of Daniel, the language of despair in Jeremiah, the parable of the good Samaritan in Luke 10, Papias's prologue, and so on. Not the pandemic. The word *pandemic* did not even appear in any of these articles. Biblical scholarship in general is still depressingly out of touch with the world around us. The focus and concerns of biblical scholarship remain largely in the past.

In this, the *Journal of Biblical Literature* is hardly unique. The *Journal for the Study of the New Testament* published a special issue in the September 2021 issue entitled "Crisis as Catalyst: Early Christian Texts and

11. Roger S. Nam, "Biblical Studies, COVID-19, and Our Response to Growing Inequality," *JBL* 139 (2020): 600–606.

12. Ying Zhang, "Reading the Book of Job in the Pandemic," *JBL* 139 (2020): 607–612.

13. Annette Weissenrieder, "The Unpleasant Sight: Vulnerability and Bodily Fragmentation," *JBL* 139 (2020): 619–24.

14. Monica J. Melanchthon and Mothy Varkey, "Teaching Biblical Studies in a Pandemic: India," *JBL* 139 (2020): 613–18.

the Covid-19 Pandemic." Unlike the *Journal of Biblical Literature* forum, in which the contributors were biblical scholars from diverse backgrounds, all the contributors to the *Journal for the Study of the New Testament* special issue were white scholars. Peter Ben-Smit of Vrije University wrote an introductory text that highlighted the Greek word κρίσις. Although he, unfortunately, did not engage Segovia's presidential address, he wrote: "The focus on 'crisis' is a very fruitful lens for researching the literary remnants of these first communities of Christ devotees." He correctly pointed out that this such attention to crises is indeed "currently… both underused and undertheorized."[15] In other words, parallel to what Segovia argued in 2014, biblical scholars should pay attention to crisis in doing their work of interpretation. Just like the *Journal of Biblical Literature*, this particular issue of *Journal for the Study of the New Testament* also contained three research articles. None of these articles discussed the global pandemic.

One can, of course, argue that those articles were probably accepted for publication long before the pandemic. But from the spring of 2019 until the winter of 2022, when the world was wrestling with the pandemic, major biblical studies journals in the West such as *Novum Testamentum*, *New Testament Studies*, *Journal for the Study of the Old Testament*, *Catholic Biblical Quarterly*, and so on all largely ignored the global pandemic. They continued to do publish scholarship that did not pay the least bit of attention to the global pandemic. Interestingly, *HTS Teologiese Studies/Theological Studies*, a journal based in South Africa, published some articles that did directly address the pandemic.[16] Johnson Thomaskutty published an article in *Biblical Studies Journal*, a journal based in India, that looked into the global pandemic in conversation with John 5:1–18.[17]

15. Peter-Ben Smit, "Crisis as a Catalyst: Early Christian Texts and the COVID-19 Pandemic," *JSNT* 44 (2021): 7.

16. See for instance, Gordon E. Dames, "Biblical Vistas of Brokenness and Wholeness in a Time Such as the Coronavirus Pandemic," *HvTSt* 76.4 (2020): art. 6160, https://doi.org/10.4102/hts.v76i4.6160; Francois Tolmie and Rian Venter, "Making Sense of the COVID-19 Pandemic from the Bible: Some Perspectives," *HvTSt* 77.4 (2021): art. 6493, https://doi.org/10.4102/hts.v77i4.6493; Lyzette Hoffman, "The Bible, Faith Formation and a Virus: Exploring the Influence of a Pandemic on Faith Formation Content and Practices for Children and Teenagers," *HvTSt* 77.4 (2021): art. 6512, https://doi.org/10.4102/hts.v77i4.6512; Sampson S. Ndoga, "Biblical Pragmatism in the Pandemic Outbreak of Numbers 25:1–18: Towards an African Paradigm," *HvTSt* 77.4 (2021): art. 6375, https://doi.org/10.4102/hts.v77i4.6375.

17. Johnson Thomaskutty, "God in the Midst of Pandemic COVID-19: Reflec-

But there is more. The biblical studies publications noted here were special issues or special forums. How do we understand this fact? What does this fact tell us about the tendency of biblical scholarship? Two things might be at work here: First, this fact points to a scholarly tendency to treat contemporary engagement as secondary work. It is not the primary work of the scholarship. It is an add-on. Responding to crisis has been and still is a sidenote, an afterthought in scholarship. Scholars do it on the side of their usual biblical studies business. It is still not yet an integral part of biblical scholarship.

Second, if one asks biblical scholars whether they are concerned about crises that the world is facing today, they will probably all say yes. One can see this in many social media discussions among biblical scholars. They are fully engaged with the global issues facing the world in which we live today. However, when they turn to the work of scholarship, they somehow become detached from these struggles. Such dissonance is appalling, but it is hardly surprising, especially knowing that the main orientation of biblical interpretation has been the ancient past. The lack of language and a theoretical framework to deal with the present world clearly leads to a sense of disengagement and detachment.

Expanding Biblical Scholarship

These two points above are precisely what Segovia was trying to address in 2014. Two duties that all biblical scholars have to bear as intellectuals are "the duty to integrate and [the duty to] respond."[18] For Segovia, doing engaging work should not be seen, placed, and treated as a secondary level of biblical scholarship. It should be not only an *integral*, but also a fundamental aspect of scholarship. Segovia points out that scholarship that responds to global affairs should cover these three aspects:

> (1) the texts and contexts of antiquity; (2) the interpretation of these texts and contexts, and the contexts of such interpretations, in the various traditions of reading the Bible, with a focus on modernity and postmodernity; and (3) the interpreters behind such interpretations, and their corresponding contexts.[19]

---

tions Based on John 5:1–18," *Biblical Studies Journal* 3.4 (2021): 1–7.

18. Segovia, "Criticism in Critical Times," 21.

19. Segovia, "Criticism in Critical Times," 26.

This call to shift and expand the scope of biblical scholarship is helpful. Segovia, after all, still acknowledges the importance of the texts and their ancient contexts. Scholars, however, should not stop there. Biblical interpretation requires a wide-angle lens. The contexts of biblical interpreters need to be interrogated as well. It is no surprise that Segovia offers a critical analysis of past presidential addresses, especially during the Great War era in which, "with one exception … none made reference to the war and the global state of affairs in their presentations."[20] That one exception was James A. Montgomery's 1918 presidential address. However, even for him, the global struggle was merely a context rather than an object of analysis, as Segovia points out.[21]

The second aspect of Segovia's presidential address is his charge to engage in *respons*ible scholarship. To be a responsible scholar means to be attentive to, and to engage the crises of, our times. The ground of biblical scholarship has to shift, in this sense, from a seminary or university setting to the public setting. A biblical scholar has to be a public-facing scholar. In the words of Francisco Lozada Jr., "The field [of biblical studies] must take responsibility for what we do and how it affects the Other. Segovia's presidential address is a call to respond to the global-systematic issues such as globalization, climate change, immigration, and now, the pandemic."[22] If one examines the works of biblical scholars through Edward Said's definition of an intellectual (based primarily on the works of Antonio Gramsci) as those who work in "the production or distribution of knowledge," then biblical scholarship is indeed in the business of both producing and distributing knowledge. Biblical scholars are intellectuals. Reflecting on the Gulf War, but making an argument applicable to every historical moment, Said insisted that the task of intellectuals is "to unearth the forgotten, to make connections that were denied, to cite alternative courses of action that could have avoided war and its attendant goal of human destruction."[23] As intellectuals, biblical scholars are

20. Segovia, "Criticism in Critical Times," 12.

21. Segovia, "Criticism in Critical Times," 12.

22. Francisco Lozada Jr., "Contemporary Biblical Interpretations: Reflections amid the Covid-19 Pandemic," in *Threshold Dwellers in the Age of Global Pandemic*, ed. Eleazar S. Fernandez (Eugene, OR: Pickwick, 2022), 114.

23. Edward W. Said, *Representations of the Intellectual: The 1993 Reith Lectures* (New York: Vintage, 1996), 22. See also Segovia's discussion on Said in Segovia, "Criticism in Critical Times," 13–16.

no exception to that. We biblical scholars should stop speaking merely to our peers and continue to expand the scope of our work by responding to the global issues we are all facing today.

Bibliography

Brett, Mark G., and Susan E. Hylen. "The JBL Forum, an Occasional Exchange: Biblical Studies in a Pandemic." *JBL* 139 (2020): 597–99.

Correia, Mariama. "Brazilian State Deputy Says She Was Sexually Assaulted by Boaventura de Sousa Santos." *Agência Pública*. 14 April 2023. https://tinyurl.com/SBL4527i.

Dames, Gordon E. "Biblical Vistas of Brokenness and Wholeness in a Time Such as the Coronavirus Pandemic." *HvTSt* 76.4 (2020): art. 6160. https://doi.org/10.4102/hts.v76i4.6160.

"Due to Allegations of Sexual Harassment, Boaventura de Sousa Santos Is Suspended from University." Euro ES Euro. 15 April 2023. https://tinyurl.com/SBL4527g.

Hoffman, Lyzette. "The Bible, Faith Formation and a Virus: Exploring the Influence of a Pandemic on Faith Formation Content and Practices for Children and Teenagers." *HvTSt* 77.4 (2021): art. 6512. https://doi.org/10.4102/hts.v77i4.6512.

Lozada, Francisco, Jr. "Contemporary Biblical Interpretations: Reflections amid the Covid-19 Pandemic." Pages 99–115 in *Threshold Dwellers in the Age of Global Pandemic*. Edited by Eleazar S. Fernandez. Eugene, OR: Pickwick, 2022.

Melanchthon, Monica J., and Mothy Varkey. "Teaching Biblical Studies in a Pandemic: India." *JBL* 139 (2020): 613–18.

Nam, Roger S. "Biblical Studies, COVID-19, and Our Response to Growing Inequality." *JBL* 139 (2020): 600–606.

Ndoga, Sampson S. "Biblical Pragmatism in the Pandemic Outbreak of Numbers 25:1–18: Towards an African Paradigm." *HvTSt* 77.4 (2021): art. 6375. https://doi.org/10.4102/hts.v77i4.6375

Segovia, Fernando F. "Criticism in Critical Times: Reflections on Vision and Task." *JBL* 134 (2015): 6–9.

Smit, Peter-Ben. "Crisis as a Catalyst: Early Christian Texts and the COVID-19 Pandemic." *JSNT* 44 (2021): 3–7.

Thomaskutty, Johnson. "God in the Midst of Pandemic COVID-19: Reflections Based on John 5:1–18." *Biblical Studies Journal* 3.4 (2021): 1–7.

Tolmie, Francois and Rian Venter. "Making Sense of the COVID-19 Pandemic from the Bible: Some Perspectives." *HvTSt* 77.4 (2021): art. 6493. https://doi.org/10.4102/hts.v77i4.6493.

Weissenrieder, Annette. "The Unpleasant Sight: Vulnerability and Bodily Fragmentation." *JBL* 139 (2020): 619–24.

Zhang, Ying. "Reading the Book of Job in the Pandemic." *JBL* 139 (2020): 607–12.

Part 3
Intercultural Readings and Transborder Cultural Readings

The Souls of Biblical Folks and the Potential for Meaning

BRIAN K. BLOUNT

In what has been called one the great books of the twentieth century, *The Souls of Black Folk*, W. E. B. Du Bois delineates the impact of otherness imposed upon African Americans.

> Between me and the other world there is ever an unasked question: unasked by some through feelings of delicacy; by others through the difficulty of rightly framing it. All, nevertheless, flutter around it. They approach me in a half-hesitant sort of way, eye me curiously or compassionately, and then, instead of saying directly, How does it feel to be a problem? they say, I know an excellent colored man in my own town; or, I fought at Mechanicsville; or, Do not these Southern outrages make your blood boil? At these I smile, or am interested, or reduce the boiling to a simmer, as the occasion may require. To the real question, How does it feel to be a problem? I seldom answer a word.
>
> And yet, being a problem is a strange experience—peculiar even for one who has never been anything else.[1]

A line was drawn. "The problem of the twentieth century," Du Bois continued, "is the problem of the color-line."[2] African Americans were and, in the twenty-first century, still are on the wrong side of that physical and existential demarcation.

To survive in this bifurcated world of imposed Otherness, African Americans, according to Du Bois, had to become bicultural. Because African Americans were not only Othered but dis-empowered and therefore dis-advantaged by their Otherness—for theirs was a societally sanctioned,

1. W. E. B. Du Bois, *The Souls of Black Folk* (Greenwich, CT: Fawcett, 1961), 15.
2. Du Bois, *Souls of Black Folk*, 23, 41.

ruthlessly enforced Other-hood—to survive, African Americans had to read and appropriately react from the space of those who had Othered them. "We who are dark can see America in a way that America cannot."[3] This prescience came with a cost. The necessity to acquire it threatened the very soul of black folks, who had to occupy and absorb the space of those who had Othered them without losing hold of the spiritual mooring of their own space.

> The Negro is a sort of seventh son, born with a veil, and gifted with second-sight in this American world,—a world which yields him no true self-consciousness, but only lets him see himself through the revelation of the other world. It is a peculiar sensation, this double-consciousness, this sense of always looking at one's self through the eyes of others, of measuring one's soul by the tape of a world that looks on in amused contempt and pity. One ever feels his twoness,—an American, a Negro; two souls, two thoughts, two unreconciled strivings; two warring ideals in one dark body, whose dogged strength alone keeps it from being torn asunder.[4]

In recognizing the struggle of his own people, Du Bois perceptively noticed that, by electrifying the color line with the charge of virulent racism, white Americans had also, ironically, Othered themselves. As a result, they limited the potential for the kind of societal evolution that would benefit all Americans. "The white man," he wrote, "as well as the Negro, is bound and barred by the color-line."[5] The remedy? Even though Du Bois knew at the time that America was not ready for it, he prophetically perceived that just societal transformation required that white Americans be as willing to cross into and respect the culture of African Americans as African Americans were required to cross into and learn, even demonstrate respect for, theirs.

> The future of the South depends on the ability of the representatives of these opposing views to see and appreciate and sympathize with each other's position.... Only by a union of intelligence and sympathy across the color-line in this critical period of the Republic shall justice and right triumph.[6]

---

3. See W. E. B. Du Bois, "Criteria of Negro Art," *The Crisis* 32 (1926): 290–97.
4. Du Bois, *Souls of Black Folk*, 16–17.
5. Du Bois, *Souls of Black Folk*, 137.
6. Du Bois, *Souls of Black Folk*, 139.

After 115 years, more than a century full of ethnic potential and promise, instead of fostering Du Bois's boundary trespass, the nation's color line has slithered into the shape and consequence of a racial line in the sand. Author Ta-Nehisi Coates reports, "In 2012, the Manhattan Institute cheerily noted that segregation had declined since the 1960s. And yet African Americans still remained—by far—the most segregated ethnic group in the country."[7] A vicious demagoguery about and violence against African Americans over the past several years requires no documentation from me.

Du Bois's question in 1903 remains demonically pertinent in 2018: "Why did God make me an outcast and a stranger in mine own house?"[8] On the whole, African Americans remain radically Other in the American context. It is the context from which I have learned to approach, analyze, and teach biblical studies.

Othering exists in the world of biblical research. That recognition is, of course, today commonplace. While the black–white dyad remains of special import in the United States, in America and around the globe the current reality is less one Other in contrast with an Other than a legion of Others operating from and confronting each Other across multiple demarcations of space and thought. Yet Du Bois's twentieth-century comments about the color line are immensely helpful for a study of global cultural hermeneutics in the twenty-first century. From his sociological study I recognize a biblical corollary. Those who hold interpretive power establish those outside their circle as Other and assign to them the status of Problem and subsequently the problematic task of working their way out of their Otherness by becoming less like themselves and more like those holding such power. In biblical studies, power has long resided in the alleged impartiality and objectivity of historical and literary methods whose positivism inoculates its practitioners from the viral infections of the space from which they conduct their biblical research. As Elisabeth Schüssler Fiorenza put it in 2010, no matter how diversified the units are on display at Society of Biblical Literature, "the discipline continues to socialize future scholars into methodological positivism and future ministers/theologians into theological positivism."[9] To accept the socialization, to

7. Ta-Nehisi Coates, "The Case For Reparations," *The Atlantic*, June 2014, https://www .theatlantic.com/magazine/archive/2014/06/the-case-for-reparations/361631/.

8. Du Bois, *Souls of Black Folk*, 16.

9. Elisabeth Schüssler Fiorenza, "Rethinking the Educational Practices of Biblical

become like such practitioners is to become less Other. Less Others learn and execute the "objective" methodologies and how biblical scholars arrive at text meaning through such methodologies while attempting simultaneously to remain fluent in the ways of reading and constructing meaning out of their own space, for their own communities. Therein, though, lies the soul-troubling dilemma.[10]

Instead of a color line, biblical operations proceed about a meaning line. Simplistically put, text meaning is determined through historical and literary engagement that uncovers text intent, or text meaning is ascertained through an engagement between the reader, reading out of her space, and the text as it is engaged in that space. There develops an interpretive veil behind which cultural interpreters are positioned and from which they must operate frequently in the shadows, as respect—and the way respect materializes in the form of promotion and publication—is to their operatives too often denied. The meaning line is destructive to readers on both sides of it. All are Othered from each Other by its very existence. It is because interpretive power rests on the historical, literary scientific side that cultural hermeneuts are required to become at the very least bicultural, knowing their own space and its influence on text meaning as well as they know the historical and literary principles that allegedly unearth static text meaning. But this prescience comes with a cost. The necessity to acquire it threatens the very soul of the cultural hermeneut, who must occupy and absorb the space of the objective Other without losing hold of the spiritual mooring of his own space. This bicultural, two-Other-ness has now expanded exponentially. Scores of readers vie for the opportunity to read rightly from their particular space and have the mean-

---

Doctoral Studies," in *Transforming Graduate Biblical Education: Ethos and Discipline*, ed. Elisabeth Schüssler Fiorenza and Kent Harold Richards, GPBS 10 (Atlanta: Society of Biblical Literature, 2010), 383.

10. See Vincent Wimbush, "Reading Darkness, Reading Scriptures," in *African Americans and the Bible: Sacred Texts and Social Textures*, ed. Vincent Wimbush (New York: Continuum, 2000), 10: "No matter what may be the actual representations in the biblical texts, the gendered and/or racial-ethnic 'Others' that were constructed by modern dominants could not either read themselves into these texts or read themselves in affirmative ways as long as they had to begin not with themselves, with their places of enunciation, in their own times, but 'with the texts,' viz. with the dominants' places of enunciation, with their constructed pasts and the hermeneutical spins that continue to give legitimacy and social and ideological power to a present that was secured and justified by those pasts."

ing derived from that cultural reading be received and engaged rather than Othered. Scores of souls are thereby troubled.

The troubling, though, can also be efficacious. Du Bois recognized that wherever Others operated with sincerity across the color line, particularly when whites engaged empathetically out of the black space, there dawned the potential for just societal transformation. *Reading from an Other's space transforms not only how one reads but how one lives.* Such cross-the-meaning-line reading in biblical studies may be of similar import. Indeed, when Schüssler Fiorenza argues that, as long as the discipline operates from a perspective of methodological positivism, "discourses and struggles for justice, radical equality, and the well-being of all will remain marginal to biblical scholarship,"[11] she, too, is implying a connection between how one exegetes in the classroom and the study and how one operates, justly or unjustly, in the world. It is a connection in need of further exploration.

1. Charging the Meaning Line: A Quick Survey of Selected Society of Biblical Literature Presidential Addresses

Selected Society of Biblical Literature presidents have meaningfully engaged this exploration. In 1988, Schüssler Fiorenza chided biblical scholarship for its refusal "to relinquish its rhetorical stance of value-free objectivism and scientific modernism."[12] She argues for a decentering, rhetorical-ethical paradigm that yields two key conclusions. First, context is critical to text interpretation. "What we see depends on where we stand."[13] Second, she recognizes that the manner in which we perform and, perhaps even more importantly, allow text interpretation has dramatic ramifications for how we structure, police, and/or liberate the academic environment in which that interpretation takes place. "Interpretive communities such as the SBL are not just scholarly investigative communities, but also authoritative communities. They possess the power to ostracize or to embrace, to foster or to restrict membership, to recognize and to define what 'true scholarship' entails."[14] The academy *can* cultivate interpretive endeavor on the Other's side of the meaning line that not only recognizes but values

11. Schüssler Fiorenza, "Rethinking the Educational Practices," 383.

12. Elisabeth Schüssler Fiorenza, "The Ethics of Biblical Interpretation: Decentering Biblical Scholarship," *JBL* 107 (1988): 4.

13. Schüssler Fiorenza, "Ethics of Biblical Interpretation," 5.

14. Schüssler Fiorenza, "Ethics of Biblical Interpretation," 8.

contextual influence and, in so doing, can prompt scholarly work that portends not only scholarly but, indeed, cultural transformation.

Fernando F. Segovia explores the connection between cultural interpretation and cultural construction. He argues "for a fusion of the critical and the political, the biblical and the worldly."[15] He makes the intriguing point that, when biblical interpreters attempt to do their work exclusively on the side of the meaning line that alleges value and context-free scientific interpretation, they actually speak meaningfully, if not dangerously, to the social and political world in which their interpretive work is undertaken. Silence has a message all its own.[16]

Vincent Wimbush understands that, in its quest to avoid global politics, biblical scholarship, rather than helping shape *new* politics, reaffirms the old. "The cultivated obliviousness to or silence about—if not also the ideological reflection and validation of—the larger prevailing sociopolitical currents and dynamics marks the beginning and ongoing history of this Society."[17] He posits a causal relationship between the Society's objectivity-driven avoidance of sociopolitical currents and dynamics and its lethargy in developing and then drawing into its ranks scholars of color. "I suggest that the paucity of black membership is due ultimately not to the bad faith and manners of members of the Society in the past but to something more profound—the (unrecognized, unacknowledged) racialized discursive practices and politics that have defined it."[18] By refusing to address politics, because politics are allegedly addressed only on the Other, contextually sensitive side of the meaning line, biblical scholarship finds itself shaped by politics.

Schüssler Fiorenza, Segovia, and Wimbush recognize that either engaging in or refusing to engage in culturally sensitive readings will have an impact on not only text conclusions reached but the social and political context in which those readings are done. I would like to explore further

---

15. Fernando F. Segovia, "Criticism in Critical Times: Reflections on Vision and Task," *JBL* 134 (2015): 6.

16. See Segovia, "Criticism in Critical Times," 16: "In largely pursuing pressing questions of the discipline while bypassing pressing questions of the world, as they overwhelmingly did in critical times, presidential addresses assumed a political stance of abstraction from the realm of global affairs into the realm of scholarship."

17. Vincent Wimbush, "Interpreters—Enslaving/Enslaved/Runagate," *JBL* 130 (2011): 6.

18. Wimbush, "Interpreters," 8.

their line of investigation. In so doing, I posit two primary thoughts. First, on either side of the meaning line—or on the proverbial fence trying to straddle both sides at once—what lies available to interpreters is *never* meaning but meaning potential. Second, a culturally responsive engagement of this meaning potential has profound implications for the shaping of a more just biblical society, classroom, and profession.

2. The Quest for Meaning Potential

For Paul Ricoeur, language is discourse. Every discourse has a surplus of meaning. In biblical studies, we tend to view language not as discourse but as system. This is one of the reasons the cultural dynamic is so often either underappreciated or dismissed outright.[19] When discourse is marginalized, it is difficult to recognize the presence and power of surplus meaning. It is also difficult to recognize how language spills over into politics. As discourse, language intends to "do" as well as to "convey." As discourse, language is, therefore, decidedly political.

Ricoeur recognizes that there is a signal difference between discourse as spoken conversation and discourse as text. Text is discourse fixed as writing. Hermeneutics is the process of engaging text as fixed discourse, not just trying "to define understanding as the recognition of an author's intention from the point of view of the primitive addressees in the original situation of discourse."[20] This is especially the case since "with the written discourse … the author's intention and the meaning of the text cease to coincide."[21] The text develops "semantic autonomy." "The text's career escapes the finite horizon lived by its author. What the text means now matters more than what the author meant when he wrote it."[22] This surplus of meaning is amplified when the reading audiences engaging the text are directly considered. In live discourse, the communication is generally limited to the speaker and the hearer. In the fixed discourse of a written text,

19. Paul Ricoeur, *Interpretation Theory: Discourse and the Surplus of Meaning* (Fort Worth: Texas Christian University Press, 1976), 2: "If discourse remains problematic for us today, it is because the main achievements of linguistics concern language as structure and system and not as used. Our task therefore will be to rescue discourse from its marginal and precarious exile."

20. Ricoeur, *Interpretation Theory*, 22.

21. Ricoeur, *Interpretation Theory*, 29.

22. Ricoeur, *Interpretation Theory*, 30.

the audience is universalized. The text addresses an indefinite number of readers and thereby opens itself up to an indefinite number of interpretive possibilities. "The opportunity for multiple readings is the dialectical counterpart of the semantic autonomy of the text."[23] When one combines the text's semantic autonomy with the access of that text by an indefinite number of readers, one opens up the possibility that multiple interpretations will occur not simply because some read rightly and most others read wrongly but because every reader approaches contextually and therefore sees contextually.[24]

How does one attempt to understand the reading of someone differently positioned to the fixed discourse of the biblical text and therefore likely to have arrived at a different perspective on what the text means? Ricoeur suggests for interpreters what Du Bois suggested for black and white Americans: a crossing over into the Other's frame of being and therefore reference. Ricoeur calls it empathy: "the transference of ourselves into another's psychic life."[25]

Despite his allegiance to understanding text as linguistic system rather than discourse, Rudolf Bultmann, in his existentialist approach to biblical interpretation, anticipated some of Ricoeur's conclusions about text as fixed discourse. I recognize that my mention of Bultmann is symptomatic of the troubling of my own academic soul, a troubling that demands not only a valuing of but also a constant attribution to the historicist, positivist world that Others me. And yet, as DuBois recognized, it is only by biculturally mastering that world that I have been allowed the opportunity to challenge and reposition myself alongside it. What I came to see is that Bultmann ironically laid the groundwork for an approach to biblical text as meaning potential that is engaged contextually.

> The presupposition of every comprehending interpretation is *a previous living relationship to the subject*, which directly or indirectly finds expression in the text and which guides the direction of the enquiry. Without such a relationship to life in which text and interpreter are

23. Ricoeur, *Interpretation Theory*, 32.

24. See Ricoeur, *Interpretation Theory*, 77: "The text as a whole and as a singular whole may be compared to an object, which may be viewed from several sides, but never from all sides at once. Therefore the reconstruction of the whole has a perspectival aspect similar to that of a perceived object."

25. Ricoeur, *Interpretation Theory*, 73.

> bound together, enquiry and comprehension are not possible, and an enquiry is not motivated at all.[26]

Bultmann appeals to two categories: life relation and preunderstanding. Life relation is important in establishing the questions that readers bring to the biblical text. The primary questions in a reader's life, those that motivate searches of biblical and other texts, come from particular interests in that reader's life.[27] This life relation is the presupposition for inquiry and, therefore, exegesis. This life relation also predisposes the text reader to bring certain questions to the text and thus wrest particular meaning conclusions from it. This predisposition is preunderstanding. The problem is that the ancient reader's life relation to a biblical text is quite different from the life relation of a contemporary reader. Because of that difference, it is to be expected that the contemporary reader's preunderstanding will also be different.

This would suggest that, unless there is some hermeneutical means to adjudicate between this difference, contemporary text readers will not derive the same meaning from the texts as the ancients. This is precisely Bultmann's point. There will be an interpretive impasse unless contemporary readers develop an appropriate hermeneutical tool.

As the matter of personal and communal existence before God has always been and will always remain the central focus of the biblical material, and is simultaneously the driving focus behind contemporary text readers' engagement with biblical material, the existential question is the hermeneutical link that binds text and interpreter together and thus makes inquiry and comprehension possible. Bultmann's hermeneutic is therefore to interpret the biblical material by existentially demythologizing it. In this way, the contemporary reader can interpret the mythological language in a way that makes sense in her contemporary circumstance.

Though intentionally limited, Bultmann's process is, in essence, a cultural hermeneutic. To be sure, Bultmann does not believe that every facet

26. Rudolf Bultmann, "The Problem of Hermeneutics," in *Essays, Philosophical and Theological*, LPTh (London: SCM, 1955), 252.

27. See Bultmann, "Problem of Hermeneutics," 240: "The formulation of a question, however, arises from an interest which is based in the life of the inquirer, and it is the presupposition of all interpretations seeking an understanding of the text, that this interest, too, is in some way or other alive in the text which is to be interpreted, and forms the link between the text and its expositor."

of a person's context is applicable. He is not concerned about whether one is black or white, from the United States or Latin America. There is one single contextual factor that is important: human existence. The texts yield existential answers because the text readers bring existential questions to a text that is existentially preoccupied. Text meaning results from the encounter between the text as existential meaning potential and the interpreter's existential life relation and preunderstanding. The interpretive process is existentially, that is to say, contextually conditioned.

Cultural Studies and Meaning Potential

A cultural-studies approach to biblical interpretation invests passionately in this contextual engagement with text meaning potential. Not just the existential, but every life relation and preunderstanding is a central part of the hermeneutical engagement with the text.

> It is the role assigned to the reader that, without doubt, most sharply differentiates cultural studies from other competing paradigms in contemporary biblical criticism. For cultural studies the reader does not and cannot remain in the background, even if so wished and attempted, but is actively and inevitably involved in the production and meaning of "texts" and history; who does not and cannot make any claims to objectivity and universality, but is profoundly aware of the social location and agendas of all readers and readings, including his or her own.[28]

The reader sees the meaning line and willfully transgresses it. Knowing and valuing her reading space, she pushes across the meaning line into the past, constructs the past from her space, and then interprets what has been constructed through the preunderstanding shaped by that space. In this encounter between "a socially and historically conditioned text and a historically conditioned reader," meaning materializes.[29] Segovia, therefore, concludes, "There is never a text out there but many 'texts.'"[30] I would say that there is never text meaning out there but text meaning potential.

28. Fernando F. Segovia, "Cultural Studies and Contemporary Biblical Criticism: Ideological Criticism as Mode of Discourse," in *Social Location and Biblical Interpretation in Global Perspective*, vol. 2 of *Reading from This Place,* ed. Fernando F. Segovia and Mary Ann Tolbert (Minneapolis: Fortress, 1995), 12.

29. Segovia, "Cultural Studies and Contemporary Biblical Criticism," 8.

30. Segovia, "Cultural Studies and Contemporary Biblical Criticism."

The key is determining how each access of text meaning potential might be potentially valid. Particularly if each such reading offers a different meaning conclusion. Differing conclusions may well be constructed from different parts of the text's meaning potential, which readers are differently positioned to access because of their different contextual access points. The discussion, then, should never have been between what the text meant and what the text means. Rather, the discussion should be between what the text means and what the text means.

Socially, culturally, politically situated readers engaging text meaning potential from their situated spaces will have dramatic implications for the body politic that those readers inhabit. Even with its limited appreciation for only the existential context of the reader, Bultmann's "cultural" hermeneutic had dramatic political implications. For Bultmann, one determines the meaning of a text not only by analyzing it as language but by responding to it as a crisis moment for decision. If one pushes Bultmann's categories beyond the existential to the full flowering of contextual possibilities as meaningful access points on a text's meaning potential to spur a contemporary crisis point for decision, then there are dramatic implications for thinking how many of those decisions will, of necessity, be political. This is undoubtedly why Dorothee Sölle can argue, "More and more, it appears to me that the move from existentialist theology to political theology is itself a consequence of the Bultmannian position."[31] If, as Abraham Smith correctly observes, "spaces are intricately tied to dynamics of power," then the access of text meaning potential *from* space is inevitably a political endeavor.[32]

3. Intercultural Bible Readings: Recognizing and Crossing Borders

The strategy of intercultural Bible readings demonstrates nicely the connection between the access of meaning potential from space and the political. Intercultural Bible reading presumes a multiplicity of text readings that pushes beyond the multicultural. Whereas multiculturality refers to Othered cultures reading over against the dominant culture, interculturality refers to equally positioned and empowered "groups [Western and

31. Dorothee Sölle, *Political Theology* (Philadelphia: Fortress, 1974), 2.

32. Abraham Smith, "Taking *Spaces* Seriously: The Politics of Space and the Future of Western Biblical Studies," in Schüssler Fiorenza and Richards, *Transforming Graduate Biblical Education*, 65.

non-Western, Global South and Global North] relating together in mutual interdependence."[33] The center no longer holds; multiplicity reigns. Bordered, Othered communities all seek access to text meaning potential. Bordered, Othered communities no longer fight to become "central." Furthermore, the dominant Western perspective can no longer credibly sustain its interpretive privilege. What results is more like the holy chaos of an ensemble dance troupe endeavoring to share the same choreographical construct by deploying different, equally significant movements of it. No one single movement is or could ever convey the entire choreographed meaning. No single dancer can ever be the only dancer who can interpret that entire meaning. Each dancer who has a role to play and is empowered to that role in order to convey it plays off the movement of the others in the mix. The stress is no longer on trying to get those in the center to read like those on the margins, but of pressing the case that every space, even that previously identified as the center, is a border space that is Other from every other border space. The reading strategy therefore becomes one of "intercultural encounters and transborder exchanges."[34]

Participants in an intercultural Bible reading are pressed to "read with the other."[35] Such reading is not expected to be easy; mutuality in this case is designed to trigger confrontation even as it spurs conversation. It is in the recognition and appreciation of such encounter that learning can occur.[36] In seeking such new "Othered" understanding, the intercultural interpreter is asking a particular question: "What happens when Bible readers from sometimes radically different contexts and cultures read the same Bible text and start dialoguing about its significance?"[37] In asking this question, he is implying an equally important subsequent one: "Can this way of shared Bible reading become a catalyst for more openness

---

33. Laura E. Donaldson, "Are We All Multiculturists Now? Biblical Reading As Cultural Contact," *Semeia* 82 (1998): 81.

34. Hans de Wit and Janet Dyk, "Introduction," in *Bible and Transformation: The Promise of Intercultural Bible Reading*, ed. Hans de Wit and Janet Dyk, SemeiaSt 81 (Atlanta: SBL Press, 2015), 7.

35. de Wit and Janet Dyk, "Introduction," 4.

36. Hans de Wit, "Through the Eyes of Another: Objectives and Background," in *Through the Eyes of Another: Intercultural Reading of the Bible*, ed. Hans de Wit et al. (Elkhart, IN: Institute of Mennonite Studies, 2004), 29: "the *inter* represents the insight that confrontation with the difference may lead to a new, productive understanding of texts" (italics original).

37. De Wit and Dyk, "Introduction," 1.

and transformation?"[38] This question harbors an important connection between the hermeneutical and the political: the presupposition that intercultural text readings can transfigure the reader who intentionally reads for diversity among a community of equally positioned Others.[39] "What intercultural Bible reading strives for is that, within a profoundly divided Christianity, the intercultural encounter becomes a *script* for transformation and leads to *shared* ownership and *shared* agency for justice and liberation."[40]

We are, then, examining the case for an ethics of interpretation focused on border access of text meaning potential that not only disrupts and thereby transforms how we read but also, as a liberating consequence, disrupts and thereby transforms the very contexts from which that reading occurs. It starts with a shattering of the meaning line that wants to distinguish between the text, to be objectively interrogated on the one side, and the reader, who interrogates from her space, on the other.

Instead, what is available is meaning potential that is best approached collaboratively, even combatively, through intercultural engagement, across border communities. Meaning, as approached proleptically through this border engagement, comes only when we are willing to move beyond our own boundaries and trespass the boundaries of others, and allow trespass of our own boundaries. The border-crossing engagement of meaning potential, as such, is both collaborative and intrusive; it requires a breaking and entering, even when the entrance is invited, because a break in perspective is required. Accessing meaning potential thus requires a violence of sorts, and perhaps this is why we pretend we can avoid it and go directly to meaning on our own terms, out of our own space, without having to trespass any Other contextual, communal borders. Indeed, perhaps this is exactly why Yak-hwee Tan refers to social location as dis-ease. "In using the hyphenated dis-ease, I am suggesting that social location can be an ailment, a disease that disrupts the ease of some."[41] Ultimately, it disrupts the ease of all. But this is an incredibly positive development. When engagement with meaning potential from border spaces is allowed to be invasive, to trespass boundaries we have carefully erected around our own social

38. De Wit and Dyk, "Introduction.".

39. Cf. Donaldson, "Are We All Multiculturists Now?," 81.

40. De Wit and Dyk, "Introduction," 6.

41. Yak-hwee Tan, "Social Location: Dis-Ease and/or Dis-Cover(Y)," in Schüssler Fiorenza and Richards, *Transforming Graduate Biblical Education*, 50.

location, or the social location of the positivist, scientist, historicist understanding of biblical inquiry, then the dis-ease such engagement fosters becomes transformative. Here is where and how transformational reading fosters transformational praxis.

> De Wit pointedly asks, "In which ways can an intercultural dialogue on the meaning of fundamental narratives—Holy Scripture—contribute to justice and liberation?" Such dialogue, such reading of sacred texts "through the eyes of another," across cultural and sociopolitical contexts, can lead readers of sacred texts to develop a greater understanding for one another and thus to move toward "reconciliation, peace, and justice."[42]

It is difficult to create a circumstance, particularly within a scholarly academy, that not only acknowledges but values and encourages the cultural work of those who engage meaning potential from within their own border space while simultaneously transgressing and entertaining the trespass of interpreters from other border spaces. Here, I am not suggesting something new. I am, though, trying to give added weight. I endeavor to see intercultural border transit and the transformational potential it portends progress from the study, the library, and the published piece to a liberating manifestation in the entire academic biblical exegetical industrial complex. If the intercultural border proponents are correct, how we research can, perhaps even should, transform how we teach and how we staff, thereby creating a more just classroom and a more just professoriate.[43]

Border Pedagogy

Border crossing in the classroom, as pedagogical strategy, follows naturally from border crossing as research method. The focal assumptions are the same. "The basic premise of border pedagogy is that the process of learn-

---

42. Fernando F. Segovia, "Intercultural Bible Reading as Transformation for Liberation: Intercultural Hermeneutics and Biblical Studies," in de Wit and Dyk, *Bible and Transformation*, 33.

43. See Schüssler Fiorenza, "Rethinking the Educational Practices," 392: "It insists on an ethical radical democratic imperative that compels biblical scholarship to contribute to the advent of a society and religion that are free from all forms of kyriarchal inequality and oppression."

ing entails crossing borders."[44] Just as interpreters are better positioned to engage meaning potential when they learn the access points of Other and Othered interpreters, so learners are better positioned to operate more effectively in the classroom when they are taught to cross cultural borders and then engage meaning potential from those varying viewpoints. This is how methodological transformation fosters classroom transfiguration.[45]

Border pedagogy is an insurgency that requires students to travel between cultural perspectives and confront cultural difference. It provides a theoretical road map for intercultural border crossings. In the classroom, not only must students be taught an awareness of their own contingency, the limitations of their own selves, and the narrative perspectives from which those selves operate; they must also be accorded the safety to engage other selves, to trespass the borders of fellow students and instructor alike in the engagement of text meaning potential. It is this border crossing, and the dialogue that takes place throughout, that enables a broader engagement with a text's meaning potential.

But dialogue, as critics have argued, remains problematic because it is based in Enlightenment principles of rational discourse. As the foundation of such rationalism is decidedly Eurocentric, even a border pedagogical approach that utilizes it remains mired in the metanarrative world of historical and literary positivism. Here the power implications are compelling. As Elizabeth Ellsworth notes, even though pedagogical procedure based on dialogue presumes that all members have an equal right to speak from an equally valued borderland of perspective, "dialogue in its conventional sense is impossible in the culture [or classroom] at large, because at this historical moment, power relations between raced, classed, and gendered students and teachers are unjust."[46]

Given these power dynamics, Ellsworth advocates a pedagogical practice that moves through dialogue into coalition building. In this case, individuals who represent distinct cultural perspectives are encouraged

44. D. N. Premnath, "Introduction," in *Border Crossings: Cross-Cultural Hermeneutics*, ed. D. N. Premnath (Maryknoll, NY: Orbis, 2007), 6.

45. See Premnath, "Introduction," 8: "Border pedagogy results in reshaping and reconfiguring boundaries. In [Henry] Giroux's words, 'border pedagogy decenters as it remaps.'"

46. Elizabeth Ellsworth, "Why Doesn't This Feel Empowering? Working through the Repressive Myths of Critical Pedagogy," in *Feminisms and Critical Pedagogy*, ed. Carmen Luke and Jennifer Gore (New York: Routledge, 1992), 108.

to join educational forces, or, in Ellsworth's words, formulate an "affinity grouping," with Others whose cultural position, whose border skirts (that is, empathizes with) their own. She notes that in her own experimental classroom,

> Once we acknowledged the existence, necessity, and value of these affinity groups, we began to see our task not as one of building democratic dialogue between free and equal individuals, but of building a coalition among the multiple, shifting, intersecting, and sometimes contradictory groups carrying unequal weights of legitimacy within the culture and the classroom.[47]

In such a case, the meaning acquired would not be the meaning prescribed from an instructor's metanarrative. But neither would it be a free-floating explosion of individual meanings in the kind of dialogue where some, by virtue of their proximity with the Eurocentric, historical metanarrative, retain power over Others. Instead, the truth(s) accessed from the text's surplus of meaning would be the result of a coalition-building process that developed directly from the crossing over and bridging together of diverse cultural borders. This operation of dialogue and coalition building recognizes differences, accepts differences, and promotes the kind of confrontation between those differences that can perpetually lead to new textual vision and understanding. The challenge is to teach students to cross each Other's borders and, in the process, *build* meaning. The very concept is, in the positivistic sense, irrational. But it is also precisely how the biblical classroom can have its most dramatic intercultural impact, and thereby become more politically just.[48]

---

47. Ellsworth, "Why Doesn't This Feel Empowering?," 109.

48. See Lawrence Grossberg, "Introduction: Bringin' It All Back Home—Pedagogy and Cultural Studies," in *Between Borders: Pedagogy and the Politics of Cultural Studies*, ed. Henry A. Giroux and Peter McLaren (New York: Routledge, 1994), 18. Grossberg calls this approach a pedagogy of articulation and risk. "Refusing to assume ahead of time that it knows the appropriate knowledge, language, or skills, it is a contextual practice which is willing to take the risk of making connections, drawing lines, mapping articulations, between different domains, discourses, and practices to see what will work."

Border Staffing

Transborder cultural study allied with engaged border pedagogy would at the very least, in order to create faculties that could effectively accomplish both, attract culturally diverse doctoral students who would graduate into a more culturally rich pool of faculty and administrative hires. I am fascinated by this matter not only because so much of my research is focused on factoring culture, most particularly my own, into my research, writing, and teaching, but because my own location as a scholar has shifted from academics to administration. As an administrator from a historically Othered community, I am keenly aware of the data. Current practices, methodological and professional, have yielded sparse numbers of persons representing border communities apart from those of European or Caucasian descent. As an example, the Society of Biblical Literature's current US membership figures indicate 3.4 percent African American; 3.3 percent Asian American; 2.9 percent Latin American; 1.5 percent Native American; 88.8 percent European or Caucasian.[49]

I want to know about the Other readers and the Other students, but I also want to know about the Other scholars and professors and how a more intentional cultural access into text meaning potential might encourage the building of a more culturally diverse professoriate and how the building of a more culturally diverse professoriate might widen access into the meaning potential of the biblical texts. I am suggesting that, by transforming the way we research and publish and encourage others to research and publish, we can begin the process of professionalizing a more democratized, border-crossing biblical approach, while simultaneously encouraging a more inclusive pool of professionals to teach that approach.

In looking at the way that learned societies developed, a historian recognizes the connection between the way research is done and the way the field is professionalized. "The feminist Bonnie G. Smith has argued that, for instance, the ethos of the American Historical Association cultivated a value-detached, 'gender-neutral' community of scholars and developed an 'objective' narrative in the course of professionalization as 'a modern scientific profession.'"[50] A connection is rightly drawn between research and

49. See the Society of Biblical Literature's Membership Report at https://tinyurl.com/SBL1130i.

50. Schüssler Fiorenza, "Rethinking the Educational Practices," 388.

pedagogy and institutionalization (hiring, promotion, etc.). This current, regrettable connection suggests that current patterns of professionalization can be transfigured through research and pedagogy that value the cultural location and perspective of the Other.

Tan is correct when she notes that "social location has a contributory role to play in the standards of excellence and the transformation of graduate biblical education for the educator-cum-biblical scholar, as well as his or her graduate students."[51] Social location not only plays a role in how we interpret. Because it plays a role in how we interpret, it can and should play a role in how we educate and then institutionalize the educational process. The "standards of excellence" that determine teaching viability, readiness for promotion and tenure, etc., conform to the "ethos of the discipline."[52] The problem is that the ethos of the discipline remains positivist, scientist, and elite white male oriented. Thus, so do the standards of excellence that follow the ethos of the discipline. "In short, professional ethos determines disciplinary discourses by establishing what can be said and what is *a priori* ruled out of court."[53] But if the disciplinary discourses shape professional ethos, then the transformational interruption starts with a border–Other oriented interpretive approach to accessing text meaning potential. A more just interpretive process fosters a more just cadre of interpreters to execute that process.

As Du Bois recognized, when social location is valued, the interpretive work of the investigator can claim neither scientific neutrality nor political disinterest.

> At the very time when my studies were most successful, there cut across this plan which I had as a scientist, a red ray which could not be ignored. I remember when it first, as it were, startled me to my feet: a poor Negro in central Georgia, Sam Hose, had killed his landlord's wife. I wrote out a careful and reasoned statement concerning the evident facts and started down to the Atlanta *Constitution* office, carrying in my pocket a letter of introduction to Joel Chandler Harris. I did not get there. On the way news met me: Sam Hose had been lynched, and they said that his knuckles were on exhibition at a grocery store farther down on Mitchell Street, along which I was walking. I turned back to the University. I began to

51. Tan, "Social Location," 47–48.
52. Tan, "Social Location," 49.
53. Schüssler Fiorenza, "Rethinking the Educational Practices," 389.

> turn aside from my work. I did not meet Joel Chandler Harris nor the editor of the *Constitution*.
>
> Two considerations thereafter broke in upon my work and eventually disrupted it: first, one could not be a calm, cool, and detached scientist while Negroes were lynched, murdered and starved; and secondly, there was no such definite demand for scientific work of the sort that I was doing.[54]

Du Bois realizes that he cannot keep working the way he has always worked, given what he knows about the realities of the spaces he and those for whom he writes exist. The space of biblical scholars and students in contemporary, Western, First World contexts contains nothing as horrible as the physical brutality about which Du Bois speaks, to be sure. That is not to say, though, that there does not exist systemic psychological and professional brutality that occur literally as well as figuratively in academia. Part of that reality develops from a systemic bias embedded in the academic system itself, such that people of color remain Othered in ways that make progress difficult. Can one continue to do one's interpretive work, one's science of biblical interpretation as one has always done it in the face of such troubling information? Certainly, in his field of sociology, Du Bois would have answered in the negative. I follow from him with an interrogative. How might intentional boundary ingress and egress into the circumstances and situations of Other spaces as we do our interpretive work impact—in a transformational way for liberation—the spaces from which most of us do that work?

Bibliography

Bultmann, Rudolf. "The Problem of Hermeneutics." Pages 234–61 in *Essays, Philosophical and Theological*. LPTh. London: SCM, 1955.

Coates, Ta-Nehisi. "The Case For Reparations." *The Atlantic*. June 2014. https://www.theatlantic.com/magazine/archive/2014/06/the-case-for-reparations/361631/.

Donaldson, Laura E. "Are We All Multiculturists Now? Biblical Reading As Cultural Contact." *Semeia* 82 (1998): 79–97.

Du Bois, W. E. B. "Criteria of Negro Art." *The Crisis* 32 (1926): 290–97.

54. W. E. B. Du Bois, *Dusk of Dawn: An Essay toward an Autobiography of a Race Concept* (repr., New Brunswick, NJ: Transaction Books, 1984), 67.

———. *Dusk of Dawn: An Essay toward an Autobiography of a Race Concept*. Repr., New Brunswick, NJ: Transaction Books, 1984.

———. *The Souls of Black Folk*. Greenwich, CT: Fawcett, 1961.

Ellsworth, Elizabeth. "Why Doesn't This Feel Empowering? Working through the Repressive Myths of Critical Pedagogy." Pages 90–119 in *Feminisms and Critical Pedagogy*. Edited by Carmen Luke and Jennifer Gore. New York: Routledge, 1992.

Grossberg, Lawrence. "Introduction: Bringin' It All Back Home—Pedagogy and Cultural Studies." Pages 1–25 in *Between Borders: Pedagogy and the Politics of Cultural Studies*. Edited by Henry A. Giroux and Peter McLaren. New York: Routledge, 1994.

Premnath, D. N. "Introduction." Pages 1–13 in *Border Crossings: Cross-Cultural Hermeneutics*. Edited by D. N. Premnath. Maryknoll, NY: Orbis, 2007.

Ricoeur, Paul. *Interpretation Theory: Discourse and the Surplus of Meaning*. Fort Worth: Texas Christian University Press, 1976.

Schüssler Fiorenza, Elisabeth. "The Ethics of Biblical Interpretation: Decentering Biblical Scholarship." *JBL* 107 (1988): 3–17.

———. "Rethinking the Educational Practices of Biblical Doctoral Studies." Pages 373–943 in *Transforming Graduate Biblical Education: Ethos and Discipline*. Edited by Elisabeth Schüssler Fiorenza and Kent Harold Richards. GPBS 10. Atlanta: Society of Biblical Literature, 2010.

Segovia, Fernando F. "Criticism in Critical Times: Reflections on Vision and Task." *JBL* 134 (2015): 6–29.

———. "Cultural Studies and Contemporary Biblical Criticism: Ideological Criticism as Mode of Discourse." Pages 1–17 in *Social Location and Biblical Interpretation in Global Perspective*. Vol. 2 of *Reading from This Place*. Edited by Fernando F. Segovia and Mary Ann Tolbert. Minneapolis: Fortress, 1995.

———. "Intercultural Bible Reading as Transformation for Liberation: Intercultural Hermeneutics and Biblical Studies." Pages 19–51 in *Bible and Transformation: The Promise of Intercultural Bible Reading*. Edited by de Hans Wit and Janet Dyk SemeiaSt 81. Atlanta: SBL Press, 2015.

Smith, Abraham. "Taking Spaces Seriously: The Politics of Space and the Future of Western Biblical Studies." Pages 59–92 in *Transforming Graduate Biblical Education: Ethos and Discipline*. Edited by Elisabeth Schüssler Fiorenza and Kent Harold Richards. GPBS 10. Atlanta: Society of Biblical Literature, 2010.

Society of Biblical Literature. "Membership Report." https://tinyurl.com/SBL1130i.

Sölle, Dorothee. *Political Theology*. Philadelphia: Fortress, 1974.

Tan, Yak-hwee. "Social Location: Dis-Ease and/or Dis-Cover(Y)." Pages 47–58 in *Transforming Graduate Biblical Education: Ethos and Discipline*. Edited by Elisabeth Schüssler Fiorenza and Kent Harold Richards. GPBS 10. Atlanta: Society of Biblical Literature, 2010.

Wimbush, Vincent. "Interpreters—Enslaving/Enslaved/Runagate." *JBL* 130 (2011): 5–24.

———. "Reading Darkness, Reading Scriptures." Pages 1–46 in *African Americans and the Bible: Sacred Texts and Social Textures*. Edited by Vincent Wimbush. New York: Continuum, 2000.

Wit, Hans de. "Through the Eyes of Another: Objectives and Background." Pages 3–53 in *Through the Eyes of Another: Intercultural Reading of the Bible*. Edited by Hans de Wit et al. Elkhart, IN: Institute of Mennonite Studies, 2004.

Wit, Hans de, and Janet Dyk. "Introduction." Pages 1–16 in *Bible and Transformation: The Promise of Intercultural Bible Reading*. Edited by de Hans Wit and Janet Dyk SemeiaSt 81. Atlanta: SBL Press, 2015.

Presidential Reflection

BRIAN K. BLOUNT

I am grateful to the Committee on Underrepresented Racial and Ethnic Minorities in the Profession (CUREMP) for the opportunity to situate my presidential address in a volume that continues the conversation in the context of biblical studies and minoritized criticism.

In my presidential address, I advocated for a transition from multicultural to intercultural readings of biblical texts. Multicultural interpretation positions the work of Othered readers against a dominant, centrist investigative perspective and agenda. Intercultural interpretation envisions equally positioned and empowered groups of readers who recognize that all readers read from within the borders of their communal perspective. All reading communities, then, are border communities, even communities previously recognized as the center. Recognizing that communities historically have centralized their identity and that interpretative privilege and perspective emanates from that identity, border communities build interpretative coalitions to challenge and decentralize such centrist perspectives and, in the process, delegitimize their interpretative conclusions.

In intercultural readings, meaning is not mandated from the center. Meaning is instead built, constructed through investigative inquiry that invites persons in different border communities to cross boundaries and learn from one another. Interpreters who construct meaning in this intercultural way invite the reading perspectives of those in other border communities. Simultaneously, such interpreters cross and, if necessary, trespass the borders of other communities to convey the meaning constructed within their borders or the meaning constructed through the building of interpretative coalition(s) with other border reading communities. In this intercultural reading perspective, no community's interpretative perspective is privileged as center while all other perspectives are doomed to reading from the so-called margins. Every reading community is an Othered reading community. Every reading community is a border community. Every reading is a border reading that, to be meaningful, requires border crossing.

Such interpretative border crossing can only have broad effect if it is followed and supported by a border pedagogy that creates classrooms dedicated to the support of boundary crossing and the encouragement of border coalitions that attack readers and communities of readers determined to invest the mantle of center on their own reading perspective and agenda. Such border pedagogy can only exist if academic institutions commit to border staffing of faculty who have themselves committed to reading interculturally.

In a very helpful Society of Biblical Literature session with members of CUREMP following the presentation of my presidential address, interlocutors appreciated my call for intercultural interpretation of texts, but they made clear that further exploration of the key power dynamic at play is essential. Colleagues noted that ethnic and racial biases operate at an unexamined level for Euro-American interpreters generally and white, male interpreters particularly—unexamined not by those who have been Othered by the assumed Eurocentrist privilege and perspective but by themselves. Having codified and empowered such perspective as objective, no need for self-examination is allegedly warranted.

Such an objective interpretative position, it was helpfully pointed out, operated in complicity with a history of white supremacy and class privilege, even, and perhaps especially within the realm of biblical investigation and damages the opportunity for true recognition of all reading communities as Othered, border communities. Othered communities remain marginalized as long as such perspective endures. One colleague noted passionately that until Eurocentric centrist biblical interpretation, disguised as objective text investigation, is rejected by Eurocentric biblical scholars themselves, border crossings run the risk of being border invasions that terrorize rather than instruct, that construct meaning for privilege and power, not for community and equity. In his challenge, Professor Miguel De La Torre said it well: "I understand the strategy to cross borders in the classroom to learn from each other. But such a strategy assumes equality and an intent to do no harm. Unfortunately, indigenous populations and those of us who hail from south of the border have always experienced a chill run up our collective spines whenever Euroamericans crossed borders.… I just fear that Euroamerican Others will fight tooth and nail not to be decentered."

In this current age of racial reckoning, I see the point all too clearly. Further study requires further examination of this power dynamic and the way it corrupts opportunity for fruitful intercultural engagement.

The Politics of Troublemaking: Biblical Studies as a Miniature Nation-State

GREGORY L. CUÉLLAR

Entering the academy as a Latino biblical scholar, I had the naïve impression that my success in the field of biblical studies depended as much on the production of original ideas as on institutional affiliations. But after attending my first few Annual Meetings of the Society of Biblical Literature, I quickly learned that the production of new biblical knowledge was (and still is) governed by a deeply rooted politics of hermeneutical authority. Within the prevailing mode of intellectual discourse—which, as Brian Blount indicated, is "historical and literary positivism"[1]—the production of new ideas that have the status of new knowledge in biblical studies remains primarily a Eurocentric white male enterprise. I knew only by observing the new books showcased in the exhibit hall and the sessions garnering large audiences that to invest my academic future in this economy of knowledge production, particularly as a Latino biblical scholar, had less to do with my original ideas than with my conformity to an established canon of Western scholarship. And yet heeding my soul's desire for unfettered creativity, I chose the path of nonconformity to the dominant intellectual discourse and its rules, language, idioms, and accepted authorities of the field.

Instead of a historical-critical study of Second Isaiah that perpetuated the authority of the field's scholarly canon, I turned to the theoretical toolchest of cultural studies—which compelled me, in turn, to privilege a different interpretive community for reading exilic poetry. Here, culture pointed to a lived experience (or what Fernando Segovia calls "flesh-and-blood" experience[2])

1. Brian K. Blount, "The Souls of Biblical Folks and the Potential for Meaning," *JBL* 138 (2019): 18.

2. Fernando F. Segovia, "In the World but Not of It: Exile as Locus for a Theology

with exile as well as its artistic expression through poetry. This theoretical framing opened up Second Isaiah to other cultural productions of exile like the immigrant experiences of Mexicans and their lyrical ballads (*corridos*) about their cyclical migration.[3] Although decentering the established canon of biblical criticism in my dissertation on Second Isaiah nourished my soul, using a cultural-studies approach did adversely affect my scholarly value in a job market calibrated to hire scholars who speak the language of the dominant intellectual discourse. Indeed, I can still remember the stack of rejection letters I received during the initial years of entering the academic job market and why I find these words by Blount particularly relevant: "Those who hold interpretive power establish those outside their circle as Other and assign to them the status of Problem and subsequently the problematic task of working their way out of their Otherness by becoming less like themselves and more like those holding such power."[4] It was precisely at this time—a newly minted PhD graduate—that I was literally "assigned to the status of Problem" during one campus visit interview at an undergraduate theological school on the West Coast. For my teaching demonstration, I introduced students and faculty to a cultural-studies reading of the wilderness wanderings in Exodus using the twentieth-century narrative paintings (*retablos*)[5] that depict the Mexican immigrant experience. The following day I met with the school's president, the final formal event of my campus interview. Upon entering his office, I remember vividly how he greeted me with a smile, saying, "So, you're the troublemaker." Later I discovered that his odd welcome was actually a response to what he had heard about my unorthodox reading of Exodus for my teaching demonstration. Hence, I was not at all surprised when, soon thereafter, I received a rejection email from the chair of the search committee—for such is the material consequence of being "assigned to the status of Problem."

Though a cultural-studies approach offered my soul a liberating terrain of knowledge production, my family and I were troubled materially by the negative economic impact of my hermeneutical troublemaking. As Edward

---

of the Diaspora," in *Hispanic/Latino Theology: Challenge and Promise*, ed. Ada María Isasi-Díaz and Fernando F. Segovia (Minneapolis: Fortress, 1996), 201–2.

3. Gregory Lee Cuéllar, *Voices of Marginality: Exile and Return in Second Isaiah 40–55 and the Mexican Immigrant Experience*, American University Studies 7.127 (New York: Lang, 2008), 5–29.

4. Blount, "Souls of Biblical Folks," 8.

5. See "Mexican Migration Project," Princeton University, https://mmp.opr.princeton.edu/.

Said describes the politics in traditional academic humanities, "opponents are therefore not people in disagreement with the constituency but people to be kept out, nonexperts and nonspecialists, for the most part."[6] Confronted with mounting student loan debt, I was eventually forced to seek employment outside of the field of biblical studies during the early years of my academic career. In a serendipitous way, the world of archives opened up as a viable field for gainful academic employment. Here, I was led to discover that I could profit financially from my diverse language skills, doctoral research instincts, and close reading abilities. As a result, for my first academic job I was hired as a curator of rare books and manuscripts at the Cushing Memorial Library and Archives at Texas A&M University.

The notion of remapping biblical studies raises questions about the specific geography of power in the guild. At an aerial level, the map of the discipline emulates the Westernized global map of nation-state boundaries. As long as the territorial nation-state remains the dominant political reality of our time, the fixed boundaries that delineate power and privilege within biblical studies will remain a dominant differentiating force that keeps all of us in our assigned places. For those in power, these boundaries are not only made to appear natural within the guild—as with nation-state borders—but equally their purpose is to protect the material benefits of privilege that their scholarly authority and whiteness afford them. In other words, their position of privilege depends on the policing of their epistemic and hermeneutical boundaries from trespassers. Like the borders of a Western nation-state that protect and sacralize its citizenry, sovereignty, and shared culture, the hierarchy of power that occupies the center of biblical studies is maintained not by transgressing its conventional boundaries of scholarly discourse but through border security against potential interpretive transgressors, trespassers, or troublemakers. The latter activity designates the realm of criminality in which those "assigned to the status of Problem"—as in the queer, indigenous, or black-brown-bodied Others—are to be rigorously excluded, for they pose a threat to the field's homogenous culture, shared identity, and common destiny.

6. Edward W. Said, "Opponents, Audiences, Constituencies, and Community," *Critical Inquiry* 9.1 (1982): 19.

Bibliography

Blount, Brian K. “The Souls of Biblical Folks and the Potential for Meaning.” *JBL* 138 (2019): 6–21.

Cuéllar, Gregory Lee. *Voices of Marginality: Exile and Return in Second Isaiah 40–55 and the Mexican Immigrant Experience*. American University Studies 7/127. New York: Lang, 2008.

Princeton University. “Mexican Migration Project.” https://mmp.opr.princeton.edu/.

Said, Edward W. “Opponents, Audiences, Constituencies, and Community.” *Critical Inquiry* 9.1 (1982): 1–26.

Segovia, Fernando F. “In the World but Not of It: Exile as Locus for a Theology of the Diaspora.” Pages 195–217 in *Hispanic/Latino Theology: Challenge and Promise*. Edited by Ada María Isasi-Díaz and Fernando F. Segovia. Minneapolis: Fortress, 1996.

Remapping Biblical Studies: Shifts, Challenges and Opportunities

Raj Nadella

Brian Blount's 2018 presidential address, "The Souls of Biblical Folks and the Potential for Meaning," masterfully explicates how interpreters' cultural contexts shape the meaning potential of biblical texts and foregrounds the extent to which one's interpretations reflect their political commitments. Blount expounds the ways in which scholars who employ vastly different methodologies in the guild can engage, transform, and be enriched by crossing into each other's interpretive spaces. In what follows, I highlight how minoritized scholars have been shaping the field of biblical studies in transformative ways in terms of methodology and the impact of biblical interpretation on people's lives. I call attention to the unique opportunities and challenges facing the field, especially for minoritized scholars.

Decentering the Hermeneutical Center

One of the insights from Blount is that our readings are descriptive of our interpretive locations but also signify how we operate in the world, with major implications for people's lives both within and outside the guild. In highlighting the link between interpreters and their locations, Blount raises questions such as: who gets to interpret, what gets highlighted (or ignored) in those readings, and why are some readings deemed more normative and legitimate than others? He is keen to analyze the role interpretive Otherness plays in delegitimizing African American readings and describes such delegitimization as the Otherhood the larger society imposes on them in ways that disadvantages the community. Building upon W. E. B. Du Bois's insights, he notes that the field of biblical studies is replicating the problematic color lines one sees on the American streets in the form of methodologies and meaning lines.[1] The meaning line *does* otherize both sides, as he astutely notes, and yet it does not, at least not in the same way or to the same extent. Some become lesser Others along the meaning line than the rest primarily because of how the guild continues to normativize a few select set of readings.

In the context of biblical studies, othering manifests itself often in the form of modifiers that are employed to refer to minoritized readings. R. S. Sugirtharajah has noted how the guild refers to Western, male interpretations as normative hermeneutics but designates all others with modifiers such as Asian American, African American, or Latinx readings. He observes that scholars from marginal spaces who want to be included in the interpretations "must conform to rules or criteria developed within the Western academic paradigm."[2] Perhaps what otherizes these readings and pushes them to peripheries is the premise that they are relevant primarily to the spaces associated with the modifiers, while Eurocentric readings that seemingly have no need of modifiers are treated as normative and central. As Ekaputra Tupamahu has noted in a blog post, Whiteness "is generally treated as a non-identity, a normal position, a transcendental self. It is the omnipresent, stubborn, grand signifier against which others are defined."[3] Just as the absence of modifiers gives Eurocentric readings privileged position in interpretive space, the modifiers move the referents away from the center and otherize them. Consequently, the work of minoritized scholars is usually engaged only in relation to their specific social location such as race and ethnicity.

A troubling consequence of othering that Blount critiques is the proclivity on the part of some minoritized scholars to work "their way out of their Otherness by becoming less like themselves and more like those holding such power" that otherized them in the first place.[4] In the realm of biblical hermeneutics, seeking to work one's way out of interpretive Otherness often takes the form of engaging and normativizing dominant readings, resulting in the loss of one's authentic voice and perspective that

---

1. Brian K. Blount, "The Souls of Biblical Folks and the Potential for Meaning," *JBL* 138 (2019): 7.

2. R. S. Sugirtharajah, *The Bible and the Third World: Precolonial, Colonial and Postcolonial Encounters* (Cambridge: Cambridge University Press, 2001), 61.

3. Ekaputra Tupamahu, "The Stubborn Invisibility of Whiteness in Biblical Scholarship," The Politics of Scripture, 11 November 2020, tinyurl.com/SBL4527f.

4. Blount, "Souls of Biblical Folks," 8.

can only be gleaned when one writes from and in conversation with their social location.

What would it look like if minoritized scholars stopped writing as if their method and insights needed to be affirmed by those occupying dominant interpretive spaces? What if we wrote primarily to the communities that sustain us and are integral to our identity? Although the realities of tenure and promotion have, at least historically, required that we write in the mode of Eurocentric methods in order to be taken seriously by dominant voices in the guild, we have an obligation to address the interpretive needs of the communities to which we are accountable. With methodologies such as womanist readings, African American readings, and postcolonial biblical criticism gaining visibility in the field and more scholars becoming intentional about writing from their locations and for their communities, there is increasing acceptance of minoritized hermeneutical methods. While this is worth celebrating, it is largely limited to certain parts of the academy. The Society of Biblical Literature must take steps to strengthen this trajectory of promoting hitherto marginal methodologies as an integral and key part of guild scholarship so that scholars operating at the margins can write from their social locations with authority and address needs of their communities without putting career advancement at risk.

Blount suggests that the interpretive center can be disrupted and decentered to everyone's advantage. Building upon Du Bois's insights about crossing the color line, he suggests that white people should cross into African American cultural spaces and learn from them just as African Americans are expected to learn from white spaces.[5] Trespassing, to use Blount's term, the space of the Other has the potential to promote better understanding on both sides and mutual transformation if done with respect for each other and genuine curiosity. With minoritized scholars long practiced at crossing over, Blount argues that scholars from dominant spaces should engage minoritized hermeneutics to create a two-way street. Often times it is the case that only one of them—the minoritized scholar—makes the effort to cross over. I was glad to see Blount engage Paul Ricoeur and Rudolf Bultmann in a conversation, but how often do scholars who write in the tradition of Ricoeur and Bultmann quote scholars such as Blount except when the discourse explicitly pertains to

5. Blount, "Souls of Biblical Folks," 12–13.

his social location? He describes interculturality as a "holy chaos of an ensemble dance troupe" where every move is essential for capturing the fullness of the text and every reading plays a part in realizing its meaning. It is an interpretive framework in which spaces previously deemed central are now bordered and everyone reads with the other from places that are simultaneously central and marginal. This interpretive paradigm shatters the established meaning line, leading to "meaning potential that is best approached collaboratively, even combatively, through intercultural engagement, across border communities."[6]

A truly intercultural interpretive exchange is not unrealistic or even improbable, but mechanisms need to be put in place to guarantee that some do not have disproportionately more power and a privileged position in the conversation. Care should be taken to raise questions such as: Who determines the borders, how are they crossed, and by whom? Who gets to be the host and sets the terms of dialogue? Are those at the margins safe when they enter dominant spaces, especially if terms of engagement are set by the latter? How do we ensure that crossing into the other's space occurs on equal terms and that the perspectives offered by African American cultural spaces and other minoritized readings are acknowledged as having the same validity as Eurocentric perspectives?

In intercultural border crossings where some hermeneutical methods are seen as less sophisticated and essential than others, it is important to ensure that interpreters from various access points engage each other as equal voices. Care should be taken to make sure that the engagement will not serve the function of minimizing interpreters from less powerful access points and place them in precarious positions. One way to facilitate an equitable engagement and safe border crossings for those south of the interpretive border is to ensure that terrain of conversation is accessible and hospitable to them. Such cross-cultural sessions are increasingly occurring at the meetings of the Society of Biblical Literature but are more often than not organized by interpreters from dominant spaces. Rather than dominant groups inviting minoritized scholars to their sessions on their terms, the conversations should be hosted by scholars from marginal spaces in order to enhance chances of an equitable engagement.

The goal is to make minoritized readings more prevalent in the guild and to facilitate conditions whereby interpreters whose readings have

6. Blount, "Souls of Biblical Folks," 16.

hitherto been treated as peripheral can trespass borders as easily as privileged interpreters and come to the table as equal partners. Going forward, a key measure of progress on this issue will be whether scholars who engage in minoritized readings will receive one of the Society's flagship awards—the David Noel Freedman Award for Excellence and Creativity in Hebrew Bible Scholarship and the Paul J. Achtemeier Award for New Testament Scholarship. A continued trend of white male scholars consistently receiving these awards accentuates the supposed normativity of their interpretive lens. The selection process is anonymous, but a pattern of granting these awards almost exclusively to scholars who engage in historical critical methods reveals a hermeneutical preference on the part of selectors. Diversifying these awards committees and populating them with scholars of disparate methodological leanings could possibly result in the awards being granted to papers that engage newer methodologies.

A Guild (with)out Modifiers—Defining Our Work on Our Own Terms

Remapping biblical studies entails carefully assessing the presumptions, methodologies, and goals of dominant hermeneutics and employing a different set of methodologies that can address issues of life and death that matter to communities at the margins. It also requires us to move past traditional sources of knowledge production and rely primarily on stories and traditions of communities to whom we are accountable and for whom we write. In the last three decades, minoritized scholars have been increasingly producing hermeneutics from their social locations, relying on their own sources and employing methods that take into account lived realities of their communities. That is, even as we acknowledge the power and influence of dominant hermeneutical spaces on our work, the goal has largely been to produce the kind of knowledge that takes place primarily on our terms and for the sake of communities at the margins.[7] Remapping biblical studies requires that minoritized scholars neither define their work in relation to Eurocentric readings in ways that continue to normativize those readings nor employ modifiers to refer to their own scholarship.

7. R. S. Sugirtharajah's *Jesus in Asia* is a recent example of knowledge production in the margins, with resources primarily from the margins, in the language of the margins and for the sake of the marginalized. R. S. Sugirtharajah, *Jesus in Asia* (Cambridge: Harvard University Press, 2018).

A dilemma pertaining to modifiers is that they do play an important role in articulating our social location and acknowledging the marginality of our approaches in the guild. Yet, it becomes necessary to challenge those modifiers when they are employed to otherize our readings and characterize them as less sophisticated or consequential. Perhaps a solution might be for all scholars—minoritized as well as white-identifying—to prefix modifiers to their methodologies in order to acknowledge their social locations and to disrupt the implied normativity of dominant hermeneutics. Such a move would actively acknowledge that all readings are culturally conditioned and reflective of interpreters' lived experiences and ideological commitments.

A second approach may also be impactful. The Society of Biblical Literature should leverage its structures and influence to undertake specific practices aimed at promoting minoritized readings as equal intellectual partners in the guild. For instance, SBL Press and other major publishers could publish a volume featuring essays exclusively from minoritized scholars without marking them with any modifiers. By not explicitly identifying the social location of the contributors, it could presume and communicate the broad relevance of their scholarship.

Given their disparate social locations, minoritized scholars are by no means a monolithic group but operate with shared goals and experiences of writing and teaching at the margins of the academy. Building upon Elizabeth Ellsworth's insights about representation and power dynamics, Blount suggests that coalition building and affinity grouping is the way forward.[8] Within this context, a key task of minoritized scholars should be to build alliances across various spaces while intentionally attending to layered power dynamics within those complex spaces. In order for such coalition building to be effective, two things need to happen: (1) The various constituent groups in the coalition need to identify common goals and aspirations that bind us so that joining forces is in everyone's best interest. (2) There needs to be enough of us for the coalition to be effective. Despite best intentions and efforts on the latter front, the number of minoritized scholars in the guild has barely increased in the last twenty-five years. This is an area where CUREMP (The Committee on Underrepresented Racial

8. Elizabeth Ellsworth, "Why Doesn't This Feel Empowering? Working through the Repressive Myths of Critical Pedagogy," in *Feminisms and Critical Pedagogy*, ed. Carmen Luke and Jennifer Gore (New York: Routledge, 1992), 90–119. See Blount, "Souls of Biblical Folks," 18.

and Ethnic Minorities in the Profession) and similar bodies within the Society of Biblical Literature should make concerted efforts to recruit more students of color into the guild and provide them networks of support so that they can thrive. Steps should be taken to provide the support systems and resources they will need in order to publish and to position themselves for career advancement. The Society of Biblical Literature should institute mechanisms and initiatives designed to guarantee that the percentage of minoritized students in the guild is at least comparable to the percentage of minoritized populations in the United States by 2030. Such an approach, however ambitious, is still limiting and problematic because of its narrow focus on the United States, but I present it as the initial, rather than the final, goal.

Biblical Scholars Engaging Lived Experiences

Blount makes the insightful observation that how one reads biblical texts is intrinsically connected to how one lives and invariably impacts people's lives, especially those at the margins. His observation is particularly relevant in light of the fact that biblical texts have historically been employed to justify the colonial project, enslavement, exploitation of Native American lands and the like. Despite the supposed notion of separation of the church and state, biblical texts continue to make it into the public square in the United States and are weaponized by politicians and religious leaders in order to justify various forms of dehumanization. Jeff Sessions's use of Rom 13 in 2018 to justify mistreatment of migrants and refugees at the Southern border is just one such example.

In some instances, biblical interpretation explicitly supports oppressive institutions and practices, but in many other instances, it fails to address problematic issues or engages in a hermeneutics of deflection by shifting the locus of conversation to abstract issues. As William H. Myers has highlighted, traditional biblical scholarship has privileged certain types of methodologies and issues that shift attention from oppressive and dehumanizing social structures.[9] It has the amazing ability to identify and analyze minute details but is not sufficiently attentive to situations of injustice that might force the scholar to reckon with troubling realities

9. William H. Myers, "The Hermeneutical Dilemma of the African American Biblical Student," in *Stony the Road We Trod: African American Biblical Interpretation*, ed. Cain Hope Felder (Minneapolis: Fortress, 1991), 41.

of communities on the other side of the meaning line. Myers helpfully notes that Eurocentric approach "is too letter-conscious and not narrative-conscious enough."[10] Yet, the guild has accorded a near canonical status to historical critical methods that have intentionally or unintentionally contributed to maintaining the status quo in the society. As Fernando Segovia has noted, "historical criticism was perceived and promoted as the proper way to read and interpret biblical texts but also as the ultimate sign of progress in the discipline."[11]

Blount helpfully reminds us to be attentive to strands of Eurocentric approaches that do indeed attend to everyday issues. He suggests crossing over into traditional interpretations by engaging, for instance, Bultmann's concept of demythologizing biblical texts that was intended to make the texts make sense in contemporary contexts, akin to cultural hermeneutics. Contemporary interpreters committed to social transformation should certainly engage Bultmann's categories beyond the existential and focus on the political. However, readers need to go beyond a general emphasis on political readings to be attentive to those at the margins and to ensure that the political reading, as transformative as it might be, does not end up highlighting as central only those concerns raised by dominant communities. Such concerns should no doubt be addressed, but they need to be looked at from the perspective of those at the margins lest it have the effect of rendering issues of marginalized communities invisible. Many communities are impacted by war and climate change, to highlight two current examples, but not every community is impacted equally by the two crises. Minoritized communities often bear the brunt of such issues and need hermeneutical lens that focus primarily on their lived experiences.

Within this context of everyday realities, numerous volumes such as Cain Hope Felder's *Stony the Road We Trod*, Fernando Segovia's *Decolonizing Biblical Studies*, and Mitzi Smith's *Womanist Sass and Talk Back: Social (In)Justice, Intersectionality, and Biblical Interpretation* have pushed biblical studies beyond its comfort zone toward addressing issues of communities at the margins.[12] Minoritized readings have influenced conversations

---

10. Myers, "Hermeneutical Dilemma," 46.

11. Fernando F. Segovia, *Decolonizing Biblical Studies: A View from the Margins* (Maryknoll, NY: Orbis, 2000), 38.

12. Felder, *Stony the Road We Trod*; Segovia, *Decolonizing Biblical Studies*; Mitzi J. Smith, *Womanist Sass and Talk Back: Social (In)Justice, Intersectionality, and Biblical Interpretation* (Eugene, OR: Cascade, 2018).

in the guild and served as positive disruptors in a field that has largely remained stale. These approaches remain at the peripheries of the guild, but they have challenged the supposed normativity of traditional readings and their issues. Even as they try to decenter dominant methodologies, the primary goal for minoritized hermeneutics should be to help disrupt systems of domination in everyday settings that engendered biblical texts in the first place.

Conclusion

Significant progress has been accomplished in the guild in the last twenty-five years in terms of facilitating systems and structures that enable scholars of color to teach and write meaningfully on issues that take their social locations seriously. Much more, however, needs to be done in order for impactful and lasting change to occur. With this goal in mind, the guild should facilitate conditions—with close attention to matters such as the Society of Biblical Literature awards and publications—whereby scholarship focusing on issues that matter to people of color will be taken more seriously not just by minoritized scholars but also by those who have access to power in the academy. Biblical interpretation has consequences for people's lives, and positive transformation becomes more possible if those in locations of power actively participate in the process of facilitating it. Such a transformation of ethos and practices has the potential to expand the horizons of conversations in the guild and is in the best interests of everyone, not just minoritized scholars.

Bibliography

Blount, Brian K. "The Souls of Biblical Folks and the Potential for Meaning." *JBL* 138 (2019): 6–21.

Ellsworth, Elizabeth. "Why Doesn't This Feel Empowering? Working through the Repressive Myths of Critical Pedagogy." Pages 90–119 in *Feminisms and Critical Pedagogy*. Edited by Carmen Luke and Jennifer Gore. New York: Routledge, 1992.

Felder, Cain Hope. *Stony the Road We Trod: African American Biblical Interpretation*. Minneapolis: Fortress, 1991.

Myers, William H. "The Hermeneutical Dilemma of the African American Biblical Student." Pages 40–56 in *Stony the Road We Trod: African*

American Biblical Interpretation. Edited by Cain Hope Felder. Minneapolis: Fortress, 1991.

Segovia, Fernando. *Decolonizing Biblical Studies: A View from the Margins*. Maryknoll, NY: Orbis, 2000.

Smith, Mitzi J. *Womanist Sass and Talk Back: Social (In)Justice, Intersectionality, and Biblical Interpretation*. Eugene, OR: Cascade, 2018.

Sugirtharajah, R. S. *The Bible and the Third World: Precolonial, Colonial and Postcolonial Encounters*. Cambridge: Cambridge University Press, 2001.

———. *Jesus in Asia*. Cambridge: Harvard University Press, 2018.

Tupamahu, Ekaputra. "The Stubborn Invisibility of Whiteness in Biblical Scholarship." The Politics of Scripture, 11 November 2020. tinyurl.com/SBL4527f.

Brought Up to Fight (and Not Be Ignored)!

ANGELA N. PARKER

Recently, I was watching an ABC miniseries entitled "Women of the Movement," which depicted events from Emmett Till's murder in 1955. Till, a fourteen-year-old child from Chicago, Illinois, was visiting relatives in Money, Mississippi, when he was murdered by two white men for the offense of whistling at a white woman, Carolyn Bryant. Seeking to put the matter away quietly, officials in Money buried Till's body without the consent of his mother, Mamie Till-Mobley. However, Till-Mobley fought hard to have her son's body exhumed and transported to Chicago for a proper burial among family and friends. Upon arrival to Chicago, Till-Mobley witnessed her child's disfigured body that suffered the beating from adult men, and she had an open-casket funeral as a way for the nation to wrestle with what grown men did to her child. Till-Mobley raised the consciousness of the world as the world witnessed the disfigurement of Till's body. The United States of America was forced to wrestle with the horrific ways in which adult men beat and murdered a child in Jim and Jane Crow South. Till's death served as a catalyst for many actions of the Civil Rights movement in the 1950s and 1960s.

As I was watching one section of the ABC miniseries, I was struck by a conversation that Till-Mobley had with her mother. The elder was trying to dissuade her daughter from speaking at an NAACP rally. Till-Mobley responded that she had to speak up for her child and then asked her mother "what if you had brought me up to fight" instead of remaining quiet and engaging what scholars now identify as respectability politics.[1]

The title of this essay came to me as I was watching "Women of the Movement" on ABC. For more on this miniseries, see https://tinyurl.com/SBLPress1130a1. In the context of this essay, I use the terms *fight* and *violence* sometimes interchangeably. A standard definition of *fight* means a violent struggle or confrontation. While not

As I engage Till-Mobley's idea of being "brought up to fight," I place Till-Mobley in conversation with Brian K. Blount's 2018 presidential address to the Society of Biblical Literature. I appreciate Blount's thesis that the problem of biblical scholarship is the meaning line, and I will respond to and extend Blount's thesis as I ponder the state of biblical studies. Essentially, I argue and advance the idea that since the continuum of a meaning potential line is often embraced by minoritized scholars, the only way forward as a guild is to fight against the idea of objective meaning while also refusing and actively blocking mainstream scholarship that continues to ignore a continuum of meaning potential. Blount states that those "who hold interpretive power establish those outside their circle as Other and assign to them the status of Problem."[2] As an Other, I had often tried to work my way out by becoming less like myself and more like those holding such power. In essence, I tried to become as close to Eurocentricity or to whiteness as possible. As a womanist scholar I have written about my own training to read as a "white male biblical scholar."[3]

In response to Blount's work, minoritized biblical scholars must continue to write about how the text has been used as a weapon of mass destruction against black and brown bodies. Moreover, Blount argues that the necessity to acquire the meaning line threatens the very soul of the cultural hermeneut, who must occupy and absorb the space of the objective Other without losing hold of the spiritual mooring of their own space.[4] I would take Blount's language further by arguing that souls have not just been troubled but defaced by violence. Black and brown biblical scholars must fight back against violence in the way of Till-Mobley.

---

advising actual physical violence, I do recognize that fighting a system entails violent confrontation in words and arguments so that the system is destroyed.

1. *Respectability politics* is a phrase coined by Evelyn Brooks Higginbotham as she conducted ethnographic research on black Baptist church women from 1880–1920. In essence, these women advocated for the reform of individual behavior and uplift of black people through the promotion of temperance, cleanliness of person and property, thrift, polite manners, and sexual purity. See Evelyn Brooks Higginbotham, *Righteous Discontent: The Women's Movement in the Black Baptist Church, 1880–1920* (Cambridge: Harvard University Press, 1993).

2. Brian K. Blount, "The Souls of Biblical Folks and the Potential for Meaning," *JBL* 138 (2019): 6–21.

3. Angela Parker, *If God Still Breathes, Why Can't I? Black Lives Matter and Biblical Authority* (Grand Rapids: Eerdmans, 2021).

4. Blount, "Souls of Biblical Folks," 9.

Therefore, I agree with Blount when he states that that readers vie for the opportunity to read rightly from their particular space while having the meaning derived from that cultural reading to be received and engaged rather than Othered.[5] Extending beyond Blount, we must fight and refuse to be ignored continually in the academic guild. Part of fighting back is making scholars who have the luxury to ignore our work uncomfortable when we bring up the fact that they have ignored our work. As I think about my own womanist identity as a contributing member to the academic guild of New Testament studies, I argue that attention to systemic violence with a willingness to fight and no longer be ignored is perhaps the only viable way forward.

Constructing a Womanist Hermeneutic of Fight

As a womanist New Testament scholar, similar to other womanist scholars, I appropriate the term *womanist* from the language of Alice Walker to situate and frame my understanding of biblical interpretation through the simultaneity of my experiences of race, class, and gender discrimination.[6] In the midst of interpreting, I must acknowledge that I struggle to love and accept my black womanhood in a world (and in an academic field) that devalues my contributions. My struggle is my continued effort to fight back against anything that seeks to destroy my livelihood and well-being while also raising the consciousness of those around me regarding my lived experiences. In essence, I have to be brought up to fight against the systemic violence of a system that chooses to ignore my own continuum of meaning potential.

While many scholars invoke the work and theories of René Girard to begin conversations about fighting or violence, I choose to think through the works of Frantz Fanon whose ideas I find helpful to fight back against

---

5. Blount, "Souls of Biblical Folks," 9.

6. As a term coined by Alice Walker, *womanism* may be defined as a type of thought pertaining to black women in order to set aside mainstream white feminists from feminists of color while also resisting antiblackness within the feminist movement. By focusing specifically on black women, womanism aims for the transformation of society and liberation of all people in the black community. Some classic texts include Jacquelyn Grant, *White Women's Christ, Black Women's Jesus: Feminist Christology and Womanist Response* (Atlanta: Scholars Press, 1989); Katie Cannon, *Black Womanist Ethics* (Atlanta: Scholars Press, 1988); Cannon, *Katie's Canon: Womanism and the Soul of the Black Community* (New York: Continuum, 1995).

the violence that academic biblical studies inflicts on my soul.[7] I have to construct ways of fighting back when others refuse to see or actively ignore the meaning potential that occurs as womanist scholars interpret biblical texts.[8] Thinking with Fanon that fighting is inherent in the colonized people who are ceaselessly exposed to the colonizer's violence, I argue that there has to be a way for those of us brought up and trained in predominantly white theological institutions to fight back against the violence perpetrated in our training.

Fanon, a noted French West Indian psychiatrist, writes about the necessary role of violence as oppressed populations seek to resist and fight back against the oppression committed by the French government. The fight becomes a liberation of being since "decolonization is the veritable creation of new men … the thing which has been colonized becomes man."[9] While I note that Fanon has masculinist ideals inherent in his writings, I do believe that his words are important. Since both the oppressor and the oppressed suffer from mental illness as a result of colonization, the fundamental solution to colonial war and mental disorders is to end colonial rule and open the way to liberation by producing greater violence that ends the colonial rule. I would also point out that Fanon does not beautify or absolutize violence when he states that "we know for sure today that in Algeria the test of force was inevitable; but other countries through politi-

---

7. In some of my other works to be published, I engage Frantz Fanon in conversation with Pierre Bourdieu. Fanon often focuses on actual violence while Bourdieu focuses on systemic violence. Combining their thoughts allows me to engage Fanon without the white fragility that I often hear when critics of Fanon claim he is "too violent." However, time limits a discussion of both theorists in the context of this response.

8. Here I specifically think about recent work by Esau McCaulley wherein he ignores the work of womanist scholars in his text until an appendix chapter entitled "Bonus Tracks." McCaulley embraces hermeneutics of retrieval and affirmation that underlies the Bible's clarity, consistency, and inherent moral goodness. As such, he ignores womanist interpretation until the appendix not because he dismisses the valid concerns of womanists but because there is a difference for McCaulley between acknowledging the social location of interpretation and letting said location eclipse the text itself. Contra McCaulley, I do not believe it is impossible for womanists to engage a constant push and pull between social location and the text that is nuanced and life-giving for contemporary readers. See Esau McCaulley, *Reading While Black: African American Biblical Interpretation As an Exercise in Hope* (Downers Grove, IL: InterVarsity Press, 2020), 181–82.

9. Frantz Fanon, *The Wretched of the Earth* (New York: Grove Press, 1963), 35–37.

cal action and through the work of clarification undertaken by a party have led their people to the same results."[10]

Thinking further with Fanon, violence (i.e., the struggle or the fight) brings about certain effects. First, violence unifies the people by binding each individual into a great chain that surges in reaction to the settler's violence in the beginning. Those in the fight begin to recognize and see each other as a unified force. The armed struggle mobilizes the people; that is, it throws them in one way and in one direction. Second, violence restores humanity: "at the level of individual, violence is a cleansing force. It frees the native from his inferiority complex and from his despair and inaction."[11] Third, violence makes people a subject of struggle: through violence (the armed struggle), the people see "that the liberation has been the business of each and all and that the leader had no special merit."[12] Fourth, violence separates the people from the leadership with a compromising attitude: "illuminated by violence, the consciousness of the people rebels against any pacification."[13]

I highlight Fanon's views concerning violence for a number of reasons. The first reason is to show that those subjugated under colonial violence must commit violence in order to become free of the initial colonial violence. Put another way, those subjugated under the violence of an academic guild that refuses to engage their meaning potential of a text must commit violence against the guild in order to liberate the guild. Thinking systemically about Fanon's actual violence, as a member of an academic guild, the power structure of the guild invokes symbolic violence upon its members when it only allows one objective meaning and not meaning potential. Is there a hermeneutic of fight that womanists can entail as we expound upon the ideas of meaning potential as identified by Blount?

Pondering Fanon's thought on violence in a systemic way helps me develop a womanist hermeneutics of fight that seeks to interrogate and break down the inequities that result to underrepresented racial and ethnic minorities in the guild. Fanon is useful as he identifies that the colonized goes through internal dynamics of racial domination wherein she or he internalizes the social structure and wrestles to find his or her place in that structure. This is very similar to Blount's idea of the troubling of the soul of

10. Fanon, *Wretched of the Earth*, 193.
11. Fanon, *Wretched of the Earth*, 93.
12. Fanon, *Wretched of the Earth*, 93.
13. Fanon, *Wretched of the Earth*, 94.

the biblical scholar who has been pigeonholed as Other. Truly, that internal struggle is part of what occurs in the academic guild for minoritized scholars who suffer with Fanon's inferiority complex. Internal struggle represents the deeper symbolic violence of racial domination. Following an idea of symbolic violence within personal struggle, I argue that a form of symbolic violence *against* oppressive structures is mandatory for liberation.

Taking the entirety of my thoughts into consideration on the work of Fanon, I offer a few insights on what a womanist hermeneutic of fight entails as I read biblical texts. First, I am reading the text and asking questions that take into consideration the lived experiences of black women in the United States of America. Second, I read the text and ask questions that center symbolic violence against the sanctioned mainstream interpretations. Third, I read the text and ask questions about consciousness raising as found in the text and in today's world. Finally, I ask questions about women's agency and the ability to be a presence that does not allow herself to be ignored even when those around her seek to do so. Thus, I now move to an example of a womanist hermeneutic of fight in action with the following case study.

A Womanist Hermeneutic of Fight: A Case Study from Mark 14:3–9

As presented in the Gospel of Mark, the story of the anointing woman occurs in Bethany, a village on the outskirts of Jerusalem.[14] As I delve into this anointing story with a womanist hermeneutic of fight, I focus on the words used around the anointing and how they show fight, resistance, and a call to remember and not ignore. Moreover, instead of focusing on the anointing and interpreting her action as a prophetic sign act alone, I will argue against most feminist scholars[15] that the anointing woman actually recognizes the feminized body of Jesus as about to enter the violence of empire, *in addition* to the prophetic sign act. Seong Hee Kim argues that taking Jesus's statement seriously about the woman anointing Jesus's body

14. See Joel Marcus, *Mark 8–16: A New Translation and Commentary* (New Haven: Yale University Press, 2009), 933.

15. For feminist scholars who interpret this act as a prophetic sign act, see Elisabeth Schussler Fiorenza, *In Memory of Her: A Feminist Theological Reconstruction of Christian Origins* (New York: Crossroad, 1982); Susan Miller, *Women in Mark's Gospel* (London: T&T Clark, 2004); and Seong Hee Kim, *Mark, Women and Empire: A Korean Postcolonial Perspective* (Sheffield: Sheffield University Press, 2010).

for burial does not allow the woman to be the subject of the Markan pericope. Contra Kim, I contend that realization of the violence inherent in the Roman imperial age similar to the violence that Fanon discusses actually allows the woman to act as an agent performing a fighting act in a highly charged context where men seek to ignore her. In order to build my argument, therefore, I will highlight how the violence allows an interpretation in the process.

The Markan narrative has set up a dilemma. In Mark 14:1–2, the chief priests had previously been conspiring about seizing Jesus in order to kill him and, particularly, at a time where the people will not riot. Thereafter, the Markan narrative transitions to a house in Bethany owned by Simon the leper. In its characterization of the anointing woman, the Markan narrative chooses precise words to portray what she does. Jesus is reclining at table when the woman approaches him from behind having an alabaster jar of perfume, pure, costly. Then suddenly at 14:3, breaking the alabaster (συντρίψασα τὴν ἀλάβαστρον), she pours it on his head.

The verb συντρίβω has a range of meaning that connotes an idea of breaking. In the context of Mark 14:3, the verb means to smash, crush or shatter into pieces. In other contexts, such as in Rom 16:20, the verb means to overcome or completely crush one's enemies. In the context of an emotional state of mind, the verb can figuratively mean to deprive someone of strength as in Luke 4:18. The only other time that the Markan narrative uses the verb συντρίβω is in Mark 5:4 as follows:

> for he had often been restrained with shackles and chains, but the chains he wrenched apart, and the shackles he broke [συντετρῖφθαι] in pieces; and no one had the strength to subdue him.[16]

Mark 5:4 is a verse found within the pericope known as the Gerasene demoniac. While some traditional scholars still write that "we have no reason to think of a covert reference to the occupation of Palestine by Roman legion," others are beginning to detect both colonial occupation and demonic possession in the text.[17] Indeed, even Stephen Moore ponders whether Mark

16. All translations of Greek texts are my own translations.

17. Robert H. Gundry, *Mark: A Commentary on His Apology for the Cross* (Grand Rapids: Eerdmans, 1993), 260. Some who read colonial oppression in this pericope include Ched Myers, *Binding the Strong Man: A Political Reading of Mark's Story of Jesus* (Maryknoll, NY: Orbis, 1988); Herman C. Waetjen, *A Reordering of Power: A*

5 can serve as a hermeneutical key for unlocking the entire narrative of Mark.[18] While I am not arguing that Mark 5 may serve as the key to unlock the entirety of Mark, I do argue that the repetition of the verb συντρίβω serves as a clue to make readers think about and connect the story of the anointing woman to Roman oppression and the violent fighting that often occurs in order to break free from such oppression.[19]

Juxtaposing the scenario between Till-Mobley and the anointing woman, I argue that both women demonstrate a consciousness raising that is vastly different from the chief priests in the Jesus context and the governing officials in the Money, Mississippi context. The anointing woman understands, I argue, that Jesus's body is about to undergo destruction at the hands of Roman imperial violence as the chief priests plot violence against Jesus. Her breaking the alabaster jar is a fighting act preparing for that violence, which Jesus recognizes as anointing his victimized and oppressed body for burial. Further, Jesus's words in 14:9 state that "wherever the gospel may be preached [κηρυχθῇ] in the whole world, even that which she did will be spoken in her memory [μνημόσυνον]." Jesus's words form a conditional clause.[20] This statement is important because here Jesus highlights the memory of a nameless woman in a conditional clause

Socio-political Reading of Mark's Gospel (Minneapolis: Fortress, 1989), 190–94; John Dominic Crossan, *The Historical Jesus: The Life of a Mediterranean Jewish Peasant* (San Francisco: Harper San Francisco, 1991), 314–18; Stephen C. Moore, *Empire and Apocalypse: Postcolonialism and the New Testament* (Sheffield: Sheffield Phoenix, 2006), 24–25; Richard Horsley, *Hearing the Whole Story: The Politics of Plot in Mark's Gospel* (Louisville: Westminster John Knox, 2001), 140–41, 147. While I am sure that there are others, this list is just a sampling of those who I am engaging in this work.

18. Moore, *Empire and Apocalypse*, 27.

19. My reading is contra other commentators who see no reason for the destructive language. For example, R. T. France states that the detail "seems an unnecessarily wasteful and inefficient means of getting the perfume out of the flask. There seems to be no basis for the common suggestion that breaking the neck of the flask was the only way to get the perfume out." See R. T. France, *The Gospel of Mark: A Commentary on the Greek Text*, NIGTC (Grand Rapids: Eerdmans; 2002), 552. He cites Robert Gundry and C. E. B. Cranfield that perhaps one idea is to demonstrate that the flask is now unusable and demonstrates the completeness of the rash act of a woman.

20. A conditional clause is a clause usually introduced by a subordinating conjunction that introduces a condition that must occur or be met before another action or event can occur. Conditional clauses may or may not reflect reality, but only the writer's presentation or perception of reality. See Daniel B. Wallace, *The Basis of New Testament Syntax* (Grand Rapids: Zondervan, 2000), 291.

in which syntactically, there is uncertainty of fulfillment though fulfillment may be likely. Therefore, the question becomes: how do you honor a memory that so often is ignored in the history of biblical interpretation?

Most scholars argue that the woman's deed, not she herself, is to be remembered with honor. I wonder if that is a reasonable reading of the text. Do we have to separate the woman from the action? I do not think so. As a woman, she took a particularly dangerous risk by walking into a house of a leper where Jesus and his disciples were having dinner, perhaps in the presence of additional men. Men often privilege other men while forgetting about women in the vicinity (or even in their academic writings and footnotes!). Even if we do not know the name of the woman anointing Jesus, her memory includes a gendered placeholder in the biblical text.

Concluding Thoughts

In the ABC miniseries, Till-Mobley wanted the world to see her boy. Violence, specifically symbolic violence, is not necessarily hitting or striking with a fist or rock. In the idea of womanist violence against systems, fighting means striking with words and truth. Violence with words and truth is necessary for breaking down the system of white supremacist academic biblical studies.

Blount argues that changing the meaning line has been addressed in recent Society of Biblical Literature Presidential addresses as submitted by Elisabeth Schüssler Fiorenza, Fernando Segovia, and Vincent Wimbush. Each recognizes that either engaging in or refusing to engage in culturally sensitive readings will have an impact on not only text conclusions reached but the social and political context in which those readings are done. Blount argues that meaning potential lies on both sides of the proverbial fence of meaning. I suggest that we have to blow up the proverbial fence by inciting violence against the objective views held by the academic guild in the first place. We cannot allow academia to forget the meaning potential found in minoritized biblical scholarship. Only then will our classrooms become a place where culturally responsive engagement of meaning potential can occur and shape a more just biblical society, classroom, and profession.

Bibliography

Blount, Brian K. "The Souls of Biblical Folks and the Potential for Meaning." *JBL* 138 (2019): 6–21.

Cannon, Katie. *Black Womanist Ethics*. Atlanta: Scholars Press, 1988.
———. *Katie's Canon: Womanism and the Soul of the Black Community*. New York: Continuum, 1995.
Cerar, Marissa Jo, et al., producers. "Women of the Movement." ABC. 6–20 January 2022.
Crossan, John Dominic. *The Historical Jesus: The Life of a Mediterranean Jewish Peasant*. San Francisco: Harper San Francisco, 1991.
Fanon, Frantz. *The Wretched of the Earth*. New York: Grove Press, 1963.
France, R. T. *The Gospel of Mark: A Commentary on the Greek Text*. NIGTC. Grand Rapids: Eerdmans, 2002.
Grant, Jacquelyn. *White Women's Christ, Black Women's Jesus: Feminist Christology and Womanist Response*. Atlanta: Scholars Press, 1989.
Gundry, Robert H. *Mark: A Commentary on His Apology for the Cross*. Grand Rapids: Eerdmans, 1993.
Higginbotham, Evelyn Brooks. *Righteous Discontent: The Women's Movement in the Black Baptist Church, 1880–1920*. Cambridge: Harvard University Press, 1993.
Horsley, Richard. *Hearing the Whole Story: The Politics of Plot in Mark's Gospel*. Louisville: Westminster John Knox, 2001.
Kim, Seong Hee. *Mark, Women and Empire: A Korean Postcolonial Perspective*. Sheffield: Sheffield University Press, 2010.
Marcus, Joel. *Mark 8–16: A New Translation and Commentary*. New Haven: Yale University Press, 2009.
McCaulley, Esau. *Reading While Black: African American Biblical Interpretation As an Exercise in Hope*. Downers Grove, IL: InterVarsity Press, 2020.
Miller, Susan. *Women in Mark's Gospel*. London: T&T Clark, 2004.
Moore, Stephen C. *Empire and Apocalypse: Postcolonialism and the New Testament*. Sheffield: Sheffield Phoenix, 2006.
Myers, Ched. *Binding the Strong Man: A Political Reading of Mark's Story of Jesus*. Maryknoll, NY: Orbis, 1988.
Parker, Angela. *If God Still Breathes, Why Can't I? Black Lives Matter and Biblical Authority*: Grand Rapids, MI: Eerdmans, 2021.
Schussler Fiorenza, Elisabeth. *In Memory of Her: A Feminist Theological Reconstruction of Christian Origins*. New York: Crossroad, 1982.
Waetjen, Herman C. *A Reordering of Power: A Socio-political Reading of Mark's Gospel*. Minneapolis: Fortress, 1989.
Wallace, Daniel B. *The Basis of New Testament Syntax*. Grand Rapids: Zondervan, 2000.

Part 4
Intersectionality

Thinking Intersectionally: Gender, Race, Class, and the Etceteras of Our Discipline

GALE A. YEE

It is a little daunting, as the first Asian American and the first woman of color, to be elected president of the Society of Biblical Literature. It is, however, this particular social location, as well as growing up in one of the poorest sections of Chicago's South Side, that influences the direction I will take in my 2019 Presidential Address. The triad of gender, race, and class—my Chinese American ethnicity, my lower-class origins, and my female gender—have made deep marks on my interpretation of the biblical text, whether I consciously knew it or not.[1] Particularly because of my class background, my profound concern about the rising inequality between the rich and the poor in today's neoliberal world compels me to examine inequality in its various forms in the Bible. I am disturbed by the compartmentalization of the poor and marginals into silos with little theorization on their unequal relationships with other institutional and economic features of society. I am acutely aware that our Annual Meeting is held here in San Diego, a border town with Mexico. In 2014, Fernando Segovia gave his own presidential address here in San Diego, describing the city as a signifier of the global divide between the haves and have-nots.[2]

1. I was recently able to reflect autobiographically on this triad in Gale A. Yee, "Negotiating Shifts in Life's Paradigms," in *Women and the Society of Biblical Literature*, ed. Nicole L. Tilford, BSNA 29 (Atlanta: SBL Press, 2019), 103–14; Yee, "The Process of Becoming for a Woman Warrior from the Slums," in *Asian and Asian American Women in Theology and Religion: Embodying Knowledge*, ed. Kwok Pui-lan, Asian Christianity in the Diaspora (New York: Palgrave Macmillan, 2020), 15–30.

2. Fernando F. Segovia, "Criticism in Critical Times: Reflections on Vision and Task," *JBL* 134 (2015): 9.

San Diego continues to be a material site where a toxic administration commits flagrant crimes against immigrants fleeing poverty and violence in their countries. Our study and interpretations of the biblical text cannot be unaware of or disinterested in the evil perpetrated at the border here so close to this convention site.

Poverty and inequality are not the same thing. While poverty focuses on the condition of the poor, inequality focuses on both the rich and the poor.[3] Inequality is embedded in power relations, forcing us to confront a question that is often avoided: How can the ways in which the rich obtain their wealth generate poverty, as evidenced in the biblical text[4] and in today's world? Poverty is primarily the result of the unequal distribution of society's goods and resources and the concentration of wealth in the hands of the few. Inequality asks us to focus on particular relations of power, whether it be economic, legal, social, ideological, et cetera—on how wealth is distributed. Power relations are secured and maintained not only among the classes (rich and poor), but also among genders, races, and the etceteras. In what specific ways do power relations among these diverse categories create poverty among the marginalized?

In wrestling theoretically with the problem of inequality and poverty, I found that the most helpful analytical tool to help me avoid compartmentalizing gender, race, class, et cetera was "intersectionality." Intersectionality has been used as a hermeneutical prism for many years in a number of disciplines to study inequality by examining power dynamics in their multiplicity, complexity, and interrelations.[5] Although there have been some recent attempts at intersectional analyses, primarily in the New Testament,[6] intersectionality has not made a significant dent as a

3. I am defining inequality as institutionalized patterns and structures of unequal control over and distribution of a society's valued goods and resources such as land, property, money, food, employment, education, healthcare, and housing.

4. I made a modest attempt to address this in the Hebrew Bible in Gale A. Yee, "'He Will Take the Best of Your Fields': Royal Feasts and Rural Extraction," *JBL* 136 (2017): 821–38.

5. Bonnie Thornton Dill and Ruth Enid Zambrana, "Critical Thinking about Inequality: An Emerging Lens," in *Feminist Theory Reader: Local and Global Perspectives*, ed. Carol R. McCann and Seung-Kyung Kim, 4th ed. (New York: Routledge, 2017), 182–93.

6. Especially, Elisabeth Schüssler Fiorenza, *Democratizing Biblical Studies: Toward an Emancipatory Educational Space* (Louisville: Westminster John Knox, 2009), 106–25; Lawrence M. Wills, *Not God's People: Insiders and Outsiders in the*

conceptual framework in biblical studies, except, not surprisingly, among scholars of color.[7] Because of the vastness of the literature, I will be able

Biblical World, Religion in the Modern World (Lanham, MD: Rowman & Littlefield, 2008). See the essays in L. Juliana M. Claassens and Carolyn J. Sharp, eds., *Feminist Frameworks: Celebrating Intersectionality, Interrogating Power, Embracing Ambiguity*, LHBOTS 621 (New York: Bloomsbury T&T Clark, 2017); and, in the special issue *BibInt* 18.4/5 (2010): Denise Buell, Jennifer Glancy, Marianne Bjelland Kartzow, and Halvor Moxnes, "Introduction: Cultural Complexity and Intersectionality in the Study of the Jesus Movement," 309–12; Kartzow, "'Asking the Other Question': An Intersectional Approach to Galatians 3:28 and the Colossian Household Codes," 364–89. See also Joseph A. Marchal, "Pinkwashing Paul, Excepting Jesus: The Politics of Intersectionality, Identification, and Respectability," in *The Bible and Feminism: Remapping the Field*, ed. Yvonne Sherwood and Anna Fisk (Oxford: Oxford University Press, 2017), 433–53.

7. Among US feminist scholars of color, see Delores S. Williams, "Hagar in African American Biblical Appropriation," in *Hagar, Sarah, and Their Children: Jewish, Christian and Muslim Perspectives*, ed. Phyllis Trible and Letty M. Russell (Louisville: Westminster John Knox, 2006), 171–84; Renita J. Weems, "The Hebrew Women Are Not like the Egyptian Women: The Ideology of Race, Gender and Sexual Reproduction in Exodus 1," *Semeia* 59 (1992): 25–34; Ahida Calderón Pilarski, "A Latina Biblical Critic and Intellectual: At the Intersection of Ethnicity, Gender, Hermeneutics, and Faith," in *Latino/a Biblical Hermeneutics: Problematics, Objectives, Strategies*, ed. Francisco Lozada and Fernando F. Segovia, SemeiaSt 68 (Atlanta: SBL Press, 2014), 231–42; M. I. Rey, "Reexamination of the Foreign Female Captive: Deuteronomy 21:10–14 as a Case of Genocidal Rape," *JFSR* 32 (2016): 37–53. See the essays in the following collections: Randall C. Bailey, Tat-siong Benny Liew, and Fernando F. Segovia, eds., *They Were All Together in One Place? Toward Minority Biblical Criticism*, SemeiaSt 57 (Atlanta: Society of Biblical Literature, 2009); Gay L. Byron and Vanessa Lovelace, eds., *Womanist Interpretations of the Bible: Expanding the Discourse*, SemeiaSt 85 (Atlanta: SBL Press, 2016); Gale A. Yee, ed., *The Hebrew Bible: Feminist and Intersectional Perspectives* (Minneapolis: Fortress, 2018); Jin Young Choi and Mitzi J. Smith, eds., *Minoritized Women Reading Race and Ethnicity: Intersectional Approaches to Constructed Identity and Early Christian Texts*, Feminist Studies and Sacred Texts (Lanham, MD: Lexington, 2020).

Concepts of intersectionality have been well established in Africa, Asia, and the Pacific even if the terminology is American. Dalit women in India have been researched for many years, bringing caste into the picture. See, e.g., Anne Pattel-Gray, "Not Yet Tiddas: An Aboriginal Womanist Critique of Australian Church Feminism," in *Freedom and Entrapment: Women Thinking Theology*, ed. Maryanne Confoy, Dorothy Lee, and Joan Nowotny (Melbourne: Dove, 1995), 165–92; Monica Jyotsna Melanchthon, "Indian Dalit Women and the Bible," in *Gender, Religion and Diversity: Cross-Cultural Perspectives*, ed. Ursula King and Tina Beattie (London: Continuum, 2004), 212–24; Melanchthon, "Toward Mapping Feminist Biblical Interpretations in Asia," in *Femi-*

only to introduce you to this field of study in this address.[8] I will first discuss intersectionality in the legal field where the term was first used, consider its assumptions as an analytical tool, and finally apply it to a particular text for its potential contributions to biblical studies.

The term *intersectionality* was coined by African American lawyer Kimberlé Crenshaw in 1989.[9] However, the interconnections among gender, race, and class had been explored by African American theorists and other women of color long before the term became fashionable.[10] In the case of *DeGraffenreid v. General Motors*, involving five black women who unsuccessfully sued General Motors for race discrimination, Crenshaw argued that the single-axis framework that dominated antidiscrimination law erased the experiences of black women. Because General Motors did hire black men and did hire women—albeit *white* women, the company maintained that it did not discriminate against these black women. The company therefore saw no need to recognize black women as a distinct social group.

Crenshaw argued that both feminist theory and antiracism politics fell into single-axis thinking by equating racism with what happened to black men and by equating sexism with what happened to white women. Neither of these positions was able "to respond to the very visible invisibility

nist Biblical Studies in the Twentieth Century: Scholarship and Movement, ed. Elisabeth Schüssler Fiorenza, BW 9.1 (Atlanta: Society of Biblical Literature, 2014), 205–19; Madipoane Masenya, "The Bible, HIV/AIDS and African/South African Women: A Bosadi Approach," *Studia Historiae Ecclesiasticae* 31 (2005): 187–201.

8. See the bibliographies in Sumi Cho, Kimberlé Williams Crenshaw, and Leslie McCall, "Toward a Field of Intersectionality Studies: Theory, Applications, and Praxis," *Signs* 38 (2013): 785–810; Vivian M. May, *Pursuing Intersectionality, Unsettling Dominant Imaginaries*, Contemporary Sociological Perspectives (New York: Routledge, 2015); Patricia Hill Collins and Sirma Bilge, *Intersectionality*, Key Concepts (Oxford: Polity, 2016); Ange-Marie Hancock, *Intersectionality: An Intellectual History* (New York: Oxford University Press, 2016); Ashley J. Bohrer, "Intersectionality and Marxism: A Critical Historiography," *Historical Materialism* 26 (2018): 46–74; Jennifer C. Nash, *Black Feminism Reimagined: After Intersectionality*, Next Wave New Directions in Women's Studies (Durham, NC: Duke University Press, 2019).

9. Kimberlé Crenshaw, "Demarginalizing the Intersection of Race and Sex," *University of Chicago Legal Forum* 41 (1989): 139–67.

10. See Angela Y. Davis, *Women, Race and Class* (New York: Vintage, 1981); Audre Lorde, *Sister Outsider: Essays and Speeches*, Crossing Press Feminist Series (Trumansburg, NY: Crossing Press, 1984); bell hooks, *Feminist Theory: From Margin to Center* (Boston: South End, 1984).

of women who were not white and blacks who were not men."[11] White feminist theory in particular tended to approach multiple oppressions by ranking them hierarchically, treating one form of oppression as earlier or more significant than others. For example, Andrea Dworkin claimed that "sexism is the foundation on which all tyranny is built."[12] Another way of dealing with multiple oppressions, variously known as the "pop-bead" or "Tootsie Roll" approach, was simply adding gender, race, and class oppressions together and describing people as doubly or triply oppressed.[13] To advance beyond such thinking, Crenshaw used the concept of intersectionality to denote the various ways in which race and gender interacted to shape multiple dimensions of black women's experiences.[14]

Intersectional analyses make the fundamental point that we all have many important facets to our identities that are impacted differently by multiple interacting systems of oppression and privilege depending on the various aspects of our identities.[15] Scholars have extended intersectionality beyond race and gender to include class, sexual orientation, nation, citizenship, immigration status, disability, and religion. They have also enlisted intersectionality to investigate the various oppressions associated with these aspects: classicism, homophobia, xenophobia, nativism, ageism, ableism, and Islamophobia.[16] Intersectionality has been recog-

---

11. Kimberlé Crenshaw, "Postscript," in *Framing Intersectionality: Debates on a Multi-Faceted Concept in Gender Studies*, ed. Helma Lutz, Maria Teresa Herrera Vivar, and Linda Supik, Feminist Imagination: Europe and Beyond (London: Routledge, 2016), 225.

12. Andrea Dworkin, *Our Blood: Prophecies and Discourses on Sexual Politics* (repr. New York: Perigree, 1981), 67–68.

13. Elizabeth V. Spelman, *Inessential Woman: Problems of Exclusion in Feminist Thought* (Boston: Beacon, 1988), 114–32; Deborah King, "Multiple Jeopardy: The Context of a Black Feminist Ideology," in *Feminist Frameworks: Alternative Theoretical Accounts of Relations between Women and Men*, ed. Alison M. Jaggar and Paula S. Rothenberg, 3rd ed. (New York: McGraw-Hill, 1993), 220–36; Nira Yuval-Davis, "Intersectionality and Feminist Politics," *European Journal of Women's Studies* 13 (2006): 194–96.

14. Kimberlé Crenshaw, "Mapping the Margins: Intersectionality, Identity Politics, and Violence against Women of Color," in *Critical Race Theory: The Key Writings That Formed the Movement*, ed. Kimberlé Crenshaw et al. (New York: New Press, 1995), 357–83.

15. Ann Garry, "Intersectionality, Metaphors, and the Multiplicity of Gender," *Hypatia* 26 (2011): 827.

16. Devon W. Carbado, "Colorblind Intersectionality," *Signs* 38 (2013): 814–15.

nized as a productive model in a number of disciplinary fields such as history, sociology, literature, philosophy, and anthropology, in addition to feminist studies, ethnic studies, queer studies, as well as legal studies, where the term was coined.

1. Assumptions

Given the wide range of disciplines adopting intersectional thinking into their methodologies, African American sociologist Patricia Hill Collins provides a helpful provisional list of the assumptions guiding different intersectional analyses.[17] You will note how these assumptions build on each other regarding their analyses of power.

- Race, class, gender, sexuality, age, ability, nation, ethnicity, and similar categories of analysis are best understood in relational terms rather than in isolation from one another.
- These mutually constructing categories underlie and shape intersecting systems of power; the power relations of racism and sexism, for example, are interrelated.
- Intersecting systems of power, such as racism and sexism, catalyze social formations of complex social inequalities. These social formations are organized by means of unequal material realities and the distinctive social experiences for people who live within them.
- Because social formations of complex social inequalities are historically contingent and cross-culturally specific, unequal material realities and social experiences vary across time and space.
- Individuals and groups who are placed differently within intersecting systems of power have diverse points of view on their own and others' experiences with complex social inequalities, typically advancing projects that reflect their social locations within power relations.
- The complex social inequalities fostered by intersecting systems of power are fundamentally unjust, shaping projects and/or political engagements that uphold or contest the status quo.[18]

17. Patricia Hill Collins, "Intersectionality's Definitional Dilemmas," *Annual Review of Sociology* 41 (2015): 1–20, here 14.

18. We can see some of these assumptions at work in the opening statement of the Declaration of the NGO (Nongovernmental Organization) Forum of the UN

Individual endeavors will embody one, some, or all of these assumptions in their intersectional analyses. I especially draw your attention to the last assumption: that the complex social inequalities fostered by intersecting systems of power are fundamentally unjust. Intersectionality has deep activist roots to combat these unjust systems of power.[19] Vivian May is quite explicit about intersectionality as being a "justice-oriented approach" for social analysis and critique and for political strategizing and organizing.[20] Intersectionality grew out of movements with a social justice agenda such as those focused on civil rights and women's rights.[21] It should not be depoliticized simply as a general abstract theory, as it has been in some learned sectors, neutralizing its political edge and its potential for social justice–oriented change.[22] It is this activist element of intersectionality that impels my work toward disrupting dominance and challenging systemic inequality in today's world.

2. No Escaping Intersectionality

In a 2006 essay, I maintained that one of the challenges in counteracting the racism against and the internalized oppression of Asian Americans was making "whiteness" visible as a culturally constructed ethnic identity. Many white people do not consciously see themselves or their conceptual

---

Conference on Racism in 2001 under the topic of gender: "119. An intersectional approach to discrimination acknowledges that every person be it man or woman exists in a framework of multiple identities, with factors such as race, class, ethnicity, religion, sexual orientation, gender identity, age, disability, citizenship, national identity, geopolitical context, health, including HIV/AIDS status and any other status are all determinants in one's experiences of racism, racial discrimination, xenophobia and related intolerances. An intersectional approach highlights the way in which there is a simultaneous interaction of discrimination as a result of multiple identities" (quoted in Dill and Zambrana, "Critical Thinking about Inequality," 191).

19. Hancock, *Intersectionality*, 37–72.

20. May, *Pursuing Intersectionality*, 228; also Sirma Bilge, "Intersectionality Undone: Saving Intersectionality from Feminist Intersectionality Studies," *Du Bois Review: Social Science Research on Race* 10 (2013): 407.

21. Dill and Zambrana, "Critical Thinking about Inequality," 183–84.

22. Bilge, "Intersectionality Undone," 405–6; Gail Lewis, "Unsafe Travel: Experiencing Intersectionality and Feminist Displacements," *Signs* 38 (2013): 869–92. However, see Jennifer Nash's critique of the "intersectionality wars," in which black feminists develop a defensive proprietary attachment to intersectionality, because of its origins in African American feminism (*Black Feminism Reimagined*, 33–58).

frameworks as raced. Instead of acknowledging its own sociohistorical production, whiteness sets itself up as *the* universal norm, disparaging all others as aberrations. Those who are white often fail to see how their racial position (pre)determines the social realities of which they are a part. Because whiteness functions incognito in our society, the burden of explaining and justifying racial differences is placed upon the hyphenated, racialized individuals themselves. I concluded this essay by stating that because Asian American biblical hermeneutics does not develop in a vacuum but is conducted within larger white institutional—and often racist—contexts, it is vital that Asian American biblical scholars make whiteness visible as a culturally constructed and racialized category.[23]

African American professor of law Devon Carbado employs the term "colorblind intersectionality" to describe any analysis that leaves whiteness as intersectionally unmarked or overlooked. Its invisibility anchors whiteness as the default and normative racial category through which gender, race, class, et cetera are expressed. In so doing, color-blind intersectionality also externalizes nonwhiteness as the racial modifier of gender, sexuality, class, and so forth. When whiteness is framed outside of intersectionality, those who are black, Asian, Latinx, et cetera are the only ones who are raced.[24]

The emphasis on interlocking relations among systems of domination therefore underscores the necessity of investigating the privileged as well as the disadvantaged, in order to attend fully to the complex and multifaceted dynamics of inequality.[25] This especially involves investigating the ideologies of white privilege and white supremacy and the structures that legitimate and sustain them.[26] The inclusion of both privilege and

---

23. Gale A. Yee, "Yin/Yang Is Not Me: An Exploration into an Asian American Biblical Hermeneutics," in *Ways of Being, Ways of Reading: Asian-American Biblical Interpretation*, ed. Mary F. Foskett and Jeffrey K. Kuan (Saint Louis: Chalice, 2006), 161–62.

24. Carbado, "Colorblind Intersectionality," 823–24.

25. Patricia Hill Collins and Valerie Chepp, "Intersectionality," in *The Oxford Handbook of Gender and Politics*, ed. Georgina Waylen et al. (Oxford: Oxford University Press, 2013), 65; Hae Yeon Choo and Myra Marx Ferree, "Practicing Intersectionality in Sociological Research: A Critical Analysis of Inclusions, Interactions, and Institutions in the Study of Inequalities," *Sociological Theory* 28 (2010): 139–42.

26. Angelina E. Castagno coined the term *powerblindness* to refer to the reluctance and avoidance of race, social class, language, gender, sexuality, and other politicized aspects of identity that are linked to power and the distribution of resources in

oppression in intersectionality demands that white members of dominant groups must consider the factors of privilege in their own identity and positionality. Intersectionality applies to *everyone*, not only to members of subordinated and marginalized groups.[27] "Addressing underprivilege requires identifying and dismantling overprivilege, within and between groups."[28] This insight is critical in approaching the initial question on inequality in the Bible that I posed at the beginning of this essay: How can the ways in which the rich obtain their wealth generate poverty, as evidenced in the biblical text and today's world?

3. The Domains of Power

According to Collins, power was basically a taken-for-granted concept in prior sociological analyses. One either had or did not have power. Intersectional sociological investigations, however, have located power relationally and complexly across multiple intersecting categories, such as race, class, and gender, which operate within different domains of social organization.[29] Investigating the different interlocking domains of power, Collins developed Crenshaw's intersectionality with her own theory of "the matrix of domination," which delineates how these intersecting oppressions are actually organized.[30]

As its name implies, the *structural* domain of power involves the institutional structures of society in arenas such as the legal, economic, and educational, and how they reproduce the subordination of peoples over time. For ancient Israelite women, it would include the patriarchal family,

---

the United States. "The notion of power and the distribution of resources are crucial in that some aspects of identity are minimally (if at all) linked to one's access to public goods and power structures. By using the term 'powerblindness,' I mean to reference those identity categories that are intimately linked to access and the distribution of power" ("Multicultural Education and the Protection of Whiteness," *American Journal of Education* 120 [2013]: 108).

27. Garry, "Intersectionality, Metaphors," 829; Sylvia Walby, Jo Armstrong, and Sofia Strid, "Intersectionality: Multiple Inequalities in Social Theory," *Sociology* 46 (2012): 230.

28. May, *Pursuing Intersectionality*, 23; See also Mary E. Hobgood, *Dismantling Privilege: An Ethics of Accountability* (Cleveland, OH: Pilgrim, 2000).

29. Collins and Chepp, "Intersectionality," 8.

30. Patricia Hill Collins, *Black Feminist Thought: Knowledge, Consciousness, and the Politics of Empowerment*, 2nd ed. (New York: Routledge, 2009), 21.

the state, the priesthood, and the scribal schools, along with the particular economic institutional forms in which these structures were situated (subsistence survival, kinship household, patronage, the [e]states, and tribute exchange).[31]

The *disciplinary* domain of power involves the ideas and practices that characterize and sustain hierarchies, the most obvious of these today are legal systems, the criminal justice system, and the police and military. As a way of governing that relies on bureaucratic hierarchies and techniques of surveillance, the disciplinary domain *manages* power relations, the goal of which is to create quiet, orderly, docile, and disciplined populations.[32] Ancient Israelite society provided its own mechanisms of surveilling its population, particularly through its religious laws that regulated women's behavior.[33] Moreover, in the separate world of Israelite women, women had their own ways to surveil and deal with their own members.[34]

The *hegemonic* domain consists of the ideas, symbols, and ideologies that shape consciousness. In order to sustain their power, dominant groups produce and disseminate a system of "reasonable" and consistent mindsets that uphold and legitimate their status and leadership.[35] These mindsets circulate in families, religious teachings, and community cultures, so much so that they become deeply entrenched and difficult to dislodge. The hegemonic domain has an important function in linking the domains of power. "By manipulating ideology and culture, the hegemonic domain acts as a link between social institutions (structural domain), their organizational practice (disciplinary domain), and the level of everyday social

31. See Roland Boer, *The Sacred Economy of Ancient Israel*, LAI (Louisville: Westminster John Knox, 2015).

32. Collins, *Black Feminist Thought*, 299–302.

33. Carolyn Pressler, *The View of Women Found in the Deuteronomic Family Laws*, BZAW 216 (Berlin: de Gruyter, 1993); Cynthia Edenburg, "Ideology and Social Context of the Deuteronomic Women's Sex Laws (Deuteronomy 22:13–29)," *JBL* 128 (2009): 43–60.

34. Gale A. Yee, *Poor Banished Children of Eve: Woman as Evil in the Hebrew Bible* (Minneapolis: Fortress, 2003), 36–56.

35. These mindsets have been described as the public transcript. See esp. James C. Scott, *Domination and the Arts of Resistance: Hidden Transcripts* (New Haven: Yale University Press, 1990), 45–69; See also Gale A. Yee, "Recovering Marginalized Groups in Ancient Israel: Methodological Considerations," in *To Break Every Yoke: Essays in Honor of Marvin L. Chaney*, ed. Robert B. Coote and Norman K. Gottwald, SWBA 2/3 (Sheffield: Sheffield Phoenix, 2007), 15–18.

interaction (interpersonal domain)."[36] My work on the symbolization of woman as evil, embedded in ideologies of kinship and honor/shame, was an attempt to analyze how this gendered and racialized abstraction was utilized in different sociopolitical arenas of power at different periods of Israelite history.[37]

The *interpersonal* domain of power refers to the interactions of people at the day-to-day microlevels of social organization. While the structural domain organizes the macrolevel with the disciplinary domain managing its operations, the interpersonal domain functions through the routine practices of how people habitually treat each other. Because of the pervasiveness of racist or sexist ideologies in the other domains, these ideologies might be so familiar and common that they are undetected in daily interactions.[38] At the interpersonal level, individual biographies are located in all domains of power, reflecting their interconnections and contradictions, and therefore they vary tremendously.

In sum, then, any particular matrix of domination was organized through four interrelated domains of power: the *structural*, the *disciplinary*, the *hegemonic*, and the *interpersonal*. "Each domain serves a particular purpose. The structural domain organizes oppression, whereas the disciplinary domain manages it. The hegemonic domain justifies oppression, and the interpersonal domain influences everyday lived experience and the individual consciousness that ensues."[39] Depending on one's social location as a gendered, raced, classed and etcetera'd individual, one must recognize that she could simultaneously be both oppressor and oppressed, powerful and powerless, because of her different and shifting locations in a matrix of domination. In a personal reflection, for example, June Jordan had different experiences of being a raced woman in the United States and then attending a resort serviced by lower-class Afro-Caribbeans in the Bahamas.[40] Collins maintains that, "once we realize that there are few pure victims or oppressors, and that each one of us derives varying amounts of penalty and privilege from the multiple systems of oppression that frame our lives, then we will be in a position to see the need for new ways of

36. Collins, *Black Feminist Thought*, 302.

37. Yee, *Poor Banished Children of Eve*.

38. Collins, *Black Feminist Thought*, 306–7.

39. Collins, *Black Feminist Thought*, 294.

40. June Jordan, "Report from the Bahamas," in McCann and Kim, *Feminist Theory Reader*, 304–12.

thought and action."[41] The simplistic model of oppressors and oppressed does not adequately deal with the complexity of the matrix of domination, which works not only along certain axes—race, gender, class, sexuality—but also through the four interconnected domains of power. Just as oppression is complex, so must resistance aimed at fostering empowerment demonstrate a similar complexity.[42] This also means that one's political activism to end oppression depends on the honest acknowledgment and exercise of one's privilege within and along these axes. Intersectionality thus not only becomes a tool to analyze oppressive domains of power but can provide the means of defying and nullifying them.

4. Application

Using 2 Kgs 4:1–7 as a springboard, I would now like to demonstrate an intersectional exploration of widows in ancient Israel by analyzing this marginal population within two of these domains of power. Because men were usually older than their wives when they married, marriages were shorter, and widowhood was commonplace.[43] I have a particular affinity for widows, because my mother became a widow upon the death of my father, leaving her a single mom with twelve children. I was twenty-four at the time, in the second year of my master's program. My youngest brother was only two years old.

In the 2 Kings narrative, a woman from the wives of Elisha's sons (or company) of prophets (בני הנביאים) appeals to Elisha, because her husband has died, and a creditor of her husband threatens to take her two children as slaves to repay her husband's debt. After learning that she only has a jar of oil in her house, Elisha instructs her to borrow many empty vessels from all her neighbors and begin filling them with the oil. The widow shuts herself and her children inside her house and begins pouring. Her son

41. Patricia Hill Collins, "Toward a New Vision: Race, Class, and Gender as Categories of Analysis and Connection," in *Social Class and Stratification: Classic Statements and Theoretical Debates*, ed. Rhonda F. Levine, 2nd ed. (Lanham, MD: Rowan & Littlefield, 2006), 232.

42. Collins, *Black Feminist Thought*, 308–9.

43. Marten Stol, *Women in the Ancient Near East*, trans. Helen Richardson and Mervyn Richardson (Berlin: de Gruyter, 2016), 277; Martha T. Roth, "The Neo-Babylonian Widow," *JCS* 43–45 (1991–1993): 4–5.

informs her that there are no more vessels, so she returns to Elisha, who tells her to sell the oil to pay her debts and live on the rest of the proceeds.

Intersectionality is concerned with relations of power, and the ways that systems of power are implicated in the development, organization, and maintenance of social inequalities. So, let us begin at the *interpersonal* domain of power in this story, which deals with the day-to-day interactions between individuals and groups. Unlike Elijah's widow in 1 Kgs 17, who is a foreigner, we do not know the ethnicity of the widow of 2 Kgs 4. We will therefore assume she is Israelite and just focus on gender and class relations here. With respect to gender, the widow in ancient Israel is not a fixed identity. She was not born a widow but was created one by the death of her husband. How she negotiates this transition will depend deeply on the ways in which structural, disciplinary, hegemonic, and interpersonal domains of power have intersectedly affected, and continue to impinge upon, her life.

Let us lay out the power configurations of dominance and subordination among these characters just within the interpersonal domain of this little story. We have relations of power between the widow and her now deceased husband, with her two children, with the creditor who wants to confiscate them, with the company of prophets,[44] with Elisha himself, with her neighbors who donate their vessels, and with the buyers who will purchase her oil and provide enough for her to repay her debt and support her and her children. We have the dead husband's relations with his creditor. A debtor, we know, works for the creditor to pay off his debt, but with the husband's death, his debt adversely affects his wife and children. We have the connections between the husband and the company of prophets to which he belonged, and the husband's relationship with Elisha and with God himself, as we will soon discover. We have Elisha's relationship with the widow and with his company of prophets. Finally, we have the power dealings of the creditor with the widow's deceased husband and with the widow and her children themselves. Each of these characters has specific locations within the power dynamics of this story.

You will notice that it will be difficult to isolate gender from economic class in this text. You have the widow's own desperate economic position, caused by her husband's death and his debt; his affiliation with the "sons

44. Wilda Gafney speculates that the wife of the dead man herself may have been a prophetic member of the sons/disciples of the prophet (*Daughters of Miriam: Women Prophets in Ancient Israel* [Minneapolis: Fortress, 2008], 39–40).

of the prophets," who are usually located by scholars on the lower, distressed rungs of society.[45] The moneylender himself is male (הנשה, *qal* ptc. masc. sg. of נשה II). At least one of the widow's children is male (2 Kgs 4:6), who would be in a position to support her economically later in life but is now able to assist her only in bringing the vessels. The deity whom the dead husband feared is male. The gender of the charitable neighbors is not specified, but one may assume that they are female by the fact that household vessels usually appear in the domain of the female.[46] We do not know the gender or the economic context of the buyers of the widow's sale of oil.[47] It is the male prophet Elisha who holds the highest socioeconomic position of power in this text, as the one to whom the widow appeals in her predicament, and who seems to be a patron supporting his clients: the company of prophets.[48]

While the ties connecting male gender and economic status are fluid in this story, it is clear that the widow is disadvantaged with respect to her gender and class within the interpersonal domain of power. Exceptions could perhaps be in her relations with her charitable neighbors and the purchasers of her oil. The widow is able to negotiate the disruptive events of her husband's death and her children's near confiscation by recognizing

---

45. Roy L. Heller, *The Characters of Elijah and Elisha and the Deuteronomic Evaluation of Prophecy: Miracles and Manipulation*, LHBOTS 671 (London: Bloomsbury T&T Clark, 2018), 115; Wesley J. Bergen, *Elisha and the End of Prophetism*, JSOTSup 286 (Sheffield: Sheffield Academic, 1999), 57–62; Norman K. Gottwald, "The Plot Structure of Marvel or Problem Resolution Stories in the Elijah-Elisha Narratives and Some Musings on *Sitz Im Leben*," in *The Hebrew Bible in Its Social World and in Ours*, SemeiaSt 25 (Atlanta: Scholars Press, 1993), 119–30; Tamis Hoover Rentería, "The Elijah/Elisha Stories: A Socio-cultural Analysis of Prophets and People in Ninth-Century B.C.E. Israel," in *Elijah and Elisha in Socioliterary Perspective*, ed. Robert B. Coote, SemeiaSt 22 (Atlanta: Scholars Press, 1992), 114–16.

46. Thus Carol L. Meyers, "Guilds and Gatherings: Women's Groups in Ancient Israel," in *Realia Dei: Essays in Archaeology and Biblical Interpretation in Honor of Edward F. Campbell, Jr. at His Retirement*, ed. Prescott H. Williams Jr. and Theodore Hiebert, Scholars Press Homage Series 23 (Atlanta: Scholars Press, 1999), 175.

47. Roger S. Nam, *Portrayals of Economic Exchange in the Book of Kings*, BibInt 112 (Leiden: Brill, 2011), 16.

48. Gale A. Yee, "The Elijah and Elisha Narratives: An Economic Investigation," in *Honouring the Past, Looking to the Future: Essays from the 2014 International Congress of Ethnic Chinese Biblical Scholars*, ed. Gale A. Yee and John Y. H. Yieh, Chuen King Lectures Series 12 (Shatin N. T., Hong Kong: Divinity School of Chung Chi College, The Chinese University of Hong Kong, 2016), 40.

her best hope, namely, appealing to her husband's male economic patron. She does this by cleverly working to her advantage the inequitable relations of the patron/client system[49] and religious ideologies of her time. To remind Elisha of his responsibilities for her husband as patron, she informs Elisha that her husband, "your servant," has died, and that Elisha *knows* "that your servant feared the Lord." She then galvanizes Elisha's conscience as a "man of God" (4:7) by informing him that a creditor "has come to take my two children as slaves" (4:1). As was previously mentioned, individual biographies vary considerably at the interpersonal domain of power. Because of interconnections with her husband's membership in the company of prophets, the widow is able to secure Elisha's patronage through her rhetorical dexterity. Under his direction, she finds resources among her neighbors, is able to sell her oil, and ultimately resolves her impoverishment and the threat of losing her children.

Not all narratives about widows end positively, however. The widow's story in 2 Kgs 4:1–7 was added primarily to exalt Elisha's wondrous power as Elijah's prophetic successor.[50] When one moves to the three other domains of power—the structural, disciplinary,[51] and hegemonic[52]—the

49. Ronald A. Simkins, "Patronage and the Political Economy of Monarchic Israel," *Semeia* 87 (1999): 123–44; Boer, *Sacred Economy of Ancient Israel*, 105–8; James Scott, "Patronage or Exploitation?," in *Patrons and Clients in Mediterranean Societies*, ed. Ernest Gellner and John Waterbury (London: Duckworth, 1977), 21–39.

50. Steven L. McKenzie, *1 Kings 16–2 Kings 16*, IECOT (Stuttgart: Kohlhammer, 2019), 281–83; Walter Brueggemann, *1 and 2 Kings*, SHBC (Macon, GA: Smyth & Helwys, 2000), 319.

51. Regarding the disciplinary domain, see the laws about the widow in Ronald A. Simkins, "The Widow and Orphan in the Political Economy of Ancient Israel," *Journal of Religion and Society* 10 (2014): 20–33; Roy L. Heller, "'The Widow' in Deuteronomy: Beneficiary of Compassion and Co-Option," in *The Impartial God: Essays in Biblical Studies in Honor of Jouette M. Bassler*, ed. Calvin J. Roetzel and Robert L. Foster, New Testament Monographs (Sheffield: Sheffield Phoenix, 2007), 1–11; Harold V. Bennett, *Injustice Made Legal: Deuteronomic Law and the Plight of Widows, Strangers, and Orphans in Ancient Israel*, Bible in Its World (Grand Rapids: Eerdmans, 2002); Mark Sneed, "Israelite Concern for the Alien, Orphan, and Widow: Altruism or Ideology?," *ZAW* 111 (1999): 498–507.

52. Regarding the ideologies about widows in the hegemonic domain, see Marjo Buitelaar, "Widows' Worlds: Representations and Realities," in *Between Poverty and the Pyre: Moments in the History of Widowhood*, ed. Jan Bremmer and Lourens van den Bosch (London: Routledge, 1995), 1–18; and, in the same volume, Karel van der Toorn, "The Public Image of the Widow in Ancient Israel," 19–30. See also Van

social disadvantages of the Israelite widow become more complex and multidimensional. Let us discuss her positionality within the *structural* domains of power. Fortunately, much research has already been done on the structural location of the widow in the institutions of the patriarchal family in ancient Israel[53] and Southwest Asia.[54] Instead, let us contextualize the widow within the power structures of the Israelite state that is implied in this story. Because 2 Kgs 4:1–7 was set during the time of Elisha, let us for the sake of argument situate the ancient Israelite widow in the socioeconomic conditions during the preexilic monarchy.[55]

During this period, two economic systems conflicted with each other, the allocative subsistence survival and the extractive state.[56] The state extracted a significant portion of goods from the villages and the agricultural estates, which were then redistributed upward to the rich and powerful of the court, temple, army, and other state institutions.[57]

der Toorn, "Torn between Vice and Virtue: Stereotypes of the Widow in Israel and Mesopotamia," in *Female Stereotypes in Religious Traditions*, ed. Ria Kloppenborg and Wouter J. Hanegraaff, SHR 66 (Leiden: Brill, 1995), 1–13.

53. Pnina Galpaz-Feller, "The Widow in the Bible and in Ancient Egypt," *ZAW* 120 (2008): 232–40; Naomi Steinberg, "Romancing the Widow: The Economic Distinctions between the *'Almānâ,* the *'Iššâ-'almānâ* and the *'Ēšet-Hammēt,*" in *God's Word for Our World*, ed. J. Harold Ellens et al., 2 vols., JSOTSup 388, 389 (London: T&T Clark, 2004), 327–46; Carolyn S. Leeb, "The Widow: Homeless and Post-Menopausal," *BTB* 32 (2002): 160–62; John Rook, "When Is a Widow Not a Widow? Guardianship Provides an Answer," *BTB* 28 (1998): 4–6; Rook, "Making Widows: The Patriarchal Guardian at Work," *BTB* 27 (1997): 10–15; Paula S. Hiebert, "'Whence Shall Help Come to Me?' The Biblical Widow," in *Gender and Difference in Ancient Israel*, ed. Peggy L. Day (Minneapolis: Fortress, 1989), 125–41.

54. Stol, *Women in the Ancient Near East*, 275–95; Jonathan S. Tenney, *Life at the Bottom of Babylonian Society: Servile Labour at Nippur in the Fourteenth and Thirteenth Centuries BC*, CHANE 51 (Leiden: Brill, 2011), 78–79, 90–91; Galpaz-Feller, "Widow in the Bible," 240–50; Hennie J. Marsman, *Women in Ugarit and Israel: Their Social and Religious Position in the Context of the Ancient Near East*, OtSt 49 (Leiden: Brill, 2003), 299–320; Roth, "Neo-Babylonian Widow," 1–26.

55. See Rentería, "Elijah/Elisha Stories," 114–15.

56. See Boer, *Sacred Economy of Ancient Israel*, 110–45.

57. Regarding the royal estates, see Izabela Jaruzelska, *Amos and the Officialdom in the Kingdom of Israel: The Socio-economic Position of the Officials in the Light of the Biblical, the Epigraphic and Archaeological Evidence*, Seria Socjologia 25 (Poznán: Adam Mickiewicz University, 1998), 169–75; see also Yigal Moyal and Avraham Faust, "Jerusalem's Hinterland in the Eighth-Seventh Centuries BCE: Towns, Villages, Farmsteads, and Royal Estates," *PEQ* 147 (2015): 283–98.

The royal estates were farmed by tenants or indentured servants, many of whom were debt slaves unable to keep up with tax payments, which forced them to lose their land.[58] The husband of the widow in 2 Kgs 4:1–7 was probably one of these. Besides the extraction of material goods, state economics would also be based on the extraction of male labor from the villages as farmers for the royal plantations, as workers for the king's building projects, as soldiers for his military campaigns, and other ventures of the court (see 1 Sam 8:11–18).[59] Along with the natural vagaries of farming, such as drought, blight, and the like, the diversion of labor from the villages to service the royal farms, the kings' building ventures, their wars, and so on, put a significant strain on the rural sectors of the nation. This strain intensified when the state had to increase the taxation of the people in order to meet the tribute demands of Assyrian imperialism (2 Kgs 15:19–20, 18:13–16).[60] The tax collectors and other officials functioning in the disciplinary domain often used coercive and violent means to keep up the extraction.[61]

The narratives were usually silent about how women became widows, but we can speculate on the socioeconomic conditions that created and oppressed them during this period. In the case of the foreign widow of 1 Kgs 17, her husband might have died of illness or malnutrition from the famine in the Levant that threatened her son. That particular drought lasted three years (1 Kgs 18:1; cf. Luke 4:25). Although we know that famine can be the result of environmental factors, it is often the result of human political strife, such as war.[62] The narratives of Elijah and Elisha were full of accounts of Israel's battles with its neighbors, some of which can be confirmed archaeologically.[63] Such wars wreaked havoc on Israel's

58. Gregory C. Chirichigno, *Debt-Slavery in Israel and the Ancient Near East*, JSOTSup 141 (Sheffield: JSOT Press, 1993), 142–44.

59. Boer, *Sacred Economy of Ancient Israel*, 118–21; Jaruzelska, *Amos and the Officialdom*, 166–69.

60. Boer, *Sacred Economy of Ancient Israel*, 146–56.

61. Jaruzelska, *Amos and the Officialdom*, 146–52.

62. Carlo Zaccagnini, "War and Famine at Emar," *Or* 64 (1995): 92–109; Peter Garnsey, "Responses to Food Crisis in the Ancient Mediterranean World," in *Hunger in History: Food Shortage, Poverty, and Deprivation*, ed. Lucile F. Newman (Oxford: Blackwell, 1995), 1–2.

63. Amihai Mazar, "The Divided Monarchy: Comments on Some Archaeological Issues," in *The Quest for the Historical Israel: Debating Archaeology and the History of Early Israel; Invited Lectures Delivered at the Sixth Biennial Colloquium of the Inter-*

fragile ecosystem, causing famine and starvation, especially when springs of water were stopped, fruitful trees cut down, and the land despoiled (2 Kgs 3:18–19, 25). During these wars, husbands might have perished as soldiers or as victims of the numerous military conflicts that swept through the land (1 Kgs 20; 22; 2 Kgs 6:24–7:20). The cannibal women of 2 Kgs 6:24–30 could very well have been widows who lost their husbands to the siege, famine, and disease of Samaria.

On the other hand, husbands might have died in the corvée (unpaid) labor camps of the state. Building the palaces, fortresses, and cities of kings required an enormous investment of male labor in particular (1 Kgs 16:24, 32; 22:39).[64] According to 1 Kgs 5:13–18, Solomon conscripted thirty thousand men for his building projects, sending them to Lebanon in shifts of ten thousand to cut cedar, spending one month in Lebanon and two months at home.[65] He also had seventy thousand laborers and eight thousand stonecutters, with three thousand three hundred overseeing their work.

One could infer from the texts that a considerable portion of the male population was diverted from food production to the king's military campaigns and building projects, putting a significant stress on the agrarian basis of Israel's economy. Men's untimely deaths resulting from famine, war, backbreaking labor in foreign lands or in domestic building ventures, and other demands of male state power undoubtedly increased the number of destitute widows in ancient Israel.[66] Moreover, if the corvée labor was

---

national Institute for Secular Humanistic Judaism, Detroit, 2005, by Israel Finkelstein, Amihai Mazar, and Brian B. Schmidt, ABS 17 (Atlanta: Society of Biblical Literature, 2007), 169–74.

64. Regarding the building projects of the Omrides, see Israel Finkelstein, *The Forgotten Kingdom: The Archaeology and History of Northern Israel*, ANEM 5 (Atlanta: Society of Biblical Literature, 2013), 85–105.

65. J. Alberto Soggin, "Compulsory Labor under David and Solomon," in *Studies in the Period of David and Solomon and Other Essays: Papers Read at the International Symposium for Biblical Studies, Tokyo, 5–7 December, 1979*, ed. Tomoo Ishida (Winona Lake, IN: Eisenbrauns, 1982), 259–67; Serge Frolov, "'They Will Be Yours for Corvée and Serve You': Forced Labor in the Hebrew Bible, Modern America, and Twentieth-Century Communist States," in *La Violencia and the Hebrew Bible: The Politics and Histories of Biblical Hermeneutics on the American Continent*, ed. Susanne Scholz and Pablo R. Andiñach, SemeiaSt 82 (Atlanta: SBL Press, 2016), 163–84, on Deut 20:10–14 in particular.

66. See Zaccagnini, "War and Famine at Emar," 100–101.

composed of ethnically diverse populations in the north who were subjected to discriminatory treatment, the "foreignness" of the widows must be considered in the power relations of the state, along with her gender and class.[67]

The אלמנה was a woman who had sunk to the lowest economic level of widows in ancient Israel.[68] She might have had living male relatives, but they were either too poor to help or unwilling to offer her financial support.[69] Holding no family plots, she could not subsist off the land. Within the structural domain of male state power, how did the landless אלמנה support herself economically? How could the אלמנה negotiate the power structures that engendered widowhood and her vulnerable status?

If she was childless, she could return to her paternal kin (cf. Gen 38:11), who really had no legal obligations to support her.[70] The same is true if she had children. Her parents may not see themselves accountable for the offspring of another man's patriline.[71] An אלמנה could beg (Job 22:9, 31:16–17). She could try to remarry[72] or maybe find a man to live with.[73] If it happened to be harvest time, she could go out to glean in the fields, or into the vineyards, or gather from the olive trees (Deut 24:19–21,

67. Walter J. Houston, "Corvée in the Kingdom of Israel: Israelites, 'Canaanites', and Cultural Memory," *JSOT* 43 (2018): 29–44.

68. Steinberg, "Romancing the Widow," 1–2. The widow of 2 Kgs 4:1–8 would have been designated an אשה אלמנה, a widow who has redemption rights in her husband's ancestral estate which she exercises through her son. However, the husband seems to have forfeited his land to his creditor and was trying to pay off his debt. One hopes that the oil that the widow sells not only pays off the debt but secures the land again for her son.

69. Regarding the unwillingness of a *levir* to marry the widow of his male relative, see Dvora E. Weisberg, "The Widow of Our Discontent: Levirate Marriage in the Bible and Ancient Israel," *JSOT* 28 (2004): 403–29; Ayelet Seidler, "The Law of Levirate and Forced Marriage—Widow vs. Levir in Deuteronomy 25.5–10," *JSOT* 42 (2018): 435–56.

70. In contrast to a priest's daughter or a divorced woman, who may return to her father's house and eat of her father's food, "as in her youth" (Lev 22:13).

71. Galpaz-Feller, "Widow in the Bible," 237.

72. Cf. Abigail (2 Sam 25:39–42) and Ruth (Ruth 4). If she was a widow of a layman, she was out of luck if she wanted to marry a priest (Lev 21:14).

73. In a Middle Assyrian law book §34: "If a man has taken a widow, but no binding agreement has been made, and she has lived for two years in his house, then she is his wife. She shall not leave." Cited in Stol, *Women in the Ancient Near East*, 290. There is no comparable law in the Hebrew Bible.

Lev 19:9–10). Along with the Levites, resident aliens, and orphans, widows were entitled to a tithe of all produce and could eat their fill every three years (Deut 14:28–29, 26:12–15). Even if these laws of the disciplinary domain sought to protect and provide for the widow, they did not address the socioeconomic conditions of the state that created the widow in the first place. The laws sought only to maintain the existing socioeconomic order rather than transform it.[74] Moreover, what if it was not harvest time or what if the land was going through a drought, plague, or famine, and gleaning in the field was not an option? Or what if the third year of tithe was two years in the offing? Instead of waiting two years, what else could an אלמנה do to feed herself and her children? In the intersectional economics of widowhood, what manner of work was open to her?

I am sure that, for many of you, the world's oldest profession sprang to mind. Prostitution did indeed exist particularly in societies, like ancient Israel's, in which marriage was central and women's premarital chastity and marital fidelity were mandated.[75] It was a common resort of women in economic straits, normally associated with widowhood or loss of family support, through the death of a responsible male or separation from the household.[76] Prostitution was thus interconnected with structural conditions of economic and gender inequality, which were reinforced in the hegemonic domain by various ideologies.[77] When most women were sexually unavailable, the demand by men for extramarital sex was there. "On the supply side, there were destitute vulnerable women—the widows and orphan girls whom rulers traditionally claimed to protect—as well, no doubt, as wives and daughters from impoverished families who saw no other alternative, and dependent women whose parents or owners might earn income from their sale of sexual favors."[78] Gerhard Lenski included

---

74. Simkins, "Widow and Orphan," 28–29.

75. Phyllis A. Bird, "Prostitution in the Social World and Religious Rhetoric of Ancient Israel," in *Prostitutes and Courtesans in the Ancient World*, ed. Christopher A. Faraone and Laura K. McClure, Wisconsin Studies in Classics (Madison: University of Wisconsin Press, 2006), 40–58; Bird, "The Harlot as Heroine: Narrative Art and Social Presupposition in Three Old Testament Texts," *Semeia* 46 (1989): 119–39; Bird, "'To Play the Harlot': An Inquiry into an Old Testament Metaphor," in Day, *Gender and Difference*, 75–94.

76. Phyllis Bird, "Of Whores and Hounds: A New Interpretation of the Subject of Deuteronomy 23:19," *VT* 65 (2015): 356–57.

77. Van der Toorn, "Torn between Vice and Virtue," 1–13.

78. Jerrold S. Cooper, "The Job of Sex: The Social and Economic Role of Pros-

prostitutes in the degraded class of persons in agrarian societies who had only their bodies to sell and were forced to accept occupations that quickly destroyed them.[79]

Besides prostitution, there were other forms of labor open to the אלמנה trying to survive in an extractive state and having no recourse to the resources of the kinship household. The administrative records of the palace, temple, and estates in Mesopotamia detailed the numerous jobs and activities of female labor needed to keep the institutions running and the number of rations that kept these women at subsistence level.[80] Unfortunately, we do not have similar records for ancient Israel. We have only clues in the biblical texts. The prophet Samuel warned the people that a king would seize their sons for his military machine and to farm his estates. Their daughters would staff the royal kitchens as "flavorers,[81] cooks, and bakers" (1 Sam 8:11–13). I have already detailed the backbreaking labor of female grain grinders for these kitchens.[82] According to Karel van der Toorn, many destitute widows found work in mill houses grinding flour for the Mesopotamian temple and palace, but "life there was hardly pleasant."[83] Commenting on the picture of the large grain-grinding installation at Ebla, Jerrold Cooper remarks that it exhibited one of the most depressing glimpses of the life of ancient women, who spent their days at hard, monotonous labor turning grain into flour.[84] Although there is no

---

titutes in Ancient Mesopotamia," in *The Role of Women in Work and Society in the Ancient Near East*, ed. Brigitte Lion and Cécile Michel, Studies in Ancient Near Eastern Records 13 (Berlin: de Gruyter, 2016), 210–11.

79. Gerhard Lenski, *Power and Privilege: A Theory of Social Stratification* (Chapel Hill: University of North Carolina Press, 1966), 281.

80. See the various essays in Lion and Michel, *Role of Women in Work and Society in the Ancient Near East*, and note the thirteen-page Index of Professions and Activities (366–78). Stol, *Women in the Ancient Near East*, 339–90; Marsman, *Women in Ugarit and Israel*, 404–37.

81. See Nathan MacDonald, "Feasting Fit for a King," in *Not Bread Alone: The Uses of Food in the Old Testament* (Oxford: Oxford University Press, 2008), 164.

82. Yee, "'He Will Take the Best,'" 834–37.

83. Van der Toorn, "Torn between Vice and Virtue," 3–4; See also Robert K. Englund, "Hard Work—Where Will It Get You? Labor Management in Ur III Mesopotamia," *JNES* 50 (1991): 270–73; Francis Joannès, "Historiography on Studies Dedicated to Women and Economy during the Neo-Babylonian Period," in Lion and Michel, *Role of Women in Work and Society in the Ancient Near East*, 466–67.

84. Cooper, "Job of Sex," 210. The picture of the Ebla grinding room can also be viewed in Stol, *Women in the Ancient Near East*, 350.

archaeological evidence for them, milling houses may have operated in Judah. Judean prisoners of war were sent to work in such mills in Babylonia (Isa 42:7, Ps 107:10–16, Lam 5:13). Samson was sent to grind in such a prison in Gaza (Judg 16:21).[85]

The temple played a social role in sixth-century Babylonia, where dependent elderly persons could finish out their lives.[86] Van der Toorn thinks that the Jerusalem temple could have provided similar shelter for widows. The prophet Anna in Luke 2:36–38 was a widow who supposedly "never left the temple."[87] According to 1 Chr 9:28–32, 23:29, Levitical gatekeepers[88] were responsible for the choice flour (סלת; cf. 1 Kgs 3:22), flat-cakes (חבתים), unleavened bread (מצות) and rows of bread (לחם) for the temple services. As we saw in our discussion of how women become widows, intersectionality involves a creative imagination to recognize how gender, race, class, et cetera are interwoven within the interpersonal and structural domains of power. Imagination can be a critical skill for seeing the possibility of certain experiences even if we cannot know the specificity of them.[89] Might we then imagine many widows included in the hundreds of women deployed in milling grain into choice flour, and in the kitchens baking the cakes and bread daily used in the Jerusalem temple? Might we then imagine widows with other women grinding grain for bread sold

85. Jennie R. Ebeling and Yorke M. Rowan, "The Archaeology of the Daily Grind: Ground Stone Tools and Food Production in the Southern Levant," *NEA* 672 (2004): 109.

86. Joannès, "Historiography on Studies Dedicated to Women," 466; Martha Roth has suggested that widows could be sheltered in a social institution called *bīt mār banî* (Martha T. Roth, "Women in Transition and the *Bīt Mār Banî*," *RA* 82 [1988]: 131–38; Roth, "Neo-Babylonian Widow," 24–2).

87. Van der Toorn, "Torn between Vice and Virtue," 4.

88. Regarding the "gaters," see Marty E. Stevens, *Temples, Tithes, and Taxes: The Temple and the Economic Life of Ancient Israel* (Peabody, MA: Hendrickson, 2006), 71–75.

89. See Jacqueline Jones Royster, *Traces of a Stream: Literacy and Social Change among African American Women*, Pittsburgh Series in Composition, Literacy, and Culture (Pittsburgh: University of Pittsburgh Press, 2000), 83–84: "As Erna Brodber, sociologist and novelist from Jamaica, has said: 'We must imagine the truth until a better truth comes along.' This strategy for inquiry claims a valuable place for imagination in research and scholarship—imagination as a term for a commitment to making connections and seeing possibility. So defined, imagination functions as a critical skill in questioning a viewpoint, an experience, an event, and so on, and in remaking interpretive frameworks based on that questioning."

in the city on Baker's Street (Jer 37:21)? In my speculations, I was able only to touch on three types of labor available for the אלמנה—prostitution, grain grinding, and baking. Much more intersectional work still needs to be done on widows and lower-class women in their specificities as they try to survive and live in the extractive state.

5. Conclusion

I asserted at the beginning of this address that, because inequality is embedded in intertwined relations of power, intersectionality provided me with the most useful analytical frame to investigate those complex relations of power and the inequities that arise from them. Intersectionality arose in the theorizing of black feminist intellectuals and activists on the multiple oppressions that beset black women's lives. It argued against single-axis or siloed thinking regarding gender, race, and class and other oppressions by insisting on their interconnections and mutual reinforcements. Intersectionality locates these oppressions within different domains of power: the structural, the disciplinary, the hegemonic, and the interpersonal. It investigates and unmasks relations of domination and subordination, privilege and agency, the ideologies that shape social consciousness, and the ways in which we personally interact with each other.

What I am suggesting for biblical studies is that we think "intersectionally" in our own methodological approaches to the biblical text. Thinking "intersectionally" is an invitation to rethink the main assumptions and paradigms of our field to reveal the interconnections of various forms of power. It encourages us to think beyond the familiar (or perhaps more entrenched) boundaries of biblical studies to expose the diverse power relations of oppression and uncover subjugated voices that were previously invisible or unheard. In trying to comprehend how all forms of subordination are interconnected, Asian American lawyer Mari Matsuda uses a method she calls "ask the other question":

> When I see something that looks racist, I ask, "Where is the patriarchy in this?" When I see something that looks sexist, I ask, "Where is the heterosexism in this?" When I see something that looks homophobic, I ask, "Where are the class interests in this?" Working in coalition forces us to look for both the obvious and non-obvious relationships of domination, helping us to realize that no form of subordination ever stands alone.[90]

---

90. Mari J. Matsuda, "Beside My Sister, Facing the Enemy: Legal Theory out of Coalition," *Stanford Law Review* 43.6 (1991): 1189.

Asking the other question in our biblical interpretations will assist us in thinking intersectionally. With respect to my analysis of 2 Kgs 4:1–7, I asked the other question: Where was the male power of the state in the economics of widowhood?

An intersectional hermeneutics would interrogate the social locations of the writers and how their gender, ethnicity, class, et cetera shaped their writings, reproducing and disseminating power to preserve the status quo or, as in the case of the prophets, to resist, protest, and denounce it. As a method of interpretation, intersectionality presumes that our own unique social locations, our own distinctive amalgams of gender, race, class, religion, et cetera, influence our readings of texts and our writing. Thinking "intersectionally" compels us to reflect seriously on how these fusions influence why and in what specific ways we study the Bible. It may presume that biblical scholars, like myself, want to move beyond the "academic" study of the Bible to incorporate intersectional thinking as a tool for "justice-oriented" social action and transformation. The Bible has played a major role in legitimating matrices of power across different categories of identity. My own political commitments to help eradicate inequality in our day and the matrices of power that the create it compels me to think about the Bible intersectionally. In this endeavor, I invite you to join me.

Bibliography

Bailey, Randall C., Tat-siong Benny Liew, and Fernando F. Segovia, eds. *They Were All Together in One Place? Toward Minority Biblical Criticism*. SemeiaSt 57. Atlanta: Society of Biblical Literature, 2009.

Bennett, Harold V. *Injustice Made Legal: Deuteronomic Law and the Plight of Widows, Strangers, and Orphans in Ancient Israel*. Bible in Its World. Grand Rapids: Eerdmans, 2002.

Bergen, Wesley J. *Elisha and the End of Prophetism*. JSOTSup 286. Sheffield: Sheffield Academic, 1999.

Bilge, Sirma. "Intersectionality Undone: Saving Intersectionality from Feminist Intersectionality Studies." *Du Bois Review: Social Science Research on Race* 10 (2013): 405–24.

Bird, Phyllis A. "The Harlot as Heroine: Narrative Art and Social Presupposition in Three Old Testament Texts." *Semeia* 46 (1989): 119–39.

———. "Of Whores and Hounds: A New Interpretation of the Subject of Deuteronomy 23:19." *VT* 65 (2015): 352–64.

———. "Prostitution in the Social World and Religious Rhetoric of Ancient Israel." Pages 40–58 in *Prostitutes and Courtesans in the Ancient World*. Edited by Christopher A. Faraone and Laura K. McClure. Wisconsin Studies in Classics. Madison: University of Wisconsin Press, 2006.

———. "'To Play the Harlot': An Inquiry into an Old Testament Metaphor." Pages 75–94 in *Gender and Difference in Ancient Israel*. Edited by Peggy L. Day. Minneapolis: Fortress, 1989.

Boer, Roland. *The Sacred Economy of Ancient Israe*. LAI. Louisville: Westminster John Knox, 2015.

Bohrer, Ashley J. "Intersectionality and Marxism: A Critical Historiography." *Historical Materialism* 26 (2018): 46–74.

Brueggemann, Walter. *1 and 2 Kings*. SHBC. Macon, GA: Smyth & Helwys, 2000.

Buell, Denise, Jennifer Glancy, Marianne Bjelland Kartzow, and Halvor Moxnes. "Introduction: Cultural Complexity and Intersectionality in the Study of the Jesus Movement." *BibInt* 18.4–5 (2010): 309–12.

Buitelaar, Marjo. "Widows' Worlds: Representations and Realities." Pages 1–18 in *Between Poverty and the Pyre: Moments in the History of Widowhood*. Edited by Jan Bremmer and Lourens van den Bosch. London: Routledge, 1995.

Byron, Gay L., and Vanessa Lovelace, eds. *Womanist Interpretations of the Bible: Expanding the Discourse*. SemeiaSt 85. Atlanta: SBL Press, 2016.

Calderón Pilarski, Ahida ."A Latina Biblical Critic and Intellectual: At the Intersection of Ethnicity, Gender, Hermeneutics, and Faith." Pages 231–42 in *Latino/a Biblical Hermeneutics: Problematics, Objectives, Strategies*. Edited by Francisco Lozada and Fernando F. Segovia. SemeiaSt 68. Atlanta: SBL Press, 2014.

Carbado, Devon W. "Colorblind Intersectionality." *Signs* 38 (2013): 811–45.

Castagno, Angelina E. "Multicultural Education and the Protection of Whiteness." *American Journal of Education* 120 (2013): 101–28.

Chirichigno, Gregory C. *Debt-Slavery in Israel and the Ancient Near East*. JSOTSup 141. Sheffield: JSOT Press, 1993.

Cho, Sumi, Kimberlé Williams Crenshaw, and Leslie McCall. "Toward a Field of Intersectionality Studies: Theory, Applications, and Praxis." *Signs* 38 (2013): 785–810.

Choi, Jin Young, and Mitzi J. Smith, eds. *Minoritized Women Reading Race and Ethnicity: Intersectional Approaches to Constructed Identity and*

Early Christian Texts. Feminist Studies and Sacred Texts. Lanham, MD: Lexington, 2020.

Claassens, L. Juliana M., and Carolyn J. Sharp, eds. *Feminist Frameworks: Celebrating Intersectionality, Interrogating Power, Embracing Ambiguity*. LHBOTS 621. New York: Bloomsbury T&T Clark, 2017.

Collins, Patricia Hill. *Black Feminist Thought: Knowledge, Consciousness, and the Politics of Empowerment*. 2nd ed. New York: Routledge, 2009.

———. "Intersectionality's Definitional Dilemmas." *Annual Review of Sociology* 41 (2015): 1–20.

———. "Toward a New Vision: Race, Class, and Gender as Categories of Analysis and Connection." Pages 243–58 in *Social Class and Stratification: Classic Statements and Theoretical Debates*. Edited by Rhonda F. Levine. 2nd ed. Lanham, MD: Rowan & Littlefield, 2006.

Collins, Patricia Hill, and Sirma Bilge. *Intersectionality*. Key Concepts. Oxford: Polity, 2016.

Collins, Patricia Hill, and Valerie Chepp. "Intersectionality." Pages 57–87 in *The Oxford Handbook of Gender and Politics*. Edited by Georgina Waylen et al. Oxford: Oxford University Press, 2013.

Crenshaw, Kimberlé. "Demarginalizing the Intersection of Race and Sex." *University of Chicago Legal Forum* 41 (1989): 139–67.

———. "Mapping the Margins: Intersectionality, Identity Politics, and Violence against Women of Color." Pages 357–83 in *Critical Race Theory: The Key Writings That Formed the Movement*. Edited by Kimberlé Crenshaw et al. New York: New Press, 1995.

———. "Postscript." Pages 221–33 in *Framing Intersectionality: Debates on a Multi-Faceted Concept in Gender Studies*. Edited by Helma Lutz, Maria Teresa Herrera Vivar, and Linda Supik. Feminist Imagination: Europe and Beyond. London: Routledge, 2016.

Cooper, Jerrold S. "The Job of Sex: The Social and Economic Role of Prostitutes in Ancient Mesopotamia." Pages 209–27 in *The Role of Women in Work and Society in the Ancient Near East*. Edited by Brigitte Lion and Cécile Michel. Studies in Ancient Near Eastern Records 13. Berlin: de Gruyter, 2016.

Davis, Angela Y. *Women, Race and Class*. New York: Vintage, 1981.

Dill, Bonnie Thornton and Ruth Enid Zambrana. "Critical Thinking about Inequality: An Emerging Lens." Pages 182–93 in *Feminist Theory Reader: Local and Global Perspectives*. Edited by Carol R. McCann and Seung-Kyung Kim. 4th ed. New York: Routledge, 2017.

Dworkin, Andrea. *Our Blood: Prophecies and Discourses on Sexual Politics.* Repr. New York: Perigree, 1981.

Ebeling, Jennie R., and Yorke M. Rowan. "The Archaeology of the Daily Grind: Ground Stone Tools and Food Production in the Southern Levant." *NEA* 672 (2004): 108–17.

Edenburg, Cynthia. "Ideology and Social Context of the Deuteronomic Women's Sex Laws (Deuteronomy 22:13–29)." *JBL* 128 (2009): 43–60.

Englund, Robert K. "Hard Work—Where Will It Get You? Labor Management in Ur III Mesopotamia." *JNES* 50 (1991): 270–73.

Finkelstein, Israel. *The Forgotten Kingdom: The Archaeology and History of Northern Israel.* ANEM 5. Atlanta: Society of Biblical Literature, 2013.

Frolov, Serge. "'They Will Be Yours for Corvée and Serve You': Forced Labor in the Hebrew Bible, Modern America, and Twentieth-Century Communist States." Pages 163–84 in *La Violencia and the Hebrew Bible: The Politics and Histories of Biblical Hermeneutics on the American Continent.* Edited by Susanne Scholz and Pablo R. Andiñach. SemeiaSt 82. Atlanta: SBL Press, 2016.

Gafney, Wilda. *Daughters of Miriam: Women Prophets in Ancient Israel.* Minneapolis: Fortress, 2008.

Galpaz-Feller, Pnina. "The Widow in the Bible and in Ancient Egypt." *ZAW* 120 (2008): 232–40.

Garnsey, Peter. "Responses to Food Crisis in the Ancient Mediterranean World." Pages 1–2 in *Hunger in History: Food Shortage, Poverty, and Deprivation.* Edited by Lucile F. Newman. Oxford: Blackwell, 1995.

Garry, Ann. "Intersectionality, Metaphors, and the Multiplicity of Gender." *Hypatia* 26 (2011): 826–50.

Gottwald, Norman K. "The Plot Structure of Marvel or Problem Resolution Stories in the Elijah-Elisha Narratives and Some Musings on *Sitz Im Leben.*" Pages 119–30 in *The Hebrew Bible in Its Social World and in Ours.* SemeiaSt 25. Atlanta: Scholars Press, 1993.

Hancock, Ange-Marie. *Intersectionality: An Intellectual History.* New York: Oxford University Press, 2016.

Heller, Roy L. *The Characters of Elijah and Elisha and the Deuteronomic Evaluation of Prophecy: Miracles and Manipulation.* LHBOTS 671. London: Bloomsbury T&T Clark, 2018.

———. "'The Widow' in Deuteronomy: Beneficiary of Compassion and Co-Option." Pages 1–11 in *The Impartial God: Essays in Biblical Studies in Honor of Jouette M. Bassler.* Edited by Calvin J. Roetzel and Robert

L. Foster. New Testament Monographs. Sheffield: Sheffield Phoenix, 2007.

Hiebert, Paula S. "'Whence Shall Help Come to Me?' The Biblical Widow." Pages 125–41 in *Gender and Difference in Ancient Israel*. Edited by Peggy L. Day. Minneapolis: Fortress, 1989.

Hobgood, Mary E. *Dismantling Privilege: An Ethics of Accountability*. Cleveland, OH: Pilgrim, 2000.

hooks, bell. *Feminist Theory: From Margin to Center*. Boston: South End, 1984.

Houston, Walter J. "Corvée in the Kingdom of Israel: Israelites, 'Canaanites', and Cultural Memory." *JSOT* 43 (2018): 29–44.

Jaruzelska, Izabela. *Amos and the Officialdom in the Kingdom of Israel: The Socio-economic Position of the Officials in the Light of the Biblical, the Epigraphic and Archaeological Evidence*. Seria Socjologia 25. Poznán: Adam Mickiewicz University, 1998.

Joannès, Francis. "Historiography on Studies Dedicated to Women and Economy during the Neo-Babylonian Period." Pages 459–72 in *The Role of Women in Work and Society in the Ancient Near East*. Edited by Brigitte Lion and Cécile Michel. Studies in Ancient Near Eastern Records 13. Berlin: de Gruyter, 2016.

Jordan, June. "Report from the Bahamas." Pages 304–12 in *Feminist Theory Reader: Local and Global Perspectives*. Edited by Carol R. McCann and Seung-Kyung Kim. 4th ed. New York: Routledge, 2017.

Kartzow, Marianne Bjelland. "'Asking the Other Question': An Intersectional Approach to Galatians 3:28 and the Colossian Household Codes." *BibInt* 18.4–5 (2010): 364–89.

King, Deborah. "Multiple Jeopardy: The Context of a Black Feminist Ideology." Pages 220–36 in *Feminist Frameworks: Alternative Theoretical Accounts of Relations between Women and Men*. Edited by Alison M. Jaggar and Paula S. Rothenberg. 3rd ed. New York: McGraw-Hill, 1993.

Leeb, Carolyn S. "The Widow: Homeless and Post-Menopausal." *BTB* 32 (2002): 160–62.

Lenski, Gerhard. *Power and Privilege: A Theory of Social Stratification*. Chapel Hill: University of North Carolina Press, 1966.

Lewis, Gail. "Unsafe Travel: Experiencing Intersectionality and Feminist Displacements." *Signs* 38 (2013): 869–92.

Lion, Brigitte, and Cécile Michel, eds. *The Role of Women in Work and Society in the Ancient Near East*. Studies in Ancient Near Eastern Records 13. Berlin: de Gruyter, 2016.

Lorde, Audre. *Sister Outsider: Essays and Speeches*. Crossing Press Feminist Series. Trumansburg, NY: Crossing Press, 1984.

MacDonald, Nathan. "Feasting Fit for a King." Pages 134–65 in *Not Bread Alone: The Uses of Food in the Old Testament*. Oxford: Oxford University Press, 2008.

Marchal, Joseph A. "Pinkwashing Paul, Excepting Jesus: The Politics of Intersectionality, Identification, and Respectability." Pages 433–53 in *The Bible and Feminism: Remapping the Field*. Edited by Yvonne Sherwood and Anna Fisk. Oxford: Oxford University Press, 2017.

Marsman, Hennie J. *Women in Ugarit and Israel: Their Social and Religious Position in the Context of the Ancient Near East*. OtSt 49. Leiden: Brill, 2003.

Masenya, Madipoane. "The Bible, HIV/AIDS and African/South African Women: A Bosadi Approach." *Studia Historiae Ecclesiasticae* 31 (2005): 187–201.

Matsuda, Mari J. "Beside My Sister, Facing the Enemy: Legal Theory out of Coalition." *Stanford Law Review* 43.6 (1991): 1183–92.

May, Vivian M. *Pursuing Intersectionality, Unsettling Dominant Imaginaries*, Contemporary Sociological Perspectives. New York: Routledge, 2015.

Mazar, Amihai. "The Divided Monarchy: Comments on Some Archaeological Issues." Pages 159–80 in *The Quest for the Historical Israel: Debating Archaeology and the History of Early Israel; Invited Lectures Delivered at the Sixth Biennial Colloquium of the International Institute for Secular Humanistic Judaism, Detroit, 2005*. By Israel Finkelstein, Amihai Mazar, and Brian B. Schmidt. ABS 17. Atlanta: Society of Biblical Literature, 2007.

McKenzie, Steven L. *1 Kings 16–2 Kings 16*. IECOT. Stuttgart: Kohlhammer, 2019.

Melanchthon, Monica Jyotsna. "Indian Dalit Women and the Bible." Pages 212–24 in *Gender, Religion and Diversity: Cross-Cultural Perspectives*. Edited by Ursula King and Tina Beattie. London: Continuum, 2004.

———. "Toward Mapping Feminist Biblical Interpretations in Asia." Pages 205–19 in *Feminist Biblical Studies in the Twentieth Century: Scholarship and Movement*. Edited by Elisabeth Schüssler Fiorenza. BW 9.1. Atlanta: Society of Biblical Literature, 2014.

Meyers, Carol L. "Guilds and Gatherings: Women's Groups in Ancient Israel." Pages 154–84 in *Realia Dei: Essays in Archaeology and Biblical Interpretation in Honor of Edward F. Campbell, Jr. at His Retirement*. Edited by Prescott H. Williams Jr. and Theodore Hiebert. Scholars Press Homage Series 23. Atlanta: Scholars Press, 1999.

Moyal, Yigal, and Avraham Faust. "Jerusalem's Hinterland in the Eighth-Seventh Centuries BCE: Towns, Villages, Farmsteads, and Royal Estates." *PEQ* 147 (2015): 283–98.

Nam, Roger S. *Portrayals of Economic Exchange in the Book of Kings*. BibInt 112. Leiden: Brill, 2011.

Nash, Jennifer C. *Black Feminism Reimagined: After Intersectionality*. Next Wave New Directions in Women's Studies. Durham, NC: Duke University Press, 2019.

Pattel-Gray, Anne. "Not Yet Tiddas: An Aboriginal Womanist Critique of Australian Church Feminism." Pages 165–92 in *Freedom and Entrapment: Women Thinking Theology*. Edited by Maryanne Confoy, Dorothy Lee, and Joan Nowotny. Melbourne: Dove, 1995.

Pressler, Carolyn. *The View of Women Found in the Deuteronomic Family Laws*. BZAW 216. Berlin: de Gruyter, 1993.

Rentería, Tamis Hoover. "The Elijah/Elisha Stories: A Socio-cultural Analysis of Prophets and People in Ninth-Century B.C.E. Israel." Pages 75–126 in *Elijah and Elisha in Socioliterary Perspective*. Edited by Robert B. Coote. SemeiaSt 22. Atlanta: Scholars Press, 1992.

Rey, M. I. "Reexamination of the Foreign Female Captive: Deuteronomy 21:10–14 as a Case of Genocidal Rape." *JFSR* 32 (2016): 37–53.

Rook, John. "Making Widows: The Patriarchal Guardian at Work." *BTB* 27 (1997): 10–15.

———. "When Is a Widow Not a Widow? Guardianship Provides an Answer." *BTB* 28 (1998): 4–6.

Roth, Martha T. "The Neo-Babylonian Widow." *JCS* 43–45 (1991–1993): 1–26.

———. "Women in Transition and the *Bīt Mār Banî*." *RA* 82 (1988): 131–38.

Royster, Jacqueline Jones. *Traces of a Stream: Literacy and Social Change among African American Women*. Pittsburgh Series in Composition, Literacy, and Culture. Pittsburgh: University of Pittsburgh Press, 2000.

Schüssler Fiorenza, Elisabeth. *Democratizing Biblical Studies: Toward an Emancipatory Educational Space*. Louisville: Westminster John Knox, 2009.

Scott, James C. *Domination and the Arts of Resistance: Hidden Transcripts*. New Haven: Yale University Press, 1990.

———. "Patronage or Exploitation?" Pages 21–39 in *Patrons and Clients in Mediterranean Societies*. Edited by Ernest Gellner and John Waterbury. London: Duckworth, 1977.

Segovia, Fernando F. "Criticism in Critical Times: Reflections on Vision and Task." *JBL* 134 (2015): 6–29.

Seidler, Ayelet. "The Law of Levirate and Forced Marriage—Widow vs. Levir in Deuteronomy 25.5–10." *JSOT* 42 (2018): 435–56.

Simkins, Ronald A. "Patronage and the Political Economy of Monarchic Israel." *Semeia* 87 (1999): 123–44.

———. "The Widow and Orphan in the Political Economy of Ancient Israel." *Journal of Religion and Society* 10 (2014): 20–33.

Sneed, Mark. "Israelite Concern for the Alien, Orphan, and Widow: Altruism or Ideology?" *ZAW* 111 (1999): 498–507.

Soggin, J. Alberto "Compulsory Labor under David and Solomon." Pages 259–67 in *Studies in the Period of David and Solomon and Other Essays: Papers Read at the International Symposium for Biblical Studies, Tokyo, 5–7 December, 1979*. Edited by Tomoo Ishida. Winona Lake, IN: Eisenbrauns, 1982.

Spelman, Elizabeth V. *Inessential Woman: Problems of Exclusion in Feminist Thought*. Boston: Beacon, 1988.

Steinberg, Naomi. "Romancing the Widow: The Economic Distinctions between the *'Almānâ*, the *'Iššâ-'almānâ* and the *'Ēšet-Hammēt*." Pages 327–46 in *God's Word for Our World*. Edited by J. Harold Ellens et al. 2 vols. JSOTSup 388, 389. London: T&T Clark, 2004.

Stevens, Marty E. *Temples, Tithes, and Taxes: The Temple and the Economic Life of Ancient Israel*. Peabody, MA: Hendrickson, 2006.

Stol, Marten. *Women in the Ancient Near East*. Translated by Helen Richardson and Mervyn Richardson. Berlin: de Gruyter, 2016.

Tenney, Jonathan S. *Life at the Bottom of Babylonian Society: Servile Labour at Nippur in the Fourteenth and Thirteenth Centuries BC*. CHANE 51. Leiden: Brill, 2011.

Toorn, Karel van der. "The Public Image of the Widow in Ancient Israel." Pages 19–30 in *Between Poverty and the Pyre: Moments in the History of Widowhood*. Edited by Jan Bremmer and Lourens van den Bosch. London: Routledge, 1995.

———. "Torn between Vice and Virtue: Stereotypes of the Widow in Israel and Mesopotamia." Pages 1–13 in *Female Stereotypes in Religious Tra-*

ditions. Edited by Ria Kloppenborg and Wouter J. Hanegraaff. SHR 66. Leiden: Brill, 1995.

Walby, Sylvia, Jo Armstrong, and Sofia Strid. "Intersectionality: Multiple Inequalities in Social Theory." *Sociology* 46 (2012): 224–40.

Weems, Renita J. "The Hebrew Women Are Not like the Egyptian Women: The Ideology of Race, Gender and Sexual Reproduction in Exodus 1." *Semeia* 59 (1992): 25–34.

Weisberg, Dvora E. "The Widow of Our Discontent: Levirate Marriage in the Bible and Ancient Israel." *JSOT* 28 (2004): 403–29.

Williams, Delores S. "Hagar in African American Biblical Appropriation." Pages 171–84 in *Hagar, Sarah, and Their Children: Jewish, Christian and Muslim Perspectives*. Edited by Phyllis Trible and Letty M. Russell. Louisville: Westminster John Knox, 2006.

Wills, Lawrence M. *Not God's People: Insiders and Outsiders in the Biblical World*. Religion in the Modern World. Lanham, MD: Rowman & Littlefield, 2008.

Yee, Gale A. "The Elijah and Elisha Narratives: An Economic Investigation." Pages 21–50 in *Honouring the Past, Looking to the Future: Essays from the 2014 International Congress of Ethnic Chinese Biblical Scholars*. Edited by Gale A. Yee and John Y. H. Yieh. Chuen King Lectures Series 12. Shatin N. T., Hong Kong: Divinity School of Chung Chi College, The Chinese University of Hong Kong, 2016.

———. "'He Will Take the Best of Your Fields': Royal Feasts and Rural Extraction." *JBL* 136 (2017): 821–38.

———, ed. *The Hebrew Bible: Feminist and Intersectional Perspectives*. Minneapolis: Fortress, 2018.

———. "Negotiating Shifts in Life's Paradigms." Pages 103–14 in *Women and the Society of Biblical Literature*. Edited by Nicole L. Tilford. BSNA 29. Atlanta: SBL Press, 2019.

———. *Poor Banished Children of Eve: Woman as Evil in the Hebrew Bible*. Minneapolis: Fortress, 2003.

———. "The Process of Becoming for a Woman Warrior from the Slums." Pages 15–30 in *Asian and Asian American Women in Theology and Religion: Embodying Knowledge*. Edited by Kwok Pui-lan. Asian Christianity in the Diaspora. New York: Palgrave Macmillan, 2020.

———. "Recovering Marginalized Groups in Ancient Israel: Methodological Considerations." Pages 15–18 in *To Break Every Yoke: Essays in Honor of Marvin L. Chaney*. Edited by Robert B. Coote and Norman K. Gottwald. SWBA 2/3. Sheffield: Sheffield Phoenix, 2007.

———. "Yin/Yang Is Not Me: An Exploration into an Asian American Biblical Hermeneutics." Pages 152–63 in *Ways of Being, Ways of Reading: Asian-American Biblical Interpretation*. Edited by Mary F. Foskett and Jeffrey K. Kuan. Saint Louis: Chalice, 2006.

Yeon Choo, Hae, and Myra Marx Ferree, "Practicing Intersectionality in Sociological Research: A Critical Analysis of Inclusions, Interactions, and Institutions in the Study of Inequalities." *Sociological Theory* 28 (2010): 129–49.

Yuval-Davis, Nira. "Intersectionality and Feminist Politics." *European Journal of Women's Studies* 13 (2006): 193–209.

Zaccagnini, Carlo. "War and Famine at Emar." *Or* 64 (1995): 92–109.

Presidential Reflection

GALE A. YEE

I would like to thank Mary Foskett and Stephanie Crowder for inviting me to contribute to *Remapping Biblical Studies: CUREMP's Thirtieth Anniversary*. This volume celebrates the central and key significance that CUREMP has played in the lives of racial and ethnic biblical scholars for the past thirty years. I was asked to reflect back on my presidential address in the context of biblical studies and minoritized criticism.

I concluded my book *Poor Banished Children of Eve: Woman as Evil in the Hebrew Bible* with these words:

> Writing this book was not simply an intellectual, academic enterprise for me. I found in the biblical text what I had already experienced in real life: that there are insidiously complex interconnections among religion—based on the biblical text—and the "'isms": sexism, racism, classism, colonialism, heterosexism, fundamentalism and so forth. The Bible continues to be used to legitimate sinful realities. As biblical scholars, we are obligated ethically to challenge and confront social, economic, and religious systems that make it impossible for the majority of our families, congregations, and nations to experience the *shalom* that the Scriptures promise.[1]

I published this book in 2003, and, at the time, I did not know the word *intersectionality*. This was a term that was brought to my attention many years later by one of the graduate students in my Feminist Theory and Theologizing course. What I had been doing for a long time as a biblical scholar became the basis of my 2019 presidential address: "Thinking Inter-

1. Gale A. Yee, *Poor Banished Children of Eve: Woman as Evil in the Hebrew Bible* (Minneapolis: Fortress, 2003), 165.

sectionally: Gender, Race, Class, and the Etceteras of Our Discipline."[2] So, as I reflect back on my presidential address, I had to go back further to the many years that I had struggled to put my thoughts on paper for that 2003 book. I was an intersectional biblical scholar long before I delivered my presidential address. And indeed, by struggling with race/ethnicity and the et ceteras in the biblical guild, those who attended CUREMP lunches and gave papers in the Society of Biblical Literature groups—Asian and Asian American Biblical Hermeneutics; The African-American Biblical Hermeneutics; Islands, Islanders, and Scriptures; Latino/a and Latin American Biblical Interpretation; and Minoritized Criticism and Biblical Interpretation; Racism, Pedagogy and Biblical Studies—*all* were involved in intersectional analysis in some form, whether they knew it or not.

When I was able to put a name on what I had been doing for many years, I now had to go forward and write a presidential address. Therefore, after I was nominated to be president-elect in 2018, I immersed myself in the wealth of literature on intersectionality. While on this interdisciplinary journey, I was introduced to many essays and books on intersectionality in critical race theory, the social sciences, feminist theory, and cultural studies by many brilliant racial/ethnic scholars. The footnotes of my address reveal the wide range of study that I embarked upon. I even read some illuminating critiques of Swedish hegemonic whiteness by a Korean professor in intercultural studies there. I encouraged racial/ethnic biblical scholars to move beyond the traditional modes and methods of biblical interpretation and put their toes into more interdisciplinary waters. At a time when Critical Race Theory (CRT) is erroneously kicked around like a football by the rightwing Republicans, let's start actually reading some CRT![3]

During this COVID time of anti–Asian American hate and inequality, when 12 percent of Asian Americans live below the federal poverty line,[4] when white supremacy revealed its true colors in the January 6 insurrection, it is crucial that Asian American biblical scholars along with their

2. Published as Gale A. Yee, "Thinking Intersectionally: Gender, Race, Class, and the Etceteras of Our Discipline," *JBL* 139 (2020): 7–26.

3. A good place to start is Kimberlé Crenshaw et al., *Critical Race Theory: The Key Writings That Formed the Movement* (New York: The New Press, 1995).

4. This is particularly the case among the Southeast Asian American refugees: the Hmong, Burmese, Cambodian, Laotian, and Vietnamese. See the work of The Southeast Asian Resource Action Center (https://www.searac.org/) and Asian Americans Advancing Justice (https://www.advancingjustice-aajc.org/).

African American, Latino/a American, and all minoritized colleagues in this volume, continue to provide rigorous intersectional and interdisciplinary scholarship, examine the multiple subject positions of our biblical exegesis and hermeneutics, and make it our *praxis* as we encounter our turbulent world.

Bibliography

Crenshaw, Kimberlé, et al. *Critical Race Theory: The Key Writings That Formed the Movement.* New York: The New Press, 1995.

Yee, Gale A. *Poor Banished Children of Eve: Woman as Evil in the Hebrew Bible.* Minneapolis: Fortress, 2003.

———. "Thinking Intersectionally: Gender, Race, Class, and the Etceteras of Our Discipline." *JBL* 139 (2020): 7–26.

Learning to Read the Bible

LESLIE D. CALLAHAN

My love for the Bible and commitment to its study began in the pews of a tiny, approximately twenty-member Pentecostal church in the coal fields of West Virginia in the 1970s and 1980s. Before I even had consciousness that I was learning, my family and community of origin showed me how to take the Bible seriously. While songs from the hymnal sourced our expression of worship, the Bible was *the source* of faith, and its application facilitated embodied experience. The Bible played a significant role in our congregation, almost itself a living character, acting as the conduit for everything from prayer to preaching and even humor.

The lay and clergy leaders from whom I first learned scripture lacked formal education, but they read the Bible meaningfully and prayerfully, always seeking and sometimes wrestling to discern the sense of what they read. Some of the wrestling took place aloud in the community, as members argued passionately for one interpretation over another, debating and drawing attention again and again to the words of the text. They showed me how to read closely. So central to our conversation was the biblical text that, if a preacher began to quote a verse, she or he could rely on the congregation in unison to finish the sentence from the King James Version. Assent to the truth of scripture was guaranteed.

Even as I learned to love the Bible as a child, I also learned early the power of its words to do harm. The occasion for this awareness is graven indelibly on my memory. In the nightstand by my mother's bed lay the Scofield Reference Bible that she prized above all the other Bibles in her collection. I, too, gravitated toward this particular Bible with its supple leather cover and thin, fragile pages. In later years, when I was teenager practicing my preaching in the mirror, I often chose this Bible for the way it opened and laid flat. But my painful encounter with the text occurred at a much younger age, in early elementary school, when I sat on the floor of the bedroom and the page fell open to Deut 23:2 "A bastard shall not enter into the congregation of the Lord; even to his tenth generation shall he not enter into the congregation of the LORD" (KJV).

For as long as I live and do ministry, I will never forget the horror of that moment, the brutal power that came from believing that all the words of this ancient text applied to me. For a few hours or perhaps even more than a few days, I wondered whether I, born of a young woman who got pregnant in college, was permanently and irrevocably excluded from "the congregation of the LORD." I read the words over and over, using a concordance to find the word *bastard* when I didn't remember chapter and verse. And I asked hard questions: Why didn't it matter that I loved God? Why didn't it matter that I was baptized? The resolution came when I reasoned that it was possible that not every word on the page was meant for me. Out of that painful encounter with the text, my work of interpretation began in earnest.

In her presidential address charting the development of intersectionality, Gale Yee applies the analysis of intersectionality, particularly the exercise of power in various domains, to the story of the widow in 2 Kgs 4: "Intersectionality is concerned with relations of power, and the ways that systems of power are implicated in the development, organization, and maintenance of social inequalities."[1] For Yee, attention to the status of widows is traceable to the widowhood of her own mother when Yee was twenty-four years old. That attention yields insight into the text that has meaning for scholarship in the academy. It also reveals possibilities and pitfalls in the application of scripture to devotional life, either through preaching or teaching. Yee's analysis demonstrates that the reading of scripture differs according to the position of the person doing the reading.

To acknowledge that we read through our own locations also offers us opportunities. Yee challenges us to read scripture in ways that refuse to take for granted the social arrangements either in the text or in our contemporary contexts. She pushes us to consider the myriad ways that unjust systems get support sometimes even from the other systems that arise to ameliorate the stress of oppression. Provision of charity for widows without actually addressing the socioeconomic system that rendered the widow vulnerable further supports the system of inequity.

1. Published as Gale A. Yee, "Thinking Intersectionally: Gender, Race, Class, and the Etceteras of Our Discipline," *JBL* 139 (2020): 17.

What are we to do? In her conclusion, Yee offers the best practical advice for those who seek to read, interpret, and apply scripture in ways that do not reinforce oppression. Citing Asian American lawyer Mari Matsuda, Yee challenges us to "ask the other question."[2] For Yee, this means using intersectional hermeneutics to interrogate the ways writers reinforced or undermined the status quo of power dynamics in their time. Intersectional readings also expose how the ways we engage and interpret texts in our own time either reestablish or undermine current power relationships.

The capacity to question how power is wielded in the interpretation of the biblical text draws me back to my time growing up in West Virginia. As I indicated above, our congregation responded audibly to the preaching and teaching of scripture, and we saw ourselves as responsible for what we said amen to. A teaching, sermon, or interpretation that we regarded as unfaithful or errant would encounter resistance expressed through silence. We withheld the expected celebration. At that time, our resistance was quiet. Now our resistance to oppressive readings can and must be explicit.

I now serve a congregation distant in a time and a place from those early years in my home church. Our relationship to the Bible is not as intimate, the commitment to its reading and application not nearly as deep. When I preach or teach, I can take nothing for granted when it comes to the hearer's knowledge of the text or commitment to its message. Silence may represent dissent and resistance, or it might equally be a sign of deep thinking and engagement. A child growing up in my congregation would never assume that *every word* of the biblical text applies to them. Yet I can still take for granted that most people have encountered the Bible's power deployed for and against them. Now my call as a responsible reader, interpreter, and proclaimer is to bring all the tools I have to the work of empowering other readers to claim the power and initiative to dismantle the forms oppression takes.

Bibliography

Matsuda, Mari J. "Beside My Sister, Facing the Enemy: Legal Theory out of Coalition," *Stanford Law Review* 43.6 (1991): 1183–92.

2. Mari J. Matsuda, "Beside My Sister, Facing the Enemy: Legal Theory out of Coalition," *Stanford Law Review* 43.6 (1991): 1189, quoted in Yee, "Thinking Intersectionally," 26.

Yee, Gale A. “Thinking Intersectionally: Gender, Race, Class, and the Etceteras of Our Discipline.” *JBL* 139 (2020): 7–26.

Minor Feelings and Embodied Strategies in Doctoral Biblical Education

JANETTE H. OK

In her presidential address to the Society of Biblical Literature, Gale A. Yee urges the guild to think beyond the familiar or more entrenched boundaries, assumptions, and paradigms of our discipline. She invites us to think "intersectionally" about own methodological approaches to the biblical text.[1] This essay takes up Yee's charge by reexamining doctoral education in biblical studies through the lens of intersectionality and maps minor feelings and embodied marginalities onto student formation. In doing so, I seek to challenge faculty and administrators to reimagine and promote more humanizing and socially just experiences for underrepresented racial and ethnic doctoral students in our discipline.[2]

It is commonly known that doctoral students face high cognitive and personal demands throughout their course of study.[3] For students of color, however, race, racialization, and racism inherent in higher educational and professional structures complicate the stages of growth. They frequently

1. Gale A. Yee, "Thinking Intersectionally: Gender, Race, Class, and the Etceteras of Our Discipline," *JBL* 139 (2020): 7–26.

2. I use *underrepresented* and *minoritized* interchangeably throughout this essay in reference to racialized doctoral students of color, with the understanding that these adjectives serve as umbrella terms and that students do not have the same experience with racism and injustice.

3. Solveig Cornér et al., "The Relationships between Doctoral Students' Perceptions of Supervision and Burnout," *International Journal of Doctoral Studies* 12 (2017): 91–106; Benjamin A. Pyykkonen, "Cognitive Processes and the Impact of Stress upon Doctoral Students: Practical Applications for Doctoral Programs," *Christian Higher Education* 20 (2021): 28–37; Jenny Hyun et al., "Mental Health Need, Awareness, and Use of Counseling Services among International Graduate Students," *Journal of American College Health* 56 (2007): 109–18.

deal with the tension between how their peers and professors perceive them to be and what they are actually capable of doing and being.[4] They may feel unwelcome and invisible and at other times feel overly visible and tokenized. They often lack the mentoring needed to navigate departmental, institutional, and academic cultures and also struggle to find diverse epistemological perspectives in the curriculum. For international students, especially Asian female scholars, their embodied marginalities of race/ethnicity are complicated by the intersectionality of multiple factors, such as gender, foreign nationality and accent, struggles with linguistic proficiency, and psychological or sociocultural adaption.[5]

Cathy Park Hong, in referring to the Asian American psyche, describes "minor feelings" as "emotions that are negative, dysphoric, and therefore untelegenic, built from the sediments of everyday racial experience and the irritant of having one's perception of reality constantly questioned or dismissed."[6] Minor feelings arose in me when a professor advised me to "do work that has a long shelf life," rather than the interdisciplinary, explicitly engaged/contextual readings I sought to offer. My exegesis was, to borrow language from Hong, "too ethnicky."[7] I felt the impact of minor feelings when my department rejected my first dissertation research proposal because there was no longer an adviser qualified to support such a project. Must students of color with interests and commitments that differ from their white professors wait to find an advisor to help them to do work in biblical studies that matters to them?

4. Ryan E. Gildersleeve et al., '"Am I Going Crazy?!': A Critical Race Analysis of Doctoral Education," *Equity and Excellence in Education* 44 (2011): 93–114. Gender and class exacerbate these challenges. See Marjorie C. Shavers and James L. Moore III, "The Perpetual Outsider: Voices of Black Women Pursuing Doctoral Degrees as Predominantly White Institutions." *Journal of Multicultural Counseling and Development* 47 (2019): 210–26.

5. In addition to institutional and cultural constraints, complex power dynamics as Asian female professors are the least recognized for their academic expertise and instructional authority, even in disciplines where they are not underrepresented (Jae Hoon Lim et al., "Walking on Gender Tightrope with Multiple Marginalities: Asian International Female Students in STEM Graduate Programs," *Journal of International Students* 11 [2021]: 647–65).

6. Cathy Park Hong, *Minor Feelings: An Asian American Reckoning* (New York: One World, 2020), 55.

7. Hong, *Minor Feelings*, 17.

Hong goes on to explain how "minor feelings arise, for instance, upon hearing a slight, knowing it's racial, and being told, Oh, that's all in your head."[8] How many times during my PhD coursework did I ask myself "Am I crazy?" Am I crazy for feeling that I have to prove myself in way that my white peers do not?[9] Am I crazy for sensing that I genuinely surprise my professors when I meet or exceed their expectations? Am I crazy to think that my textual concerns are legitimate when no one else at the table or in the course syllabi voices or shares them? Am I crazy to be one of the few doctoral students to voice concerns about the lack of racial-ethnic diversity among our Bible faculty? Turns out, I was not crazy, but the nagging question did wear down my confidence and deteriorate my sense of belonging.

The social narrative, "Am I going crazy?!" has been documented as a persistent and pervasive question asked by students of color in predominantly white institutions across genders, discipline, and institutions.[10] It reflects how the experiences of students of color are shaped by the "the tentativeness, insecurity, and doubt" often projected on and felt by them and also the resiliency required for their survival.[11] It is exacerbated by the ways they must defend the merits and legitimacy of their work if it falls outside the dominant scholarship model.[12]

The focus on Diversity, Equity, and Inclusion (DEI) in higher education is often too limited to the physical presence of diverse bodies devoid of what makes them unique. Diversity in our institutions and doctoral programs needs to go beyond functionalism (enlightening white students to people of color) and addition (adding students who are different from the dominant racial-ethnic makeup of the student body).[13] To provide a more

---

8. Hong, *Minor Feelings*, 55.

9. When an MDiv classmate of mine, a white male who also happened to be interested in doctoral studies, confessed to me, "I wish I were an Asian woman or a black man. I'd be so much more likely to get into a PhD program," minor feelings gnawed at me.

10. Gildersleeve et al., "Am I Going Crazy?!," 97–99.

11. Gildersleeve et al., "Am I Going Crazy?!," 100.

12. Michelle A. Holling and Amardo Rodriguez, "Negotiating Our Way through the Gates of Academe," *Journal of Latinos and Education* 5 (2006): 51.

13. While Yee's presidency has given Asian American women more visibility in the Society of Biblical Literature, it should be noted that the actual number of and Asian American women in biblical studies remains relatively low. For example, in the 2019 member profile, only 3.99 percent of all Society members in 2018 indicated that

holistic, humanizing, and justice-oriented graduate biblical education, diversity needs also to be ontological (encouraging learners to express new and different ways of being and ways of reading) and epistemic (allowing for different hermeneutical horizons and reservoirs of knowledge to inform learners' ways of interpreting and knowing).[14] It also needs to be material (acknowledging the economic dimensions of structural racism).

How might we take seriously the minor feelings and multiple marginalities often experienced by students of color in their doctoral training and formation? Here I offer some embodied strategies:

1. Develop targeted initiatives to identify potential underrepresented racial and ethnic minorities students at the MA level or MDiv level in seminaries to encourage and support their trajectory toward pursuing doctoral education in biblical and theological studies.
2. Recruit and hire faculty, staff, and administrators and appoint board members who embody racial-ethnic and gender diversity and ontological and epistemic diversity.
3. Commit to fostering and advocating for the diverse approaches, viewpoints, concerns, and interests of minoritized doctoral students.
4. Prepare and equip underrepresented doctoral students to navigate and negotiate the complex and often-conflicting dilemma unique to their embodied pressures, burdens, desires, and commitments, such as the inordinate demands of professional service that serves the needs and interests of their institutions and yet places undue

they were of Asian descent, and 24.22 percent of all responders indicated that they were female. See Society of Biblical Literature, "2019 SBL Membership Data," https://www.sbl-site.org/assets/pdfs/sblMemberProfile2019.pdf.

14. Holling and Rodriguez, "Negotiating Our Way through the Gates," 51; Franziska Dübgen, "Scientific Ghettos and Beyond: Epistemic Justice in Academia and Its Effects on Researching Poverty," *Dimensions of Poverty: Measurement, Epistemic Injustices, Activism*, ed. Valentin Beck et al. (Cham, Switzerland: Springer, 2020), 79. See also Xin Xu, "Epistemic Diversity and Cross-Cultural Comparative Research: Ontology, Challenges, and Outcomes," *Globalisation, Societies and Education* 20.2 (2022): 36–48. The ways in which philosophers and educational researchers use the terms *ontological* and *epistemic* or *epistemological* differ significantly. I employ these terms informed by research that focuses on educational diversity.

stress on them and potentially disadvantage their chances for job security, tenure, and/or promotion.

5. Provide and facilitate culturally relevant support systems, such as peer mentoring and professional mentoring that focus on identity and account for the distinct fusions of gender, race/ethnicity, class, foreign nationality, et cetera within the institution and outside the institution.[15]
6. Support the research and writing of students and provide what I call "advocacy-oriented doctoral advising" that recognizes the impact of the multiple identity dimensions and oppressions on underrepresented students' scholarly, professional, and personal development and promotes structures, relational networks, and pathways that contribute to their academic success and overall thriving.

Thinking intersectionally, as Yee explains, interrogates how the social location and gender, race, class, et cetera of the biblical authors shape their writings and our own interpretation and scholarship on these texts. It also leads to justice-oriented approaches and change.[16] By mapping the ways minor feelings and multiple marginalities impact the intersectional identities of underrepresented and/or minoritized doctoral students, I seek to locate some of the areas in which we members of the Society of Biblical Literature can reimagine, institute, and promote more humanizing, socially just, culturally relevant, and multidimensional programs of study for the next generation of diverse scholars.

Bibliography

Cornér, Solveig, et al., "The Relationships between Doctoral Students' Perceptions of Supervision and Burnout." *International Journal of Doctoral Studies* 12 (2017): 91–106.

15. Studies show the benefits of such support systems, such as peer mentoring, professional mentoring, and group counseling to improve learning experiences and program completion. See, e.g., Lim et al., "Walking on Gender Tightrope," 649; Marjorie C. Shavers and James L. Moore III, "Black Female Voices: Self-Presentation Strategies in Doctoral Programs at Predominantly White Institutions," *Journal of College Student Development* 44 (2014): 391–407.

16. Yee, "Thinking Intersectionally," 12, 15.

Dübgen, Franziska. "Scientific Ghettos and Beyond: Epistemic Justice in Academia and Its Effects on Researching Poverty." Pages 77–96 in *Dimensions of Poverty: Measurement, Epistemic Injustices, Activism.* Edited by Valentin Beck et al. Cham, Switzerland: Springer, 2020.

Gildersleeve, Ryan E., et al. '"Am I Going Crazy?!': A Critical Race Analysis of Doctoral Education." *Equity and Excellence in Education* 44 (2011): 93–114.

Holling Michelle A., and Amardo Rodriguez. "Negotiating Our Way through the Gates of Academe." *Journal of Latinos and Education* 5 (2006): 49–64.

Hong, Cathy Park. *Minor Feelings: An Asian American Reckoning.* New York: One World, 2020.

Hyun, Jenny, et al. "Mental Health Need, Awareness, and Use of Counseling Services among International Graduate Students." *Journal of American College Health* 56 (2007): 109–18.

Lim, Jae Hoon, et al. "Walking on Gender Tightrope with Multiple Marginalities: Asian International Female Students in STEM Graduate Programs." *Journal of International Students* 11 (2021): 647–65.

Pyykkonen, Benjamin A. "Cognitive Processes and the Impact of Stress upon Doctoral Students: Practical Applications for Doctoral Programs." *Christian Higher Education* 20 (2021): 28–37.

Shavers, Marjorie C., and James L. Moore III. "Black Female Voices: Self-Presentation Strategies in Doctoral Programs at Predominantly White Institutions." *Journal of College Student Development* 44 (2014): 391–407.

———. "The Perpetual Outsider: Voices of Black Women Pursuing Doctoral Degrees as Predominantly White Institutions." *Journal of Multicultural Counseling and Development* 47 (2019): 210–26.

Society of Biblical Literature. "2019 SBL Membership Data." https://www.sbl-site.org/assets/pdfs/sblMemberProfile2019.pdf.

Xu, Xin. "Epistemic Diversity and Cross-Cultural Comparative Research: Ontology, Challenges, and Outcomes." *Globalisation, Societies and Education* 20.2 (2022): 36–48.

Yee, Gale A. "Thinking Intersectionally: Gender, Race, Class, and the Etceteras of Our Discipline." *JBL* 139 (2020): 7–26.

Intersectionality of Intersectionalities in Biblical Studies

AHIDA CALDERÓN PILARSKI

In her presidential address to the Society of Biblical Literature, Gale Yee—"the first Asian American and the first women of color … to be elected president"[1]—focused on the concept of intersectionality. The aim of my essay here is to join her in a conversation about this concept and, from a Latina perspective, to add additional epistemological elements/concepts for consideration as we—minoritized[2] scholars and others—strive for a better future for the discipline of biblical studies.

Two keywords in Yee's presidential address turned her presentation into a hopeful crossroads for me. The first keyword is *intersectionality*, which she fully developed in her address. The second keyword is *stance*, which appeared in an essay she referenced in a footnote. In that essay, which includes her autobiography as an Asian American biblical scholar, she uses the term stance when defining the cultural/ethnic identity of a biblical scholar. These two keywords formed a hopeful crossroads for me, pointing to the intersecting roads (metaphorically and epistemologically) of a Latina woman (Calderón Pilarski), an Asian American woman (Yee),

1. Her presidential address is included in this volume. References here follow the article published in *the Journal of Biblical Literature*: Gale A. Yee, "Thinking Intersectionally: Gender, Race, Class, and the Etceteras of Our Discipline," *JBL* 139 (2020): 7–26. This is how she identified herself in the very first sentence of the presidential address (7).

2. For a definition of *minoritized* biblical criticism, see Randall C. Bailey, Tat-siong Benny Liew, and Fernando F. Segovia, "Toward Minority Biblical Criticism: Framework, Contours, Dynamics," in *They Were All Together in One Place? Toward Minority Biblical Criticism*, ed. Randall C. Bailey, Tat-siong Benny Liew, and Fernando F. Segovia, SemeiaSt 57 (Atlanta: Society of Biblical Literature, 2009), 3–43.

and a black woman (Patricia Hill Collins)—an intersectionality of intersectionalities. In my own journey, more than a decade ago, I wrote an essay where I reflected about my own identity as a Latina biblical scholar, and I used the same concepts—intersectionality and stance.[3]

My essay here—a conversation at the crossroads—delves deeper into the realm of the identity of critics, especially minoritized women critics in biblical studies. To this end, the essay is divided into two main parts. The first part elaborates further on the relevance of the two terms, intersectionality and stance, for my transition to a new phase in reflecting on my stance as a Latina biblical critic, one that still includes intersectionality but has evolved. The second part brings to the fore two epistemological elements/concepts from decolonial thinking that have contributed to the evolution in my own thinking about intersectionality: colonial semiosis and decolonizing turn.

Intersectionality and Stance

In 2008, a couple of panels were organized to inaugurate the "Latino/a and Latin American Biblical Interpretation" section at the Society of Biblical Literature. This was a historic moment for all minoritized scholars in the guild. For this occasion, the invited Latinx panelists were asked to reflect on the question of "What does it mean to be a Latino/a biblical critic?" I was invited to participate in the panel of junior scholars then. Eventually, in 2014, many of these presentations were developed into essay published in the volume *Latino/a Biblical Hermeneutics: Problematics, Objectives, Strategies*.[4] The title of my essay in that volume (which was also the title of my original presentation at the Society of Biblical Literature in 2008) was "A Latina Biblical Critic and Intellectual: At the *Intersection* of Ethnicity, Gender, Hermeneutics, and Faith."[5] My response to the central question addressed to the panel was then (and still is now) that "to be a Latin*a* biblical critic is to take, through a process of conscientization…, a well-informed and well-engaged *stance* in the inquiry process. This par-

3. See below.

4. Francisco Lozada Jr. and Fernando F. Segovia, eds., *Latino/a Biblical Hermeneutics: Problematics, Objectives, Strategies*, SemeiaSt 68 (Atlanta: SBL Press, 2014).

5. Ahida Calderón Pilarski, "A Latina Biblical Critic and Intellectual: At the Intersection of Ethnicity, Gender, Hermeneutics, and Faith," in Lozada and Segovia, *Latino/a Biblical Hermeneutics*, 231–48, emphasis added.

ticular stance, I argued, should be informed by at least four distinct but intersecting perspectives: ethnicity, gender, hermeneutics, and faith."[6] At that early phase of my scholarship as a Latina, I found the concept of intersectionality—as developed by African American sociologist Patricia Hill Collins[7]—to be the most adequate epistemological platform to speak about the different aspects/dimensions that were part of my stance as a Latina biblical critic.

I complemented my experience of intersectionality with the process of having, or taking, a stance that I defined at that point in my journey as "a sustainable hermeneutical platform that can allow a Latino/a[/x] biblical critic (or any biblical critic conscious of his or her ethnic heritage) to incorporate a critical and constructive vision [or analytical lens] into the analysis of the biblical text as well as to the analysis of the different coordinates left by Latina and Latino communities (or other ethnic groups) in their historical continuum."[8] It was empowering to see that Yee, in her autobiography, described similarly her journey of becoming an Asian American biblical scholar using the term stance. She says, "I realized ... that Asian American identity and biblical hermeneutics would only be created by ethnic Asian individuals, who have consciously adopted an Asian American advocacy *stance* at some point in their histories here in the United States."[9] Hence, a critical awareness of both, intersectionality and stance, constitute key elements in a process of thinking about one's continuously evolving identity as a critic. I agree with Yee that it is a process of becoming.[10]

At the basis of the concept of intersectionality is Hill Collins's description of the "matrix of domination." Yee summarizes the "domains of power" involved in this matrix in the third section of her presidential address. The matrix of domination involves four interrelated domains of power: the structural, the disciplinary, the hegemonic, and the interpersonal.[11] Advancing her reflection on intersectionality in her book *Towards*

6. Calderón Pilarski, "Latina Biblical Critic and Intellectual," 231, emphasis added

7. Patricia Hill Collins, *Black Feminist Thought: Knowledge, Consciousness, and Politics of Empowerment*, 2nd ed. (New York: Routledge, 2000).

8. Calderón Pilarski, "Latina Biblical Critic and Intellectual," 232, addition mine.

9. Gale A. Yee, "Negotiating Shifts in Life's Paradigms," in *Women and the Society of Biblical Literature*, ed. Nicole L. Tilford, BSNA 29 (Atlanta: SBL Press, 2019), 107.

10. Gale A. Yee, *Towards an Asian American Biblical Hermeneutics: An Intersectional Anthology* (Eugene, OR: Cascade, 2021), 3.

11. Yee, "Thinking Intersectionally," 14–16.

an Asian American Biblical Hermeneutics: An Intersectional Anthology, Yee adds that it is the task of biblical scholars "to develop more complex notions of empowerment and resistance, by being cognizant of the ways in which a matrix of domination was structured through those domains of power."[12] Unfortunately, as Yee observed already in her presidential address, "intersectionality has not made a significant dent as a conceptual framework in biblical studies, except … among scholars of color."[13] Why that might be so? And why it should not be so?

I find it pertinent now to elaborate further on a distinction that relates to the title of my essay, "Intersectionality of Intersectionalities." Intersectionality has a complex dual dimension when applied to biblical interpretation. The matrix of domination, on the one hand, provides a framework (or as I call it, an epistemological platform) for intersectional thinking, and, on the other hand, it serves as an analytical tool to identify relevant intersecting axes (such as race, ethnicity, gender, class, hermeneutics, faith, etc.) in the realities where domains of power are at play. So, when applied to biblical interpretation, intersectionality creates a complex dual platform. On the side of the biblical critic, it provides a framework to identify the intersecting axes in the domains of power influencing (positively and/or negatively) the life of the critic as well as the critic's identity, and, on the other side, the experienced intersectionality of the critic provides a more focused and perceptive lens to identify intersecting axes in the matrix of domination existent in the biblical text and its interpretation. As the critic develops and takes a stance informed by intersectionality, the stance and lens apply to both realms.

Scholars who are consciously aware of the intersectional axes in their own identities as critics can bring a more perceptive lens—as an analytical tool—to biblical criticism. This is perhaps why scholars of color find intersectionality to be necessary. Yet, because intersectional thinking underscores how the axis of race/ethnicity includes all races/ethnicities, not just those of minoritized critics and their communities, this perspective can be of secondary importance for those who privilege dominant practices or methods that are disconnected from race/ethnicity. The fact that biblical scholars have to refer to minoritized biblical criticism, which is now a noticeable trend at the Society of Biblical Literature, signals already the asymmetrical power at play in the interpretive process. I argue

12. Yee, *Towards an Asian American Biblical Hermeneutics*, 23.

13. Yee, "Thinking Intersectionally," 8–9.

that to do intersectional thinking and to take a stance are tasks that pertain to every (biblical) scholar.

Yee mentions in her presidential address that the triad of gender, race, and class—the intersectional axes relevant to her identity—"have made deep marks on … [her] interpretation of the biblical texts."[14] She proceeds in her analysis to apply intersectionality to the study of 2 Kgs 4:1–7, a passage that refers to widows in ancient Israel. Yee's critical lens allow her to distinguish axes in at least two domains of power (the interpersonal and the structural) at play in this biblical passage.[15] Her intersectional analysis provides powerful insights into the understanding of this marginal community of widows in ancient Israel.

Looking further now into the responsibility of all biblical critics to do intersectional thinking, I bring Gregory Cuéllar to this conversation. He commends the contribution made by Yee in her presidential address as she bravely uses an intersectionalizing strategy—as a justice-oriented approach—to develop a counterdiscourse to interrogate whiteness and make it visible "as a culturally constructed and socio-historically produced racial category."[16] The spaces for interrogation that Yee opens up include biblical criticism itself and also the history of the Society of Biblical Literature, which "since its inception has been a majority white male organization."[17] Furthermore, Cuéllar observes that "the term 'white' not only refers to phenotypic whiteness but also serves as the locus of a political project of privilege and supremacy that is fueled by discursive fields (ideologies) and material dimensions (structures)."[18] These observations are critical for envisioning the future of the Society. These spaces of interrogation actually open up for all critics an adequate platform for engaging in intersectional thinking and analysis. It is the responsibility of all critics to identify axes of ideological and structural domination and to take a stance in confronting the domains of power at play in the Society of Biblical Literature and in the field of biblical studies. Yee has courageously taken a first step.

---

14. Yee, "Thinking Intersectionally," 7.

15. Yee, "Thinking Intersectionally," 16.

16. Yee, "Thinking Intersectionally," 12; Gregory Cuéllar, "Reading Yee's Intersectionality as an Intervening Counterdiscourse to Whiteness," *The Bible and Critical Theory* 17 (2021): 7.

17. Cuéllar, "Reading Yee's Intersectionality," 4.

18. Cuéllar, "Reading Yee's Intersectionality," 7.

One of Cuéllar's observations where I agree to disagree is when he criticizes Yee for applying "intersectional analyses to the ancient world," something which he is "reluctant to join."[19] His main critique focuses on two aspects: the uninterrogated use of historical criticism in Yee's analysis of the biblical text and her citing of scholars who have perpetuated the ideologies of white privilege and white supremacy. Regarding the methodological approach, Cuéllar observes that "one problematic feature of scientific-based historical criticism is its devaluation of subjectivity for both the biblical critic and the artifacts they use to support their arguments.... Intersectionality has demonstrated [that] the notion of reaching a pristine disembodied state of being when analyzing ancient texts and artifacts is not just absurd but socially destructive."[20] Regarding the second aspect, Cuéllar points to Yee's "overreliance on European male historical critics"[21] whose racial rhetoric is problematic and must be also interrogated in the process of intersectional analysis. He says that to go "uninterrogated only ensures future returns on the guild's early investments in white supremacist ideology."[22] Cuéllar convincingly argues his points, and I agree with him about the need of interrogating, as Yee said, "the ideologies of white privilege and white supremacy and the structures that legitimate and sustain them"[23] at the Society of Biblical Literature and in the field at large. However, I disagree with Cuéllar's reluctance to apply intersectionality to the analysis of ancient texts because I believe that it is still possible and necessary. This leads me to the second part of this essay.

Colonial Semiosis and Decolonizing Turn

The two epistemological elements/concepts included in the title for this section are connected to the much larger project of decolonial thinking.[24] Latinx scholars have been already engaging this project as a critical par-

19. Cuéllar, "Reading Yee's Intersectionality," 8.

20. Cuéllar, "Reading Yee's Intersectionality," 8.

21. Cuéllar, "Reading Yee's Intersectionality," 10.

22. Cuéllar, "Reading Yee's Intersectionality," 9.

23. Yee, "Thinking Intersectionally," 13.

24. A central scholar developing this project has been Walter Mignolo. See especially, *The Darker Side of the Renaissance: Literacy, Territoriality, and Colonization* (Ann Arbor: University of Michigan Press, 1995); and Mignolo, *Local Histories/Global Designs: Coloniality, Subaltern Knowledges, and Border Thinking* (Princeton: Princeton University Press, 2000).

adigm for the twenty-first century.[25] Fernando Segovia alluded to these efforts in his 2014 presidential address to the Society of Biblical Literature when he proposed a seventh paradigm in biblical interpretation which he called the "Global-Systemic paradigm" to bring awareness to epistemologies of the Global South.[26]

In a recent essay for a volume in honor of Fernando Segovia, I provide a more elaborated description of the epistemic line that divides the Global South from the Global North. Understanding the detrimental impact of this epistemic line is essential to decolonial thinking. In the referred essay, I explain that "more than five hundred years ago, when Columbus accidentally arrived in the lands that would be referred to as the New World, he opened a Trans-Atlantic commercial circuit that already came impregnated with many other types of inequalities.… Through this same event, a (detrimental and synchronous) global 'linear' thought (an epistemic line) was developed in which the colonization of the New World automatically became one more event in the history of the Old World."[27] Furthermore, I point out that the "Old World's global 'linear' thought was constructed based on assumptions and interpretations of events that saw and interpreted history in a teleological direction, that is, the goal of the Old World's 'linear' thought was (and continues to be) to expand the Western-European/Occidental culture."[28]

Walter Mignolo explains that the Global South, therefore, "is not simply a line below the equator. It is an ideological concept highlighting the economic, political, and epistemic dependence and unequal relations in the global world order, from a subaltern perspective."[29] As the Western epistemic line was drawn more than five centuries ago, the racialization of the New World happened as well. This detail is essential for intersectional thinking, especially in connection to minoritized biblical criticism,

25. See Ada María Isasi-Díaz, and Eduardo Mendieta, *Decolonizing Epistemologies: Latina/o Theology and Philosophy* (New York: Fordham University Press, 2012).

26. Fernando F. Segovia, "Criticism in Critical Times: Reflections on Vision and Task," *JBL* 134 (2015): 26.

27. Ahida Calderón Pilarski, "Latina and Mujerista Biblical Hermeneutics: A Contribution to Decolonizing the Theme of (Im)migration," in *The Critic in the World: Biblical Criticism and Glocal Realities*, ed. Francisco Lozada Jr. , Amy Lindeman Allen, and Yak-hwee Tan (Atlanta: SBL Press, forthcoming).

28. Calderón Pilarski, "Latina and Mujerista Biblical Hermeneutics," n.p.

29. Walter Mignolo, "The Global South and World Dis/Order," *Journal of Anthropological Research* 67 (2011): 166.

because with that event a deep-rooted matrix of domination breached the historical continuum of the many peoples and their knowledges that became subjugated (or marginalized) through the colonial encounter. From a decolonial perspective, one can perceive that colonization produced a colonial matrix of domination that included an epistemic axis that intersected with race/ethnicity, and these axes are still at play in our times and in the field of biblical studies. Conversely, through the concept of colonial semiosis, decolonial thinking underscores how there were other emerging realities in the colonial encounter. The epistemic line of the colonizers found unintended outcomes—subaltern epistemologies or knowledges.

Mignolo explains this phenomenon through the concept of colonial semiosis. I have applied this concept heuristically to biblical criticism to illustrate the dynamics of power existent between a dominant discourse and marginalized *discours-ive* practices of resistance. To embrace the reality of verbal and nonverbal discourses and practices that emerged after the colonial encounter, I use the term *discours-ive* practice. Mignolo observes that colonial semiosis distinguishes

> the fractured semiotic [discours-ive] practices in the colonial periphery resulting from the clash between hegemonic norms and values guiding semiotic [discours-ive] practices in metropolitan centers, their extension to the colonial periphery, and the resistance and adaptation to them from the perspective of the native population to whose historical legacy the European Renaissance was quite meaningless.[30]

Colonial semiosis "speaks of what is perceived (by the dominant groups) as fractured discours-ive practices resulting from the clash … showing a spectrum of discours-ive practices going from adaptation to resistance."[31] Bringing this distinction to the current state of biblical studies, one can see in the discourses emerging out of minoritized biblical criticism a more visible articulation of marginalized discourses in the historical continuum of resistance. This is not a recent reality or trend; these subaltern knowledges

---

30. Walter Mignolo, "The Darker Side of the Renaissance: Colonization and the Discontinuity of the Classical Tradition," *RenQ* 45 (1992): 808.

31. Ahida Calderón Pilarski, "Hagar and the Well in the Wilderness (Genesis 21:9–21)," in *Reading Biblical Texts Together: Pursuing Minoritized Biblical Criticism*, ed. Tat-siong Benny Liew and Fernando F. Segovia, SemeiaSt 98 (Atlanta: SBL Press, 2022), 82.

have been latent under this matrix of domination for centuries, and intersectionality can provide a lens to deconstruct structural and epistemic domains of power in the field.

The term *decolonizing turn* informs at a deeper level the power of a stance. Nelson Maldonado-Torres explains that a decolonizing turn relates to "the emergence of consciousness about colonization as a fundamental problem and to decolonizing thought at a global level."[32] The historical trajectory of the colonizing epistemic line that has impacted academia started centuries ago. A decolonial turn involves exposing—or taking a stance—to make more visible (and to interrogating) the colonial epistemic lines of the colonizers-selves as well as bringing to light the preexistent epistemologies before colonization and those that emerged through and after the colonizing encounter, and this process has to happen at the local and global levels.

Reflecting on what a decolonizing turn would mean for an intersectional analysis of biblical criticism is in itself a critical task. An intersectionality of intersectionalities would take a conscious stance to analyze the matrix of domination to find the axes of subjugation or empowerment that pertain to a critic's individual identity as well as those that are at play in the theoretical frameworks behind paradigms of biblical criticism. This process would involve interrogating the structures and the people who keep the dynamics of (subjugating) power at play in the world in front of the text, in the world of the text, and in the world behind the text. My hope is that this conversation at the crossroad serves as a call for critics, not just minoritized biblical scholars, to engage in reflecting about intersectionality so that it can make a significant dent in biblical studies.

As Segovia pointed out in his presidential address to the Society of Biblical Literature in 2014, we are living in critical times, and our responses have to level up to the complexity of these times. I believe that intersectionality and decolonial thinking can provide some of the necessary lenses to take a critical stance. Thank you, Dr. Gale Yee, for taking a brave step of speaking about intersectionality as the first Asian American and the first women of color to be elected president of the Society of Biblical Literature.

---

32. Nelson Maldonado-Torres, "The Decolonial Turn," in *New Approaches to Latin American Studies: Culture and Power*, ed. Juan Poblete (London: Routledge, 2018), 114.

Bibliography

Bailey, Randall C., Tat-Siong Benny Liew, and Fernando F. Segovia. "Toward Minority Biblical Criticism: Framework, Contours, Dynamics." Pages 3–43 in *They Were All Together in One Place? Toward Minority Biblical Criticism*. Edited by Randall C. Bailey, Tat-siong Benny Liew, and Fernando F. Segovia. SemeiaSt 57. Atlanta: Society of Biblical Literature, 2009.

Calderón Pilarski, Ahida. "Hagar and the Well in the Wilderness (Genesis 21:9–21)." Pages 79–99 in *Reading Biblical Texts Together: Pursuing Minoritized Biblical Criticism*. Edited by Tat-siong Benny Liew and Fernando F. Segovia. SemeiaSt 98. Atlanta: SBL Press, 2022.

———. "A Latina Biblical Critic and Intellectual: At the Intersection of Ethnicity, Gender, Hermeneutics, and Faith." Pages 231–48 in *Latino/a Biblical Hermeneutics: Problematics, Objectives, Strategies*. Edited by Francisco Lozada Jr. and Fernando F. Segovia. SemeiaSt 68. Atlanta: SBL Press, 2014.

———. "Latina and Mujerista Biblical Hermeneutics: A Contribution to Decolonizing the Theme of (Im)migration." In *The Critic in the World: Biblical Criticism and Glocal Realities*. Edited by Francisco Lozada Jr., Amy Lindeman Allen, and Yak-hwee Tan. Atlanta: SBL Press, forthcoming.

Cuéllar, Gregory. "Reading Yee's Intersectionality as an Intervening Counterdisocurse to Whiteness." *The Bible and Critical Theory* 17 (2021): 4–13.

Hill Collins, Patricia. *Black Feminist Thought: Knowledge, Consciousness, and Politics of Empowerment*. 2nd ed. New York: Routledge, 2000.

Isasi-Díaz, Ada María, and Eduardo Mendieta. *Decolonizing Epistemologies: Latina/o Theology and Philosophy*. New York: Fordham University Press, 2012.

Lozada, Francisco, Jr., and Fernando F. Segovia, eds. *Latino/a Biblical Hermeneutics: Problematics, Objectives, Strategies*. SemeiaSt 68. Atlanta: SBL Press, 2014.

Maldonado-Torres, Nelson. "The Decolonial Turn." Pages 11–127 in *New Approaches to Latin American Studies: Culture and Power*. Edited by Juan Poblete. London: Routledge, 2018.

Mignolo, Walter D. "The Darker Side of the Renaissance: Colonization and the Discontinuity of the Classical Tradition." *RenQ* 45 (1992): 808–28.

———. *The Darker Side of the Renaissance: Literacy, Territoriality, and Colonization*. Ann Arbor: University of Michigan Press, 1995.

———. "The Global South and World Dis/Order." *Journal of Anthropological Research* 67 (2011): 165–88.

———. *Local Histories/Global Designs: Coloniality, Subaltern Knowledges, and Border Thinking*. Princeton: Princeton University Press, 2000.

Segovia, Fernando F. "Criticism in Critical Times: Reflections on Vision and Task." *JBL* 134 (2015): 6–29.

Yee, Gale A. "Negotiating Shifts in Life's Paradigms." Pages 103–12 in *Women and the Society of Biblical Literature*. Edited by Nicole L. Tilford. BSNA 29. Atlanta: SBL Press, 2019.

———. "Thinking Intersectionally: Gender, Race, Class, and the Etceteras of Our Discipline." *JBL* 139 (2020): 7–26.

———. *Towards an Asian American Biblical Hermeneutics: An Intersectional Anthology*. Eugene, OR: Cascade, 2021.

A Minority Report: Doing Intersectionality in Biblical Criticism

Jin Young Choi

Gale Yee's election as the president of the Society of Biblical Literature was historic. When this first Asian American and first woman president of color was invited to break the grave silence that had lasted for 139 years, what topic would she choose to address? In her 2019 presidential address, Yee challenged biblical scholarship to think of the discipline intersectionally, focusing on gender, race, class, and other social factors of oppression. For Yee, intersectionality is not only an analytical tool for interpreting the biblical text but is embodied in her personal life and professional commitments. Her multiple identities as a Chinese American woman from a lower-class background cannot be separated from her work as a biblical scholar.[1] In the following, I focus on Yee's contributions to biblical studies in terms of her commitments as an Asian American woman, her emphasis on class, and her activist oriented intersectionality. Then, guided by her distinct contributions, I reflect on the work of minoritized biblical scholars in white dominated biblical studies and propose a perspective for minoritized criticism to remap biblical studies.

Intersectional Commitments of the First Asian American Woman President

The 1960s social movements in the United States transformed academic disciplines so that, for instance, women's studies programs integrating scholarship and political action were introduced into the academy in the

1. Gale A. Yee, "Thinking Intersectionally: Gender, Race, Class, and the Etceteras of Our Discipline," *JBL* 139 (2020): 7.

1970s. African American, Asian American, Latina/o, international, and women students were accepted to doctoral programs in biblical studies in the 1970s. Since Yee, like other women scholars of color, received her training in historical criticism in male-dominated institutions, she self-studied feminist theory outside the discipline, applying it to biblical interpretation. Until that time, the overwhelming majority of feminist biblical scholars were white. As one of only few Asian American women in the guild, Yee was left out of debates on feminism and race among white and black feminist scholars in the late 1980s.[2]

Yee's position as an Asian American feminist scholar demanded multiple commitments in the 1990s. For example, while she represented women as she served on the Society of Biblical Literature's Council, she sat on the Women in the Biblical World steering committee as the only person of color. Additionally, she was one of the founding members of emerging racial/ethnic minority communities within the Society, such as the Committee on Underrepresented Racial and Ethnic Minorities in the Profession (CUREMP, founded in 1992); Asian and Asian-American Biblical Studies program unit (1995); and Ethnic Chinese Biblical Colloquium (1995).[3] Her intersectional work, which emerged from her engagements as a racialized woman biblical critic, began in the 2000s, when intersectionality became "pronounced as an act of resistance to forces of cooptation into the dominant discourse."[4] However, white feminist scholarship's inclusion of women of color is not the same as intersectionality. In fact, in her presidential address, Yee critiques the "colorblind intersectionality" that masks the whiteness of feminist criticism that needs to be made visible as a "culturally constructed ethnic identity."[5]

2. Gale A. Yee, "An Autobiographical Approach to Feminist Biblical Scholarship," *Encounter* 67 (2006): 375–90; Yee, "Negotiating Shifts in Life's Paradigms," in *Women and the Society of Biblical Literature*, ed. Nicole L. Tilford, BSNA 29 (Atlanta: SBL Press, 2019), 103–12.

3. Beside the Society of Biblical Literature, Yee has been active on the board and committee of Catholic Biblical Association of America and in Pacific Asian North American Asian Women in Theology and Ministry (PANAAWTM, founded in 1984) as a faculty advisor.

4. Susanne Scholz, "Stirring Up Vital Energies: Feminist Biblical Studies in North America (1980s–2000s)," in *Feminist Biblical Studies in the Twentieth Century: Scholarship and Movement*, ed. Elisabeth Schüssler Fiorenza, BW 9.1 (Atlanta: SBL Press, 2014), 54.

5. Yee, "Thinking Intersectionally," 13.

While her feminist critique of the "intersectional site of whiteness" is readily recognized,[6] what is not widely perceived in her intersectional discourse is her emphasis on class. Yee highlights the "material intersection of gender, race/ethnicity, economic class, and colonial relations in the production of biblical texts," which she calls ideological criticism.[7] Her own class background makes her profoundly concerned about "the rising inequality between the rich and the poor in today's neoliberal world," which in turn compels her to examine various forms of inequality in the Bible.[8] Her interpretation of 2 Kgs 4 in the address is only one example of her numerous intersectional works, which employ Marxist, feminist, and race theories, among others.[9] Yee's emphasis on material realities and socioeconomic structures of power that produce injustice should be taken seriously because of the ways that the discipline of biblical studies and its educational and publication practices appertain to academic industry in the neoliberal capitalist system. Her work challenges biblical academicians taking middle- or upper-class positions by asking if they maintain an "ethics of accountability" or if they contribute to promoting social and economic disparities.

The last notable point in Yee's address is the "activist element of intersectionality that impels my [her] work toward disrupting dominance and challenging systemic inequality in today's world."[10] Her stance resonates with Patricia Hill Collins's conceptualization of intersectionality as a critical social theory and a "knowledge project of resistance" that "both explains and critiques existing social inequalities."[11] "Thinking intersectionally," Yee urges

---

6. Gregory L. Cuéllar, "Reading Yee's Intersectionality as an Intervening Counter-discourse to Whiteness," *The Bible and Critical Theory* 17 (2021): 6–8.

7. Gale A. Yee, *Poor Banished Children of Eve: Woman as Evil in the Hebrew Bible* (Minneapolis: Fortress, 2003). Yee developed her ideological intersectional work and minoritized criticism serving as associate and general editor of Semeia Studies (2003–2009). See also Gale A. Yee, "'She Stood in Tears amid the Alien Corn': Ruth the Perpetual Foreigner and Model Minority," in *They Were All Together in One Place? Toward Minority Biblical Criticism*, ed. Randall C. Bailey, Tat-siong Benny Liew, and Fernando F. Segovia, SemeiaSt 57 (Atlanta: Society of Biblical Literature, 2009), 119–40.

8. Yee, "Thinking Intersectionally," 7–8, 13.

9. See Gale A. Yee, "She Is Not My Wife and I Am Not Her Husband: A Materialist Analysis of Hosea 1–2," *BibInt* 9 (2001): 345–83.

10. Yee, "Thinking Intersectionally," 12.

11. Patricia Hill Collins, *Intersectionality as Critical Social Theory* (Durham, NC: Duke University Press, 2019), 4, 10.

biblical scholarship to locate the role of the Bible "in legitimating matrices of power across different categories of identity" and conduct "social analysis and critique ... for political strategizing and organizing."[12] As minoritized scholars undertake the task of minoritized criticism based on race/ethnic identity toward coalition building across racial lines in an activist position, Yee's social justice-oriented intersectionality guides us to further develop transformative intersectional minoritized discourse and practices.

Contributions and Challenges of Minoritized Criticism

Minoritized biblical criticism employs the strategy of interpretive contextualization that refutes dominant historical criticism's claim of objectivity and universality, while at the same time centering the interpreter's social location and unpacking ideological-political agendas.[13] This contextual move involves racializing a minoritized critic's interpretation (e.g., African American interpretation), setting it against white dominance and racist exclusion in the discipline. A dilemma of such strategic essentialization is that it is liable to reinscribe the racial identity the dominant culture imposes. Moreover, such a racialized interpretation is often carried out in isolation in the "racial house." For instance, unmarked conference programs or book projects are willing to include nonwhite biblical scholars, but white scholars scarcely attend racially marked sessions or read and cite minoritized scholars' works. Racialized scholars are called to diversify white programs or projects. In addition to this diversity work, feminist scholars of color encounter further challenges as they do intersectional work to address both race and gender.

Minoritized scholars realize that their constructed racial identity is pragmatic and work on forming cross-racial alliances to dismantle racism and white supremacy. Minoritized criticism, which focuses on problematizing objectivity, disciplinary boundaries, and normative criticism in interdisciplinary fashion, has recently entered another phase of discourse-making.[14] Working to amplify the contributions of minoritized scholars

12. Yee, "Thinking Intersectionally," 12, 26.

13. Randall C. Bailey, Tat-siong Benny Liew, and Fernando F. Segovia, "Toward Minority Biblical Criticism: Framework, Contours, Dynamics," in Bailey, Liew, and Segovia, *They Were All Together in One Place?*, 26.

14. Bailey, Liew, and Segovia, "Toward Minority Biblical Criticism," 25–36. Cf. Tat-siong Benny Liew and Fernando F. Segovia, eds., *Reading Biblical Texts Together:*

and increase their visibility within the Society of Biblical Literature, the Minoritized Criticism and Biblical Interpretation program unit provides a discursive space for engaging the public square and social movements of the Global South.[15] Additionally, womanist and feminist scholars of color have recently made intentional efforts to build coalitions and strengthen mutual bonds for transformative intersectional work.[16]

As antiblack racism and police brutality reached a peak in 2020, the Society's Council responded to systemic and institutional racism by forming the Black Scholars Matter Task Force and offering the two-part online symposium, entitled "#BlackScholarshipMatters: Visions and Struggles."[17] It took 140 years for the Society to listen intentionally to African American members' experiences and struggles. Meanwhile, white-critical scholars have addressed problems of whiteness in biblical studies. Focusing on historical constructions of ethnicity and race in antiquity, particularly Christian identity in relation to Judaism, whiteness studies contributes to dismantling anti-Judaism embedded in the text and European modern biblical scholarship.[18] However, their critique of whiteness hardly extends to directly challenging contemporary

---

Doing Minoritized Biblical Criticism, SemeiaSt 98 (Atlanta: SBL Press, 2022); and Liew and Segovia, eds., *Reading in These Times: Purposes and Practices of Minoritized Biblical Criticism* (Atlanta: SBL Press, forthcoming).

15. For example, the unit has created the sessions responding to political challenges and social movements such as the Black Lives Matter movement (since 2013), Donald Trump's presidency buttressed by white supremacy and nationalism (2017–2021), and the coronavirus pandemic, which further fueled racism (since 2020). As a result of consistent coalitional commitment, the following volume has been published: Jin Young Choi and Gregory L. Cuéllar, eds., *Activist Hermeneutics of Liberation and the Bible: A Global Intersectional Perspective* (New York: Routledge, 2023).

16. Mitzi J. Smith and Jin Young Choi, eds., *Minoritized Women Reading Race and Ethnicity: Intersectional Approaches to Constructed Identity and Early Christian Texts* (Lanham, MD: Lexington Books, 2020).

17. The recorded sessions are available on the Society of Biblical Literature website: https://www.sbl-site.org/meetings/blackscholarsmatter.aspx. Cf. Tat-siong Benny Liew, "Black Scholarship Matters," *JBL* 136 (2017): 237–44.

18. See David G. Horrell, *Ethnicity and Inclusion: Religion, Race, and Whiteness in Constructions of Jewish and Christian Identities* (Grand Rapids: Eerdmans, 2020); Denise Kimber Buell, "Anachronistic Whiteness and the Ethics of Interpretation," in *Ethnicity, Race, Religion: Identities and Ideologies in Early Jewish and Christian Texts, and in the Traditions of Biblical Interpretation*, ed. Katherine M. Hockey and David G. Horrell (London: T&T Clark, 2018), 149–67.

racism, particularly antiblack racism.[19] Along with the emergence of whiteness studies in the discipline, Wongi Park proposes a "multiracial biblical studies" to create coalitional work across racial groups, including white scholars. He aims to "provide justifications for moving from monoracial to multiracial biblical studies" in terms of identity, method, and sources.[20] While a multiracial approach helps to make visible the unmarked methods of whiteness and break up the normative Eurocentricity of biblical studies, a cursory move toward multiracial biblical studies that does not interrogate whiteness as a structure may result in a recentering of whiteness.

Yee's justice-oriented intersectional approach, which focuses on the domains of power—structural, hegemonic, disciplinary, and interpersonal—is instructive in this regard.[21] Minoritized scholars have made efforts to decenter the identity and ideology of whiteness, diversify discursive practices, and support one another in various ways. However, if "the institutional structures of society [and the field] … reproduce the subordination of peoples over time," oppression and subordination will not cease.[22] For example, there were only eighteen Latinas in biblical studies as of 2018, and only five Latinas with full-time faculty positions in the United States in 2021.[23] How many of them teach at a PhD-granting institutions? What possibilities are there for unemployed or contingent women and minoritized scholars with PhD degrees to publish, which in turn would provide capital to

---

19. Shawn Kelley's work is exceptional in that he examines the racist legacy of modern biblical scholarship built on Enlightenment intellectual traditions and its effects on minoritized scholars. Shawn Kelley, *Racializing Jesus: Race, Ideology and the Formation of Modern Biblical Scholarship* (London: Routledge, 2002). Also see, Greg Carey, "Introduction and a Proposal: Culture, Power, and Identity in White New Testament Studies," in *Soundings in Cultural Criticism: Perspectives and Methods in Culture, Power, and Identity in the New Testament*, ed. Francisco Lozada Jr. and Greg Carey (Minneapolis: Fortress, 2013), 1–13.

20. Wongi Park, "Multiracial Biblical Studies," *JBL* 140 (2021): 438.

21. Yee, "Thinking Intersectionally," 14–16; Patricia Hill Collins, *Black Feminist Thought: Knowledge, Consciousness, and the Politics of Empowerment*, 2nd ed. (New York: Routledge, 2009), 21.

22. Yee, "Thinking Intersectionally," 14.

23. Jacqueline M. Hidalgo, "Defying the Meaning Line: Reading Brian Blount's Presidential Address alongside Lxs Atravesadxs," *The Bible and Critical Theory* 17 (2021): 36–37.

be employed? The structure of the field of biblical studies is not exempt from Yee's critique.

Doing Minoritized Criticism for Liberation

Given the impetus of Yee's address, I contend that a consideration of structural power demands an analysis of intersectionality that attends to the political economy of race, the psychological impact of structural racism, and the global reach of minoritized criticism in coalition building.

First, minoritized criticism should move beyond identity-based criticism to an intersectional approach that considers political economy. As Jonathan Tran suggests, "identarian antiracism" often reinforces the dominant logic or racial frameworks of white supremacy.[24] The black radical tradition recognizes capitalism as racial and race as commodified. Racial capitalism points to the process of extracting social and economic value from people of color through settler colonialism, genocide, chattel slavery, exclusion, segregation, internment, the prison industrial complex, and so on.[25] At the micro-level, we often see scholars of color are tokenized or commodified to diversify white institutions. Their diversity work is unpaid. Many minoritized scholars have learned that inclusion, tolerance, and multiculturalism are the language of the dominant, which serve their agenda. While the Society's policy on inclusiveness and diversity is commendable, in reality, it demands that minoritized scholars make whiteness less invisible in white spaces.

Second, interrogating the structural domain of power that sustains oppression, minoritized criticism also looks into "internalized oppression."[26] Gregory Cuéllar makes a poignant observation of the trauma-laden words uttered by minoritized and women presidents in their addresses.[27] Citing Brain K. Blount's presidential address, Jacque-

24. Jonathan Tran, *Asian Americans and the Spirit of Racial Capitalism* (Oxford: Oxford University Press, 2021), 13.

25. Cedric J. Robinson, *Black Marxism: The Making of the Black Radical Tradition* (Chapel Hill: University of North Carolina Press, 2000).

26. Yee, "Thinking Intersectionally," 13.

27. Such words include *shocking*, *woeful*, and *daunting* in Vincent L. Wimbush, "Interpreters—Enslaving/Enslaved/Runagate," *JBL* 130 (2011): 7; Elisabeth Schüssler Fiorenza, "The Ethics of Biblical Interpretation: Decentering Biblical Scholarship," *JBL* 107 (1988): 6; Yee, "Thinking Intersectionally," 7, respectively. See Cuéllar, "Reading Yee's Intersectionality," 5.

line M. Hidalgo makes a similar point that systemic violence or "academic brutality" takes various forms, such as racial gatekeeping on doctoral admissions, "dominant monocultural enforcement of the meaning line," or "metaphorical policing" of meaning-making.[28] We must address historical trauma enacted on black and other minoritized scholars both on the institutional level and among their communities. Whereas the Society can further develop spaces like the #BlackScholarshipMatters into deep listening sessions, different racial minority groups gather together to have internal conversations on difficult topics such as the black-white binary and the model-minority myth to build up antiracist coalitions to transform the field and society. Attending to systemic violence and racial trauma, Vincent L. Wimbush calls on black and white intellectuals to let go and run away from all bondage, such as "the black essential," "the white text," and the whiteness of studying "the ancient Near Eastern world as a white world in seamless historical development with the modern white world."[29] African America, symbolized by Fredrick Douglass—"a runagate before he runs away"—provides "the model of the imperative of running for life to a zone of discursive and ideological marronage" for black, white, and those in-between.[30]

Last, this running *for* life is even more urgent in critical times when crises and challenges are all connected and complicated on the global level and require the "global-systemic" analysis as an activist intervention, as Fernando F. Segovia proposes.[31] The intersectional thinking of feminist critics of color unfailingly takes this globally engaged activist position. In an international symposium, womanist biblical critic Renita J. Weems describes the transcultural engagement that made her "convinced of how important it is for African American women scholars to resist the myopisms of Western feminism by building bridges of dialogue with women from around the globe."[32] Jewish liberation theologian Marc H. Ellis also

28. Hidalgo, "Defying the Meaning Line," 36–38; Brian K. Blount, "The Souls of Biblical Folks and the Potential for Meaning," *JBL* 138 (2019): 21.

29. Wimbush, "Interpreters—Enslaving/Enslaved/Runagate," 12, 23.

30. Wimbush, "Interpreters—Enslaving/Enslaved/Runagate," 23.

31. Fernando F. Segovia, "Criticism in Critical Times: Reflections on Vision and Task," *JBL* 134 (2015): 16, 26. Segovia employs concepts of the *postglobal* from the perspective of economics; the *posthuman* from the perspective of climate change; and the *postnational* from the perspective of world migration.

32. Renita J. Weems, "Re-reading for Liberation: African American Women and the Bible," in *Feminist Interpretation of the Bible and the Hermeneutics of Liberation*,

notes that his prophetic interior, wounded by traumas from flight and exile, led him to encounter the Others and see the glimpse of the new diaspora of the global prophetic.[33] As all the Society's presidents of color charge in unison, biblical scholarship is called to engage the political economy of race, structural racism and internalized oppression, and an activist mode of biblical criticism on the global scale.

Moving Forward

Yee's call for intersectional biblical studies urges us to explore minoritized criticism in light of structural mechanisms of power. We also need to understand sexism beyond the gender binary, thus resisting the collusive powers of heteropatriarchy and white supremacy. At the center of our work stands the Bible that has been used to "sanction conquest and conversion."[34] In the era of neoliberal global capitalism, biblical scholarship is invited to visit the traumas of the Other in the formerly colonized countries and respond to global crises of democracy, racial capitalism, and climate change. At this juncture, the election of Musa Dube, the first woman president of color from the Global South, ushers in a new paradigm of biblical studies to contribute to the cause of global justice.[35]

Bibliography

Bailey, Randall C., Tat-siong Benny Liew, and Fernando F. Segovia. "Toward Minority Biblical Criticism: Framework, Contours, Dynamics." Pages 3–43 in *They Were All Together in One Place? Toward Minority Biblical Criticism*. Edited by Randall C. Bailey, Tat-siong Benny Liew, and Fernando F. Segovia. SemeiaSt 57. Atlanta: Society of Biblical Literature, 2009.

---

ed. Silvia Schroer and Sophia Bietenhard (London: Sheffield Academic, 2003), 20. This paper was first presented at the International Symposium on Feminist Exegesis and the Hermeneutics of Liberation held in Ticino, Switzerland, July 2000.

33. Marc H. Ellis, *Toward a Jewish Theology of Liberation: The Challenge of the Twenty-First Century*, 3rd ed. (Waco, TX: Baylor University Press, 2004), 199.

34. R. S. Sugirtharajah, *Voices from the Margin: Interpreting the Bible in the Third World*, 25th anniv. ed. (Maryknoll, NY: Orbis, 2016), 142.

35. I am grateful to Mary Foskett and Janette H. Ok for their careful reading of this essay and their valuable comments.

Blount, Brian K. "The Souls of Biblical Folks and the Potential for Meaning." *JBL* 138 (2019): 6–21.

Buell, Denise Kimber. "Anachronistic Whiteness and the Ethics of Interpretation." Pages 149–67 in *Ethnicity, Race, Religion: Identities and Ideologies in Early Jewish and Christian Texts, and in the Traditions of Biblical Interpretation*. Edited by Katherine M. Hockey and David G. Horrell. London: T&T Clark, 2018.

Carey, Greg. "Introduction and a Proposal: Culture, Power, and Identity in White New Testament Studies." Pages 1–13 in *Soundings in Cultural Criticism: Perspectives and Methods in Culture, Power, and Identity in the New Testament*. Edited by Francisco Lozada Jr. and Greg Carey. Minneapolis: Fortress, 2013.

Choi, Jin Young, and Gregory L. Cuéllar, eds. *Activist Hermeneutics of Liberation in the Bible*. London: Routledge, 2023.

Collins, Patricia Hill. *Black Feminist Thought: Knowledge, Consciousness, and the Politics of Empowerment*. 2nd ed. New York: Routledge, 2009.

———. *Intersectionality as Critical Social Theory*. Durham, NC: Duke University Press, 2019.

Cuéllar, Gregory L. "Reading Yee's Intersectionality as an Intervening Counterdiscourse to Whiteness." *The Bible and Critical Theory* 17 (2021): 4–13.

Ellis, Marc H. *Toward a Jewish Theology of Liberation: The Challenge of the Twenty-First Century*. 3rd ed. Waco, TX: Baylor University Press, 2004.

Hidalgo, Jacqueline M. "Defying the Meaning Line: Reading Brian Blount's Presidential Address alongside Lxs Atravesadxs." *The Bible and Critical Theory* 17 (2021): 36–45.

Horrell, David G. *Ethnicity and Inclusion: Religion, Race, and Whiteness in Constructions of Jewish and Christian Identities*. Grand Rapids: Eerdmans, 2020.

Kelley, Shawn. *Racializing Jesus: Race, Ideology and the Formation of Modern Biblical Scholarship*. London: Routledge, 2002.

Liew, Tat-siong Benny. "Black Scholarship Matters." *JBL* 136 (2017): 237–44.

Liew, Tat-siong Benny, and Fernando F. Segovia, eds. *Reading Biblical Texts Together: Doing Minoritized Biblical Criticism*. SemeiaSt 98. Atlanta: SBL Press, 2022.

———, eds. *Reading in These Times: Purposes and Practices of Minoritized Biblical Criticism*. Atlanta: SBL Press, forthcoming.

Park, Wongi. "Multiracial Biblical Studies." *JBL* 140 (2021): 435–59.
Robinson, Cedric J. *Black Marxism: The Making of the Black Radical Tradition*. Chapel Hill: University of North Carolina Press, 2000.
Segovia, Fernando F. "Criticism in Critical Times: Reflections on Vision and Task." *JBL* 134 (2015): 6–29.
Scholz, Susanne. "Stirring Up Vital Energies: Feminist Biblical Studies in North America (1980s–2000s)." Pages 53–57 in *Feminist Biblical Studies in the Twentieth Century: Scholarship and Movement*. Edited by Elisabeth Schüssler Fiorenza. BW 9.1. Atlanta: SBL Press, 2014.
Schüssler Fiorenza, Elisabeth. "The Ethics of Biblical Interpretation: Decentering Biblical Scholarship." *JBL* 107 (1988): 3–17.
Smith, Mitzi J., and Jin Young Choi, eds. *Minoritized Women Reading Race and Ethnicity: Intersectional Approaches to Constructed Identity and Early Christian Texts*. Lanham, MD: Lexington Books, 2020.
Sugirtharajah, R. S. *Voices from the Margin: Interpreting the Bible in the Third World*. 25th anniv. ed. Maryknoll, NY: Orbis, 2016.
Tran, Jonathan. *Asian Americans and the Spirit of Racial Capitalism*. Oxford: Oxford University Press, 2021.
Weems, Renita J. "Re-reading for Liberation: African American Women and the Bible." Pages 19–32 in *Feminist Interpretation of the Bible and the Hermeneutics of Liberation*. Edited by Silvia Schroer and Sophia Bietenhard. London: Sheffield Academic, 2003.
Wimbush, Vincent L. "Interpreters—Enslaving/Enslaved/Runagate." *JBL* 130 (2011): 5–24.
Yee, Gale A. "An Autobiographical Approach to Feminist Biblical Scholarship." *Encounter* 67 (2006): 375–90.
———. "Negotiating Shifts in Life's Paradigms." Pages 103–12 in *Women and the Society of Biblical Literature*. Edited by Nicole L. Tilford. BSNA 29. Atlanta: SBL Press, 2019.
———. *Poor Banished Children of Eve: Woman as Evil in the Hebrew Bible*. Minneapolis: Fortress, 2003.
———. "She Is Not My Wife and I Am Not Her Husband: A Materialist Analysis of Hosea 1–2." *BibInt* 9 (2001): 345–83.
———. "'She Stood in Tears amid the Alien Corn': Ruth the Perpetual Foreigner and Model Minority." Pages 119–40 in *They Were All Together in One Place? Toward Minority Biblical Criticism*. Edited by Randall C. Bailey, Tat-siong Benny Liew, and Fernando F. Segovia. SemeiaSt 57. Atlanta: Society of Biblical Literature, 2009.

———. “Thinking Intersectionally: Gender, Race, Class, and the Etceteras of Our Discipline.” *JBL* 139 (2020): 7–26.

Contributors

Brian K. Blount is President Emeritus of Union Presbyterian Seminary, Richmond, Virginia, and Charlotte, North Carolina. Previous to assuming the presidency, he was Richard J. Dearborn Professor of New Testament Interpretation at Princeton Theological Seminary. A past president of the Society of Biblical Literature, Blount is the sole author of six books, including *Can I Get A Witness? Reading Revelation through an African American* Lens (Westminster John Knox, 2005); *Revelation: A Commentary* in the New Testament Library series (Westminster John Knox, 2009); and *Invasion of the Dead: Preaching Resurrection* (Westminster John Knox, 2014).

Gay L. Byron is Professor of New Testament and Early Christianity at Howard University School of Divinity in Washington, DC. Her scholarship focuses on the origins of Christianity in ancient Ethiopia, cultural and womanist readings of Scripture, and race and ethnicity in early Christian writings. She is the author of *Symbolic Blackness and Ethnic Difference in Early Christian Literature* (Routledge, 2002), coeditor (with Vanessa Lovelace) of *Womanist Interpretations of the Bible: Expanding the Discourse* (SBL Press, 2016), and coeditor (with Hugh R. Page Jr.) of *Black Scholars Matter: Visions, Struggles, and Hopes in Africana Biblical Studies* (SBL Press, 2022).

Leslie D. Callahan is the pastor of the Saint Paul's Baptist Church in Philadelphia, Pennsylvania. Prior to her current appointment, she taught at New York Theological Seminary and the University of Pennsylvania. Her scholarly interests include the history of Christianity in the United States, with a focus on the black church and Pentecostal studies.

Jin Young Choi is Professor of New Testament and Christian Origins and the Baptist Missionary Training School Professorial Chair for Biblical

Studies at Colgate Rochester Crozer Divinity School. Choi is the author of *Postcolonial Discipleship of Embodiment: An Asian and Asian American Feminist Reading of the Gospel of Mark* (Palgrave Macmillan, 2015).

Stephanie Buckhanon Crowder is Professor of New Testament and Culture at Chicago Theological Seminary. She is a dually aligned National Baptist and Disciples of Christ minister. She is the author of *Simon of Cyrene: A Case of Roman Conscription* (2002) and *When Momma Speaks: The Bible and Motherhood from a Womanist Perspective* (2016).

Gregory L. Cuéllar is Associate Professor of Hebrew Bible/Old Testament at Austin Presbyterian Theological Seminary. He has been a visiting scholar at the Centre on Migration, Policy, and Society (COMPAS) and the Centre for Criminology at the University of Oxford. He is the cofounder of a refugee artwork project called Arte de Lágrimas (Art of Tears): Refugee Artwork Project. This project is a traveling art exhibit and archive that aims to create greater public awareness of the lived migratory journeys of asylum-seeking children, youth, and adults.

Mary F. Foskett is Wake Forest Kahle Professor of Religious Studies and John Thomas Albritton Fellow at Wake Forest University, where she is chair of the Department for the Study of Religions. She is the coeditor of *Ways of Being, Ways of Reading: Asian American Biblical Interpretation* (2007) and *Diverse Strands of a Common Thread: An Introduction to Ethnic Chinese Biblical Interpretation* (2014).

Jacqueline M. Hidalgo is Professor of Theology and Religious Studies at the University of San Diego, and she is the author of *Latina/o/x Studies and Biblical Studies* (Brill, 2020), as well as *Revelation in Aztlán: Scriptures, Utopias, and the Chicano Movement* (Palgrave Macmillan, 2016). With Efraín Agosto, she also coedited the collection of essays *Latinxs, the Bible, and Migration* (Palgrave Macmillan, 2018). She currently serves as general editor for the SBL Press Semeia Studies book series.

Tat-siong Benny Liew is Class of 1956 Professor in New Testament Studies at the College of the Holy Cross. He is the author of *Politics of Parousia* (Brill, 1999) and *What Is Asian American Biblical Hermeneutics?* (University of Hawai'i Press, 2008). He is coeditor (with Shelly Matthews) of *Race and Biblical Studies: Antiracism Pedagogy for the Classroom* (SBL Press,

2022) and ten other volumes. Liew is also the series editor of T&T Clark's Study Guides to the New Testament.

Velma E. Love is Associate Professor of Interdisciplinary Studies and Director of the Doctor of Ministry Program at the Interdenominational Theological Center in Atlanta, Georgia, where she teaches transdisciplinary courses related to design thinking and prophetic problem-solving through an Africentric lens. Love's primary research interests include sacred texts in society, the art of divination, ancestral knowledge systems, and the contemporary application of Ifa spiritual technology. She has published extensively on African American engagements with scriptures and sacred texts in society and is author of *Divining the Self: A Study in Yoruba Myth and Human Consciousness* (Penn State University Press, 2012).

Andrew Mbuvi is a Kenyan-American biblical scholar who currently holds the position of Visiting NEH Chair in Humanities and Associate Professor of Religion at Albright College, Reading, Pennsylvania. He has served as cochair of the Society of Biblical Literature's African Biblical Hermeneutics Unit (2010–2014) and chair of the New Testament section of the former Society of Biblical Literature South Eastern Regional meeting (SECSOR; 2010–2013). His most recent publication is *African Biblical Studies: Unmasking Embedded Racism and Colonialism in Biblical Studies* (T&T Clark Bloomsbury, 2022).

Raj Nadella is the Samuel A. Cartledge Associate Professor of New Testament at Columbia Theological Seminary. Nadella is the author of *Dialogue Not Dogma: Many Voices in the Gospel of Luke* (Bloomsbury, 2011) and coeditor of *Christianity and the Law of Migration* (Routledge, 2021). He serves on the editorial boards of *Review of Biblical Literature* and *Currents in Biblical Research* and chairs the Society of Biblical Literature's Committee on Underrepresented Racial and Ethnic Minorities in the Profession (CUREMP).

Janette H. Ok serves as Associate Professor of New Testament at Fuller Theological Seminary. She is the author of *Constructing Ethnic Identity in 1 Peter: Who You Are No Longer* (T&T Clark, 2021) and coeditor and contributor to the forthcoming *The New Testament in Color: A Multiethnic Biblical Commentary* (IVP Academic). Currently, she is writing a commentary on the Letters of John (NICNT, Eerdmans). She cochairs the Society of Biblical Literature's Asian and Asian American Hermeneutics unit and has served as a member of the Committee for the Status of Women in the Profession and on the steering committee for the Minoritized Criticism and Biblical Interpretation unit.

Angela N. Parker is Assistant Professor of New Testament and Greek at Mercer University's McAfee School of Theology. In 2018, Parker's article, "One Womanist's View of Racial Reconciliation in Galatians," earned second place in the *Journal for Feminist Studies in Religion*'s Elisabeth Schüssler Fiorenza New Scholar Award, and in 2023 she published *If God Still Breathes, Why Can't I: Black Lives Matter and Biblical Authority* (Eerdmans). Parker is ordained with the Missionary Baptist Association of North Carolina and can be found on YouTube and TikTok @BoozyBibleScholar.

Ahida Calderón Pilarski is Professor of Old Testament/Hebrew Bible at Saint Anselm College in New Hampshire. Her research focuses on the intersection of culture, race/ethnicity, and gender in biblical interpretation, especially in Latina and Mujerista Biblical Hermeneutics. She is currently the President-Elect of the Academy of Catholic Hispanic Theologians of the United States (ACHTUS), and her most recent publication is *Daughters of Wisdom: Women and Leadership in the Global Church* (Wipf & Stock, 2023).

Fernando F. Segovia holds the Oberlin Graduate Chair of New Testament and Early Christianity in the Divinity School and the Graduate Department of Religion at Vanderbilt University. He is a product of migration from the Global South to the Global North, from Latin America (Cuba) to the United States, where he has formed part of the Latinx American population. A long-time proponent of contextual, ideological, and cultural studies, Segovia is at work on global criticism. As a child of a peripheralized and minoritized diaspora, he is committed to the project of human rights and the pursuit of cosmopolitan ideals.

Abraham Smith is Professor of New Testament at Perkins School of Theology, Southern Methodist University. His research interests include ancient and modern slavery, violence studies, and African American biblical hermeneutics. His most recent publications include *Mark: An Introduction and Study Guide—Shaping the Life and Legacy of Jesus* (Bloomsbury, 2017); *Black/Africana Studies and Black/Africana Biblical Studies* (Brill,

2020); and "Incarceration on Trial: The Imprisonment of Paul and Silas in Acts 16," in *Journal of Biblical Literature* 140 (2021).

Yak-hwee Tan is an adjunct lecturer at Discipleship Training Center, Singapore. She was an Associate Professor of Biblical Studies at Tainan Theological College, Tainan, Taiwan (2018–2022) and a Tutor of New Testament Language, Literature and Theology at Westminster College, Cambridge, United Kingdom. She was also an Affiliated Lecturer of the Faculty of Divinity, University of Cambridge (2015–2018). She has written a number of articles in the area of ideological criticism, ecological concerns, and mission.

Ekaputra Tupamahu is Assistant Professor of New Testament and Director of Master's Programs at Portland Seminary in Oregon. His research on the New Testament is informed by race/ethnic theory, postcolonial studies, and immigration studies. He is the author of *Contesting Languages: Heteroglossia and the Politics of Language in the Early Church* (Oxford University Press, 2022).

Vincent L. Wimbush is founding director of The Institute for Signifying Scriptures, an independent organization for transdisciplinary research and programming. His teaching career was spent in Claremont, California (Claremont School of Theology and Claremont Graduate University), and in New York City (Union/Columbia University). He is author/editor of several books, including *Masquerade: Scripturalizing Modernities through Black Flesh* (Lexington Books, 2023); *Black Flesh Matters: Essays in Runagate Interpretation* (Lexington Books, 2022); and *White Men's Magic* (Oxford University Press, 2012). In the 1990s he served as the first chair of the Committee on Underrepresented Minorities in the Profession (CUREMP) and in 2010 as president of the Society of Biblical Literature.

Gale A. Yee is Nancy W. King Professor of Biblical Studies emerita, Episcopal Divinity School. She is the author of several books, articles, and essays. In 2019, she was the first Asian American and first woman of color president of the Society of Biblical Literature. She was awarded an honorary Doctor of Divinity from Virginia Theological Seminary in 2020. She lives at Pilgrim Place, a retirement community in Claremont, California, known for its social activism.

www.ingramcontent.com/pod-product-compliance
Lightning Source LLC
LaVergne TN
LVHW091113080826
845145LV00008B/1903

* 9 7 8 1 6 2 8 3 7 4 8 1 0 *